Wages and Labor Markets in the United States, 1820–1860

NBER Series on Long-term Factors in Economic Development

A National Bureau of Economic Research Series

Edited by Claudia Goldin

Wages and Labor Markets in the United States, 1820–1860

Robert A. Margo

The University of Chicago Press

Chicago and London

Robert A. Margo is professor of economics at Vanderbilt University and a research associate of the National Bureau of Economic Research.

The University of Chicago Press, Chicago 60637
The University of Chicago Press, Ltd., London
© 2000 by The University of Chicago
All rights reserved. Published 2000
Printed in the United States of America
09 08 07 06 05 04 03 02 01 00   1 2 3 4 5
ISBN: 0-226-50507-3 (cloth)

Library of Congress Cataloging-in-Publication Data

Margo, Robert A. (Robert Andrew), 1954–
    Wages and labor markets in the United States, 1820–1860 /
Robert A. Margo.
        p.   cm.—(NBER series on long-term factors in economic
development)
    Includes bibliographical references and index.
    ISBN 0-226-50507-3 (cloth : alk. paper)
    1. Wages—United States—History.   2. Labor supply—United
States—History.   I. Title.   II. Series.
HD4975.M33   2000
331.2′973—DC21   99-31175
                                                                            CIP

Relation of the Directors to the Work and Publications of the National Bureau of Economic Research

1. The object of the National Bureau of Economic Research is to ascertain and to present to the public important economic facts and their interpretation in a scientific and impartial manner. The Board of Directors is charged with the responsibility of ensuring that the work of the National Bureau is carried on in strict conformity with this object.

2. The President of the National Bureau shall submit to the Board of Directors, or to its Executive Committee, for their formal adoption all specific proposals for research to be instituted.

3. No research report shall be published by the National Bureau until the President has sent each member of the Board a notice that a manuscript is recommended for publication and that in the President's opinion it is suitable for publication in accordance with the principles of the National Bureau. Such notification will include an abstract or summary of the manuscript's content and a response form for use by those Directors who desire a copy of the manuscript for review. Each manuscript shall contain a summary drawing attention to the nature and treatment of the problem studied, the character of the data and their utilization in the report, and the main conclusions reached.

4. For each manuscript so submitted, a special committee of the Directors (including Directors Emeriti) shall be appointed by majority agreement of the President and Vice Presidents (or by the Executive Committee in case of inability to decide on the part of the President and Vice Presidents), consisting of three Directors selected as nearly as may be one from each general division of the Board. The names of the special manuscript committee shall be stated to each Director when notice of the proposed publication is submitted to him. It shall be the duty of each member of the special manuscript committee to read the manuscript. If each member of the manuscript committee signifies his approval within thirty days of the transmittal of the manuscript, the report may be published. If at the end of that period any member of the manuscript committee withholds his approval, the President shall then notify each member of the Board, requesting approval or disapproval of publication, and thirty days additional shall be granted for this purpose. The manuscript shall then not be published unless at least a majority of the entire Board who shall have voted on the proposal within the time fixed for the receipt of votes shall have approved.

5. No manuscript may be published, though approved by each member of the special manuscript committee, until forty-five days have elapsed from the transmittal of the report in manuscript form. The interval is allowed for the receipt of any memorandum of dissent or reservation, together with a brief statement of his reasons, that any member may wish to express; and such memorandum of dissent or reservation shall be published with the manuscript if he so desires. Publication does not, however, imply that each member of the Board has read the manuscript, or that either members of the Board in general or the special committee have passed on its validity in every detail.

6. Publications of the National Bureau issued for informational purposes concerning the work of the Bureau and its staff, or issued to inform the public of activities of Bureau staff, and volumes issued as a result of various conferences involving the National Bureau shall contain a specific disclaimer noting that such publication has not passed through the normal review procedures required in this resolution. The Executive Committee of the Board is charged with review of all such publications from time to time to ensure that they do not take on the character of formal research reports of the National Bureau, requiring formal Board approval.

7. Unless otherwise determined by the Board or exempted by the terms of paragraph 6, a copy of this resolution shall be printed in each National Bureau publication.

(Resolution adopted October 25, 1926, as revised through September 30, 1974)

To Daniel

Contents

Preface

The construction of historical time series is one of the central tasks of economic history. This book presents new series of nominal and real wages in the United States over the period 1820–60 and uses them to explore various issues in antebellum economic development. The new series dramatically expand the existing body of wage evidence for the antebellum period and should be of value to a wide variety of scholars.

This book has taken shape over an unusually long gestation period. The origins of this project date back to 1980, when, as a graduate student at Harvard University, I began looking for new antebellum wage data in response to a query from Robert Fogel. The initial data collection—which Georgia Villaflor and I supervised—was performed by the Center for Population Economics at the University of Chicago. Preliminary results were reported in a paper published in the *Journal of Economic History* in 1987 (Margo and Villaflor 1987). I collected additional data myself with the aid of a grant from the National Science Foundation (NSF) through the National Bureau of Economic Research. I am grateful to the NSF for this support. I am also grateful for additional support from the University of Pennsylvania, Colgate University, and Vanderbilt University. The final version of the manuscript was written at Harvard University and at the National Bureau of Economic Research (Cambridge, Massachusetts), for whose hospitality I am very grateful.

Over the many years of working on this project, I have accumulated intellectual debts to numerous individuals. These include Donald Adams, Lee Alston, Jeremy Atack, Price Fishback, Robert Fogel, the late Robert Gallman, Claudia Goldin, David Gray, Farley Grubb, Graham Hodges, Oswald Honkalehto, Lawrence Katz, John Komlos, Stanley Lebergott, Gloria Main, Emily Mechner, Thomas Mroz, Paul Rhode, Sherwin Ro-

sen, Kenneth Sokoloff, Richard Sylla, the late Paul Taubman, Robert To-
pel, Georgia Villaflor, David Wildasin, and Jeffrey Williamson. Versions
of chapters have been presented at many institutions, including Bard, the
University of California (Los Angeles and San Diego), Chicago, Colgate,
Dartmouth, Harvard, Illinois, Indiana, Maryland, the National Bureau
of Economic Research, Northwestern, Pennsylvania, Tufts, Vanderbilt,
Washington University at St. Louis, and Yale. I am grateful to seminar
audiences at these institutions as well as to audiences at various conferences of the American Economic Association, the Economic History Association, and the Social Science History Association. Stanley Engerman and Claudia Goldin provided very helpful comments at a late stage
in the revisions. Finally, I would like to thank Jodi Bilinkoff, Lee Brecken-
ridge, Marilyn Darling, Robert Driskill, Claudia Goldin, Lance Gunder-
son, Paul McGill, Emily Mechner, Janet Topolsky, Susan Trent, Gloria
Vachino, Leah Welch, Stanley and Becky Yates, and Donna Zerwitz for
their friendship and support while I was writing this book.

R.A.M.
Nashville, December 1998

Introduction

The period from 1820 to 1860 was one of the most tumultuous in American economic history. During these four decades—decades that led, ultimately, to the American Civil War—the political arena was beset by rancor, and the American economy was profoundly transformed. The United States experienced the onset of modern economic growth, the spread of the factory system, and fundamental improvements in productivity and in internal transportation. Vast numbers of individuals changed their place of residence. Some moved short distances—from one rural county to another or from the countryside to a town or city—whereas others migrated from the long-settled states of the Northeast and South Atlantic regions to frontier locations in the Midwest and South Central regions.[1] Still others covered extraordinary distances, braving hardship in the hopes of striking it rich when gold was discovered in California in the late 1840s. European immigrants arrived on America's shores in increasing numbers in the 1840s and 1850s, permanently altering the political, social, and economic landscape, particularly in Northeastern cities. Divisions between North and South became starker, as one part of the country began to industrialize while the other—the South—remained largely rural. In short, the antebellum period was one of enormous economic, social, and political flux, as different sections of the nation took on their distinctive structures.

Several of the changes just listed are believed to have had important and lasting effects on the standard of living of free labor. Perhaps the most interesting is the fact that, as the prevailing wisdom has it, living standards greatly improved on average from 1820 to 1860 as a consequence of technological and other changes in production (e.g., mechanization, the factory system, better agricultural land) and in distribution (e.g., the building of canals and railroads). Quantitative evidence for the prevailing wisdom has been sought in estimates of real per capita incomes. According to Thomas Weiss (1992, 27), real per capita incomes were higher in 1860 than in 1820 by approximately 62 percent.

But the fact that real per capita incomes appear to have risen by a considerable amount in the antebellum period does not fully resolve the question of whether the standard of living of the average worker rose. Many scholars have reached the opposite conclusion (see, e.g., Commons et al. 1918; Ware 1924; Sullivan 1955; Hirsch 1978; Laurie 1980; Wilentz 1984; Ross 1985; Fogel 1989). These scholars believe that gains in the standard of living of many of the antebellum "working class" may have been much more modest in the long run and that economic well-being may have stagnated or even declined during certain subperiods—as evidenced primarily, but not exclusively, by movements in real wages.

Associated with these opposing views on the growth of living standards are divergent beliefs about the ability of the antebellum labor markets to cope with economic change. Broadly speaking, the "optimist" viewpoint is that markets or market-like processes were reasonably effective in responding to economic change, with the result that growth in antebellum living standards was generally steady and that most in the working class shared in the gains. Thus, for example, when early industrialization increased the general demand for nonfarm labor at the expense of farm labor, labor shifted out of agriculture, and potential gains in real wages could be—and were—quickly realized.

The "pessimist" viewpoint is far less sanguine about how effectively antebellum labor markets coped with change. Pessimists assert, for example, that nominal wages lagged behind when the price level rose in the mid-1830s and early 1850s, producing declines in real wages and (in the earlier period) a wave of strikes and labor agitation. The influx of immigrants starting in the late 1840s is alleged to have glutted labor markets and, together with the effects of inflation via the wage lag, to have put additional downward pressure on real wages. So pronounced was that downward pressure that one scholar has dubbed the period a "hidden depression" for labor (Fogel 1989). Recent research has uncovered other evidence that appears to bolster the pessimist case or at least challenge the view that antebellum living standards were rising consistently. For example, usage of publically provided poor relief—the antebellum equivalent of today's welfare—rose markedly between 1850 and 1860 (Kiesling and Margo 1997). Nutritional status, morbidity, and mortality appear to have worsened in the period 1820–50 (Margo and Steckel 1983; Komlos 1987; Pope 1992).

Scholars of both persuasions have suggested that antebellum economic development changed the relative demand for workers with different types of skills. But these scholars do not agree on exactly how demand changed.

For some, early industrialization produced a decline in the relative demand for certain types of skilled labor via the displacement of artisanal shops by factories requiring less-skilled labor, but others believe that industrialization actually bolstered the relative demand for various skills (Williamson and Lindert 1980; Goldin and Sokoloff 1982; Sokoloff 1984). Whether the antebellum wage structure would be persistently, or only temporarily, affected by these purported shifts in relative demands, however, depended on how readily labor could adapt—by acquiring new skills or otherwise shifting out of occupations with declining relative demand toward more lucrative pursuits.

Antebellum economic development occurred against the initial condition of a vast frontier. Industrialization and, more generally, economic development did not occur uniformly across the antebellum landscape. Capitalizing on economic opportunities frequently required migration, a response that was facilitated by falling costs of internal transportation and improved access to economic information. The optimist position is that antebellum labor markets were reasonably effective in guiding labor from low- to high-value locations, as evidenced by high rates of geographic mobility that arguably produced an erosion of wage differentials between locations. The opposing viewpoint, however, is that geographic imbalances in labor demand and supply were ubiquitous and persistent before the Civil War and that the emergence of spatially integrated labor markets was a milestone of a much later period in American history.

In view of the critical role that the antebellum period played in American economic history, it might be thought that many of the issues under debate would have been long resolved in the historical literature. But they have not been. The reasons have less to do with the framing of questions or with methodology (although these aspects of the analysis are sometimes important) than with sources of evidence. Simply put, research on these (and many related) issues has been seriously hampered by a lack of suitable wage data. Contemporary economists are blessed—some might say overwhelmed—with an abundance of data on labor markets. But the student of the antebellum period—and, more generally, the nineteenth-century United States—has not been so fortunate. Historians have previously had to make do with sources of antebellum wage evidence that were severely limited in temporal, geographic, and occupational coverage; consequently, progress in illuminating many important issues has been slow or nonexistent.

This book offers a new interpretation of wages and labor markets before the Civil War. Broadly speaking, the interpretation can be seen as a synthesis of the opposing viewpoints just described, although it contains novel findings that neither could have anticipated without the availability of a substantial body of new evidence (see below). The new interpretation has three parts:

1. The Long Run. In the aggregate, between 1820 and 1860, real wages grew at about 1 percent per year, approximately the same as the growth rate of real output per worker. Thus, on average, antebellum economic growth did "trickle down" to many in the working class.

2. The Short Run. While real wages grew in the long run, pessimists are right to emphasize their erratic behavior over certain subperiods. Real wages grew less rapidly from the 1820s to the 1830s than previously thought, and the late 1840s to the mid-1850s was a period of generally declining real wages. Deviations of real wages from their long-run growth path appear to have been caused by a mixture of nominal and real shocks that were incompletely adjusted to in the short and medium run. Declines in real wages over subperiods may help explain certain declines in nutritional status and were also instrumental in the rise in pauperism in the 1850s.

3. The Effectiveness of Labor Markets. Antebellum labor markets had a reasonably good, if occasionally spotty, record of coping with economic change. Labor markets adjusted to trend growth in the general demand for nonfarm labor insofar as wage gaps between the farm and the nonfarm sectors for unskilled labor were small. Some wage differentials between locations were eroded over time in a manner consistent with simple models of labor supply and demand. However, antebellum development did alter the structure of wages, favoring educated labor at the expense of other groups; and a gap in unskilled wages emerged between the South and the North in the 1830s.

Support for the synthesis draws heavily on the analysis of two bodies of archival evidence that were newly collected for this book. The first is the *Reports of Persons and Articles Hired,* a collection of monthly payrolls documenting the wages of civilian workers employed at United States Army posts throughout the country. A sample of approximately sixty-two thousand wage observations has been collected from this source and put into machine-readable form. The second body of evidence is the manuscript Census of Social Statistics, conducted in 1850 and 1860. This source gives information at the local level on average monthly or daily wages for different types of labor and on the weekly cost of board. Data from a sample of states have been collected and computerized from this source. I also make extensive use of information on antebellum prices and on the labor force collected or produced primarily by other scholars. The tools of cliometrics—formal economic models and econometrics—are employed throughout, but I believe that the key ideas in the book can be understood without detailed knowledge of these techniques.

Chapter 2 discusses the prevailing wisdom on the growth of nominal and real wages from 1820 and 1860 and also introduces the data on which the new interpretation is based. Chapter 3 uses these and other data to construct annual series of nominal and real wages for three occupation groups (common laborers, skilled artisans, white-collar workers) in each of the four major census regions (the Northeast, Midwest, South Atlantic, and South Central states) over the period 1820–60. These series, along with related series presented in chapters 5 and 6, are the principal empirical contribution of the book.

Chapters 4–6 are concerned with the allocative effectiveness of antebellum labor markets. Chapter 4 examines gaps in wages between the farm and the nonfarm sectors because the shift of labor out of agriculture is a key feature of economic growth. The existence of wage gaps would be prima facie evidence of an impediment to growth. Data from the Censuses of Social Statistics are used to measure the size of wage gaps in 1850 and 1860.

Chapter 5 modifies the wage series produced earlier so that they can be used to study the evolution of regional differences in real wage levels by occupation group. Aggregate nominal and real wage series for common laborers, artisans, and white-collar workers are presented in this chapter. Real wages were initially higher in the Midwest than in the Northeast, but the regional wage gap declined in the North as the Midwest's share of the labor force increased. I also find, however, that a North-South gap in unskilled wages emerged in the 1830s. Using the data from the census manuscripts, I also study whether real wages at the local level remained persistently high or low between 1850 and 1860, discovering instead that wages tended to regress to the mean, as would be expected of an interlinked set of local labor markets.

Chapter 6 examines the most famous location-specific shock to labor markets in all nineteenth-century American history—the California Gold Rush. The Gold Rush is an interesting natural experiment to use to study allocative effectiveness because capitalizing on the discovery of gold required the costly reallocation of labor to a distant, and sparsely populated, area. Because the army maintained forts in the state before and after the discovery of gold, it has proved possible to construct wage series spanning the Gold Rush period. I find that real wages rose during the initial phase of the Gold Rush but subsequently declined as labor migrated into California.

Chapter 7 uses the findings of the previous chapters, along with findings presented elsewhere, to develop the new interpretation discussed earlier. Chapter 8 concludes with some brief observations on the relevance of the findings for a current audience.

The Growth of Wages in Antebellum America
A Review

This chapter reviews the economic history literature on the growth of wages before the Civil War. Although various studies point to increases in real wages over the period 1820–60, virtually all the evidence pertains to the Northeast, and it is limited in other ways (e.g., in detail about occupation). The chapter concludes with a discussion of the two new sources of wage evidence developed for this book.

2.1 Real Wages

This section surveys the literature on trends and fluctuations in nominal and real wages during the antebellum period.[1] By *real wage,* I mean the money wage (or its equivalent in money) per some unit of time (typically, a day or a month) divided by an index of prices. The end result is an index of real wages; that is, the value of the real wage is set to 100 in some base year, and the value of the real wage in other years is expressed relative to the value in the base year. There are numerous practical difficulties constructing such indices, and there are equally numerous difficulties interpreting such indices once constructed. I leave a fuller discussion of some of these difficulties to later chapters, where I present and interpret my own set of indices. For the moment, I simply assume that real wage indices provide useful information about movements in living standards for antebellum (free) labor.[2]

History has not been particularly kind to economic historians interested in the course of wages before the Civil War. The federal government attempted to collect some comprehensive, internally consistent wage information for scattered years. The earliest such documents are the 1820 manuscript Census of Manufactures and the McLane Report (McLane

1833). The purpose of both surveys was to provide information on early antebellum manufacturing enterprises, and both are sufficiently detailed to analyze, for example, the gender composition of the industrial labor force, labor productivity, and average monthly wages in manufacturing (Goldin and Sokoloff 1982; Sokoloff 1986a; Sokoloff and Villaflor 1992). The McLane Report also provided some information, albeit widely scattered geographically, on the wages of mechanics and a few other occupations. Agricultural wages at the state level were first collected by the Treasury Department in 1848 as part of its attempt to monitor crop production (Lebergott 1964).

The first serious attempts to collect national wage data occurred in 1850 and 1860 as part of the federal census. Enumerators collected "social statistics" on real and personal wealth, crop yields, churches, schools, poor relief, and crime and information on the wages of farm laborers, common laborers, carpenters, and domestics and on the cost of board. State-level averages of wages and the cost of board were published in the 1850 and 1860 censuses (DeBow 1854, 164; Secretary of the Interior 1866, 512). Manuscript schedules of the social statistics have survived for various states. Later in the chapter, I describe a sample drawn from this rich and greatly neglected source.

Both the published and the sample 1850 and 1860 census data are extremely useful in constructing benchmarks (Lebergott 1964; and chap. 3 below). Elsewhere, I use them to study the relation between wage movements and the incidence of poor relief (Kiesling and Margo 1997) and the efficiency of labor markets (chaps. 5 and 6 below). However, the census data are obviously of little use for charting long-run trends (except between 1850 and 1860) and none at all regarding cyclic fluctuations.[3] To gauge trends more accurately, and even to measure cycles, annual information on real wages is needed. Two types of annual information have been examined—retrospective surveys and archival records.

The primary sources of retrospective information are two federal government documents: the Weeks Report, published as part of the 1880 census (Weeks 1886), and the Aldrich Report, published in conjunction with a Senate investigation of tariffs in the early 1890s (Aldrich 1893). The two reports differ in detail, but their basic designs are similar. Both contain wage information culled from payroll records, and both are retrospective—the data are time series derived from the records of firms that were in existence at the time of the survey. Firms that existed prior to either survey but went out of business before the surveys were taken were not included. However, because many of the firms in both surveys had been in business for many years, either survey can be—and has been—used to estimate wage indices well back into the nineteenth century. The two reports both disaggregate average wages by firm (and hence industry), occupation, and frequency of payment (daily and hourly), but the Weeks

Report does not give the number of observations underlying the firm averages.[4]

The Weeks and Aldrich Reports are not the only retrospective surveys that cover the antebellum period. Similar retrospective data were compiled for Massachusetts by Carroll Wright when he was commissioner of labor for that state, and the entire data set was published in an annual report of the Massachusetts Bureau of Labor Statistics (Wright 1885). As in the case of the Weeks and Aldrich reports, the data were culled from the payroll records of firms. A large array of occupations—skilled laborers, common laborers, farm laborers, and manufacturing workers—is represented in the Wright survey; however, none of the occupations contain wage quotations for every year. As a result, economic historians have primarily used the Wright data to study long-term movements in skill differentials—the ratio of skilled to unskilled wages (see Grosse 1982; Lindert and Williamson 1982).

Although a case can be made that either the Weeks or the Aldrich Report can be used to study post–Civil War wage movements, their usefulness in studying antebellum patterns is another matter, especially before 1850.[5] The number of observations per year declines very sharply before 1840.[6] Whether the retrospective nature of the reports introduces any bias for the antebellum period is unclear, but selectivity is clearly a concern because the number of firms with antebellum data is small. Perhaps most important, the antebellum data in either report pertain almost solely to the Northeast before 1850; little can be gleaned about the behavior of wages in the Midwest or the South (Coelho and Shepherd 1976). By definition, the Wright survey pertains solely to Massachusetts; like the Weeks Report, it lacks information on the number of workers in the firms that were surveyed; and, worse, no information was reported on the location of the firms in the state.

These deficiencies aside, all three reports are fundamental sources of economic data for the nineteenth century. The Aldrich and Weeks Reports, in particular, have been extensively mined, starting with Abbott (1905), Mitchell (1908), and Hansen (1925). Examples of modern studies based totally or in part on either source are Coelho and Shepherd (1976), David and Solar (1977), and Williamson and Lindert (1980). The David-Solar and Williamson-Lindert wage indices are hybrids, making use of archival evidence in conjunction with the Weeks Report, so I discuss the Coelho-Shepherd study and various archival sources before reviewing the David-Solar and Williamson-Lindert indices.

Coelho and Shepherd (1976) used the Weeks Report to chart regional differences in trends and levels of nominal and real wages from 1851 to 1880. Over three-fourths of the firms canvased by Weeks and his associates were located in the Northeast or East North Central states. Because the undersampling was especially severe for the West South Central, Mountain, and Pacific regions, Coelho and Shepherd present limited estimates for these areas. For the 1850s, the sample was deemed unreliable for all but the Northeast and East North Central regions (Coelho and Shepherd 1976, 207).

After a careful discussion of biases, Coelho and Shepherd focus on six occupations—engineer, blacksmith, machinist, painter, carpenter, and common laborer. They also use the Weeks Report data to construct national and regional price deflators (their construction was described in an earlier paper, Coelho and Shepherd [1974]). Two types of regional wage series were presented. The first type combined all observations, either within a region, unweighted across occupations, or within an occupation, unweighted across regions. The second type was by region for engineers and common laborers.[7] Because my interest is in the pre–Civil War period, I focus on their estimates for the Northeast and the East North Central states as these are the series they believe to be most reliable.

The unweighted series suggest that real wages fell during the first half of the 1850s, regardless of whether the national or the regional price indices are used as the deflator.[8] Real wages then increased but were no higher in 1860 than in 1851 in any region. Thus, the Weeks Report data suggest that the 1850s was a decade of little or no overall real wage growth. The same conclusions about the 1850s hold for common laborers; for engineers, however, real wages were higher in 1860 than in 1851 in the Mid-Atlantic and East North Central states.[9]

Real wages were higher in the East North Central region than in the Northeast in the 1850s for the unweighted series and for engineers and common laborers.[10] Within the Northeast, real wages were generally higher in New England than in the Mid-Atlantic states, although the regional differences within the Northeast were generally smaller than those between the East North Central states and the Northeast.[11] The real wage advantage enjoyed by the East North Central states was a consequence of lower prices because money wages were higher in the Northeast.

Archival records have also been used to study wage movements before the Civil War. Perhaps the most famous such study is Walter B. Smith's (1963) well-known compilation of wages paid to workers on the Erie Canal. The data pertain to maintenance work performed on the canal. The bulk of the wage quotations (about 90 percent) are for common laborers. Smith also produced series for carpenters, masons, and "teamwork" (teamsters plus horses). The series for masons, however, has several gaps in it, owing to the fact that the hiring of masons was less frequent than that of the other types of workers.[12]

Although the state government in Albany appears to have been concerned with employment on the canal, it generally seemed to have left the remuneration of canal workers to local supervisors. For this reason, according to Smith (1963, 298), the "Erie Canal Papers have made it possible to compile series which are trustworthy indicators of wage levels, wage trends, and fluctuations," series that "approximate the prevailing wages in the areas adjoining the canal."

Maintenance work on the canal was organized in gangs of varying size and specialization. Two sources of wage rate statistics are available: the "checkrolls" of the gangs and workmen's receipts of pay. These were sufficient in quantity to yield about thirty thousand observations—clearly a larger sample size than that boasted by any other antebellum source, except for the data analyzed in this book.[13]

Interpretation of the Erie Canal series is complicated by the fact that Smith chose the mode as an indicator of central tendency. The mode might impart a spurious stability to nominal wages, although Smith (1963, 301) argued that the modal wage and the mean wage generally differed little from one another. Comparisons between the Erie Canal series and other sources suggest a few differences in levels, but Smith claimed that these were readily explained; he also noted that the Erie Canal series generally match "trends and turning points" in other series.

Cyclic movements in canal wages seemed dampened relative to the general course of economic activity. For example, wages did not fall until 1843, "after the worst of the depression of the 1840s was about to be over" (Smith 1963, 307). Public works spending on the canal continued unabated in the early 1840s, so it is possible that demand-side pressures kept wages up in areas surrounding the canal. Money wages did not respond much to the inflationary pressures of the 1850s after an initial increase in 1852.

To convert nominal into real wages for carpenters and common laborers, Smith used two deflators: Hoover's (1958) price index and the Federal Reserve Bank's cost-of-living index, neither of which pertained to upstate New York per se. Considerable fluctuations in real wages were evident around the upward trend. For both common laborers and carpenters, the late 1840s was a period of substantial increases in real wages. Little growth in real wages occurred, however, from 1830 to 1845 and in the 1850s.[14] Real wage growth was slightly greater for carpenters than for common laborers; the ratio of carpenters' pay to common laborers' pay rose from 1.53 in the 1830s to 1.64 in the 1850s.

In addition to Smith's work, important archival contributions have been made by Layer (1955), Lebergott (1964), Adams (1968, 1970, 1982, 1986, 1992), Zabler (1972), and Rothenberg (1988). Layer (1955) used firm payrolls to construct a long time series of wages for textile manufacturing workers beginning in the late 1830s. Lebergott's (1964) classic study of "wages in the long term" is difficult to summarize because of the wide array of sources employed. In brief, Lebergott pulled together wage estimates for various occupations. He produced fundamental annual series covering the period from 1860 to 1900, as well as benchmark estimates for various years before the Civil War, but he stopped short of constructing an annual index for the antebellum period.[15]

Zabler's (1972) paper is chiefly of interest in that Williamson and Lindert (1980) used his estimates of skilled wages in their reconstruction of skill differentials before the Civil War (see below). All Zabler's data come from payrolls of iron firms located in rural eastern Pennsylvania. Zabler constructed estimates of average monthly wages for six "skilled occupations" (clerk, keeper, carpenter, smith, miller, collier), five unskilled occupations (filler, laborer, teamster, woodcutter, banksman), and farm labor for the period 1800–1830. Since my interest is in the period after 1820, I focus on Zabler's estimates for the 1820s.

Zabler's series generally show a decline in money wages in the early 1820s, with little further change thereafter during the decade. The most important implication of Zabler's series, however, concerns levels, not trends; in particular, his series imply much lower skill differentials than do other sources for the 1820s. For example, the ratio of carpenters' to laborers' pay (using Zabler's "laborer series") averages 1.22 in the 1820s, considerably below the skilled-unskilled gap in Philadelphia as estimated by Adams (1968, 411). Zabler argues that wage differentials in the iron industry support Habakkuk's (1962) assertion that the skilled-unskilled wage gap was lower in the United States than in Great Britain in the 1820s.

In a comment on Zabler's paper, Adams (1973) argued that Zabler's estimates of skill differentials were too low. While unskilled wages in the iron industry do not appear to have been low (if anything, the opposite was true), skilled wages were. For example, on a daily basis, carpenters in the iron industry earned about $0.58 per day, compared with $1.25 for house carpenters in Philadelphia at the time.[16] Although the iron industry may have offered more secure employment, artisanal unemployment would have had to approach very high levels to equalize annual earnings between the two locations.[17] Adams (1973, 92) speculates that skilled workers may have received some form of nonwage compensation, a possibility denied by Zabler (1972, 110), except for clerks.

Without question, some of the most important archival work on antebellum wages has been done by Donald Adams. Adams (1968, 1970) used archival records for Philadelphia to chart wage trends from 1785 to 1830. The principal source was the Stephan Girard Collection, held at the American Philosophical Society library in Philadelphia. Girard, a Philadelphia financier and philanthropist, maintained meticulous records of business dealings, and his records have yielded an abundant collection of wage quotations. Since my interest in this book is the period from 1820 to 1860, I focus primarily on Adams's estimates for the 1820s. With the exception of agricultural labor, all estimates are of daily wages.

Adams constructed annual estimates of nominal and real wages for several occupations found in the Girard records. The occupations were in either shipbuilding (e.g., caulkers, ship carpenters), construction (house carpenters, bricklayers, masons), or agriculture (daily and monthly laborers, female domestics). In his appendix tables, Adams reported a single number if all wage quotations in a given occupation were the same in a given year; otherwise, a range was given. In the text of the article, however, Adams produced an average wage for "artisans"; this is simply the unweighted average of wages in the different skilled occupations. The artisanal average fluctuated a great deal from year to year because Adams did not hold constant the composition of the artisanal sample when constructing the average (i.e., he computed an unweighted average across occupations).

A feature common to almost all the occupations was a decline in the nominal wage from 1820 to 1821.[18] Nominal wages then generally rose from 1822 to 1824, remaining more or less at the 1824 level for the rest of the decade. Stability in money wage rates was not, apparently, a characteristic of just the 1820s. After reviewing patterns for the entire period, Adams (1968, 408) concluded that money wages were strikingly stable, changing only "in response to major declines or advances in the level of economic activity. . . . This 'stickiness' of wage rates is all the more surprising when we consider the lack of effective labor organizations during the period under question." Little evidence was found of a secular trend in the ratio of skilled to unskilled wages, but there was some indication of a decline in skill differentials during booms and a rise during downturns.

To estimate real wages, Adams relied on wholesale prices from Bezanson, Gray, and Hussey (1936), in conjunction with a working-class budget prepared by one Matthew Carey in 1833. Like virtually all other studies of real wages before the Civil War, Adams's ignored changes in the rental cost of housing. Since the expenditure share for housing in Carey's budget was 0.133 (13.3 percent), Adams (1968, 413) argued that excluding housing would not alter his basic findings.[19]

In brief, Adams found substantial increases in real wages during the 1820s for common laborers. Using 1821 as the base year, the growth rate of real wages for common laborers was 4.3 percent per year. About 28 percent of this growth rate reflected a decline in prices in the early 1820s; the remainder was a jump in the money wage (from $0.75 to $1.00 per day). Virtually all the increase in real wages occurred before 1824, which suggests a delayed response to the economic downturn that followed the War of 1812. Consistent with Adams's inferences about movements in skill differentials during booms and recessions, growth rates of real wages were somewhat lower over the 1820s for artisans than for common laborers (the 1820s were boom years). Again, the choice of a base year was crucial. Real wage growth was more substantial choosing 1821 as the base year than it was choosing 1820.[20]

On the basis of his estimates, Adams drew three conclusions. First, real wage growth was considerable before 1830, which is consistent with the view that per capita income growth was also substantial. Second, money wages were rigid, and this rigidity was found in all occupations, skilled and unskilled. Third, there was little evidence of a sustained trend, upward or downward, in skill differentials before 1830.

Adams (1982) examined payroll and other records of manufacturing establishments in the Brandywine region of southeastern Pennsylvania, near Philadelphia and Baltimore. Manufacturing took hold relative early in the Brandywine (the area has many sites that can provide waterpower), and thus wage trends in the region should shed useful light on early industrialization. Most of the data were drawn from the records of two companies: DuPont and a textile firm, Bancroft, Simpson, and Eddystone.

Converting Adams's annual estimates to decadal averages, the monthly wages of male manufacturing employees increased at an average rate of 0.3 percent per year from the 1820s to the 1850s. Adams found, however, that growth in money wages understated growth in annual earnings; the latter increased at an average pace of 1.3 percent per year from the 1820s to the 1850s. The explanation for this (very) large difference, according to Adams, was a decline in seasonality (firms were open on a more regular basis at the end of the period) and an increase in hours of work in the 1850s. Some fluctuations in money wages were evident in Adams's series, but these were relatively modest compared to the fluctuations in real wages. To compute real wages, he deflated by the David-Solar (1977) price index (see below). Because this index shows very steep price declines over time, the modest growth in money wages translated into substantial gains in real earnings.

Adams also investigated wage differentials between agriculture and industry, an issue that I consider in chapter 4. The computation of farm-nonfarm wage gaps was complicated by the fact that farm labor received perquisites, like board, but Adams's data were sufficient to place a value on board. Again computing decadal averages, Adams found that the ratio of monthly wages of agricultural and manufacturing labor was about 91 percent in the 1820s and 1830s. The ratio fell to 84 percent in the 1840s, before returning to about 92 percent in the 1860s. Similar evidence of integration was apparent for female labor: the wages of female domestics and female manufacturing operatives were quite similar throughout the period. Given the difficulties of valuing farm perquisites, this evidence suggests that the farm and nonfarm labor markets in the Brandywine region were closely integrated—any deviations from equilibrium (as in the 1840s) were swiftly followed by a return to equilibrium (the 1850s). Because the markets appear to have been well integrated, a substantial shift in labor out of agriculture was accommodated. Efficiency also implies that productivity gains in one sector (in this case, manufacturing) were quickly diffused (in the form of higher wages) throughout the labor force.

Sufficient information was available on the sectoral composition of the Brandywine labor force to compute estimates of aggregate "full-time-equivalent" earnings (assuming a twelve-month workyear). Because there was a slight gap in favor of manufacturing wages over farm wages, intersectoral reallocation of the labor force raised average earnings. About 26 percent of the growth in average annual earnings between the 1820s and the 1850s was due to the shift of labor out of agriculture, the remainder to within-sector growth in earnings. Although it is difficult to make comparisons because there are no per capita income estimates for the Brandywine region, the import of Adams's calculation is that intersectoral reallocation was less important in raising wages than in raising per capita income before the Civil War.

The DuPont (and other) firm records also yield insights into working-class budgets before the Civil War. Using the estimates of the monthly cost of board provided by Adams, I computed the ratio of board to monthly wages of manufacturing workers (male only); this ratio is an estimate of the budget share for food of an adult male. For the 1820s and 1830s, the budget share remained constant at 0.39 (39 percent); it declined slightly in the 1840s (to 38 percent) and then rose in the 1850s (to 42 percent). In fact, combining Adams's estimates of room and board for the 1840s and 1850s, "real" monthly wages (the money wage deflated by the combined cost of room and board) of manufacturing workers fell from the 1840s to the 1850s. But, as Adams (1982, 915) notes, real annual wages in manufacturing rose from the 1840s to the 1850s. As a result, Adams concludes that workers were better off in the 1850s than in the 1840s.

This conclusion, however, does not follow necessarily from the evidence presented in the paper. The reason why real *annual* earnings were higher in the 1850s is that labor spent more time on the job. Unless manufacturing workers were constrained in the 1840s, working less than they wished, labor welfare (defined to be a function of the real monthly wage and annual "leisure"—time not spent working) was lower in the 1850s than in the 1840s.[21]

Adams (1986) tracked prices and wages in Maryland agriculture from 1750 to 1850 drawing on account books. Average annual prices were computed for twelve agricultural commodities, chiefly meats and grains. The account books also yielded an abundant collection of wage quotations. Like the Rothenberg study discussed below, Adams focused primarily on wages for unspecified farm labor, using these to construct nominal wage indices for monthly and daily labor.

Labor hired on a daily basis received a higher wage than the average daily wage paid to labor hired on a monthly basis, a fact that Adams attributes to greater regularity of employment with monthly contracts and to additional nonwage compensation given to workers who were hired monthly. Harvest labor also commanded a premium; in many contracts, workers reserved the right to hire themselves out on a daily basis on those occasions in which premia could be had (such as the harvest). Female and child labor earned about 60 percent of the daily wage of adult males, with little evidence of a long-term trend. The account books also provide information on the value of board, which appears to have averaged about 50 percent of total expenditure for a typical adult male.

The basic finding is that money wages in Maryland agriculture increased only slightly from the 1820s to the 1850s. If the period is extended to encompass 1800–1850, nominal wages grew at about 0.3 percent per year. Using his agricultural commodity price series as the deflator, Adams computes a real wage index, which is better labeled a *real cost of labor* index (as in Rothenberg 1988). This real wage series registers a decline from the 1820s to the 1850s (and even from the 1800s to the 1850s). As pointed out below in the discussion of Rothenberg (1988), the real wage of farm labor might still have risen if the relative price of nonfarm goods fell in Maryland after 1820.[22] At the very least, however, the failure of real wages to rise (when defined in Adams's terms) suggests little or no productivity growth in Maryland agriculture during the first half of the nineteenth century.

Finally, Adams (1992) used account books to chart prices and wages in the western counties of Virginia from 1790 to 1860. The price series refer solely to basic foodstuffs (imported and locally produced). The "common labor" series reported in the appendix refers solely to agricultural labor (which the text makes clear), although Adams provided decadal averages of money wages for skilled workers in the building trades.

Although West Virginia counties were clearly isolated geographically, changes in the price level evident in the major wholesale markets in seaboard cities (e.g., Philadelphia or New York) matched those in West Virginia. There were, however, significant differences in the level of commodity prices. Food prices were lower in West Virginia than in Northeastern cities—not surprising since, over time, food was being exported from West to East. Consistent with Berry's (1943) evidence on food prices in Cincinnati, prices in West Virginia rose over time relative to prices on the coast, which Adams attributes to declining costs of internal transportation. On the basis of the price evidence, Adams (1992, 207) concludes that "a national commodity market was beginning to develop very early in the nation's history."

For agricultural labor, the daily wage ranged from $0.47 to $0.58 between the 1820s and the 1850s. Money wages actually fell from the 1820s to the 1850s, while food prices rose. Adams defined the real wage of agricultural labor to be the daily (money) wage divided by his price index; using this definition, real wages in West Virginia agriculture fell in the four decades before the Civil War (from an index number of 92.6 in the 1820s to 79.1 in the 1850s). The decline in real wages is consistent with the western

path of internal migration and with commodity price equalization between regions, but Adams does not speculate on the sources of the decline.

Although the decline in real wages suggests little or no agricultural productivity growth in West Virginia before the war, Adams is somewhat cau-
tious in drawing firm conclusions because the price deflator is produced
from individual commodity price series by weighting by consumption
shares—that is, it is not a producer price index. Later in the paper, however, he shows that prices of locally produced foodstuffs were rising (prices
of imported foods were falling), which does suggest a stagnant agricultural
economy. Ignoring trends, Adams compares cycles in real wages in West
Virginia with his earlier estimates of real agricultural wages in the Brandywine region and Maryland and with the Margo-Villaflor (1987) real wage
index for common labor in the Northeast, again finding a good deal of
cyclic synchronicity.

Adams was able to measure the secular trend in skill differentials where,
as noted above, *skilled* means artisans in the building trades. The level of
the skill differential between the 1820s and the 1850s (these are ratios of
decadal average wage rates of artisans to those of agricultural laborers)
ranged from 2.1 to 2.4. Skill differentials rose in the 1830s, but declined
between the 1830s and the 1850s, and were no higher at the end of the
1850s than in the 1820s.

Winifred Rothenberg's (1992) important study of Massachusetts agriculture provided valuable data on farm wages. Rothenberg (1988) used
farm account books to examine the development of an agricultural labor
market in rural Massachusetts from the mid-eighteenth to the mid-
nineteenth centuries. Along the way, she also presented a time series of
nominal and real wages. The ninety account books examined in the study
covered sixty-five New England towns, 80 percent of which were located
in Massachusetts. Rothenberg's goals were two: to date the "emergence"
of a market for farm labor and to measure the trend in "real labor cost,"
from which inferences can be made about movements in labor productivity. The unit of observation was the daily wage by "task"; an example
would be mowing and threshing.

By *real labor cost,* Rothenberg meant the money wage of farm labor
divided by a (farm-gate) price index of agricultural output (from Rothenberg 1979). Rothenberg estimated a time-series regression of real labor
cost on a polynomial time trend. The regression coefficients (and an ac-
companying figure) suggested rising labor productivity from the 1820s to
the 1840s but a decline from the 1840s to the first half of the 1850s. In
fact, computation of decadal averages from the annual figures provided
in an appendix to Rothenberg (1988) indicates that labor productivity in
Massachusetts agriculture in the early 1850s was no higher, on average,
than it was during the 1820s.[23] However, the nominal wage was about 31
percent higher in the 1850s than it was in the 1820s. Thus, while agricul-

tural productivity did not rise appreciably in Massachusetts in the four decades before the Civil War, the real wages of agricultural labor arguably did. Such gains in real wages occurred as the relative price of nonfarm products (i.e., relative to farm-gate prices of agricultural goods) declined as a consequence of productivity growth in the nonfarm sector and improved internal transportation (Taylor 1951; Sokoloff 1986b).[24]

The studies reviewed thus far make use of either retrospective surveys or archival evidence but not both. Two important studies have attempted to splice together longer time series drawing on the Weeks or the Aldrich Reports, and various archival series are David and Solar (1977) and Williamson and Lindert (1980).

David and Solar (1977) is a widely cited paper on (very) long-term movements in the wages of unskilled labor. David and Solar attempted to trace these movements from 1774 to 1974, in both nominal and real terms. The primary sources of wage evidence for the antebellum period are Wright (1885), the Weeks Report, Smith (1963), and Lebergott (1964).

The period from 1800 to 1830 is covered by the data compiled by Wright (1885). David and Solar (1977) prefer the Massachusetts data to Adams's (1968) compilation of common laborers' pay for Philadelphia on two grounds: the Massachusetts data stretch back further into the eighteenth century, and they themselves believe that the Massachusetts sample was larger and more diverse geographically.[25] To compute daily wages, they simply averaged the quotations in the Massachusetts report for any particular year.

The period from 1830 to 1860 combines estimates from Lebergott (1964), the Weeks Report, and the Erie Canal series. The 1850 and 1860 figures were benchmarked to Lebergott and thus pertain to national average daily wages of common labor derived from the federal Censuses of Social Statistics.[26] The 1830 and 1840 figures were also benchmarked to Lebergott and thus pertain to the McLane Report and the 1840 census. Lebergott's 1830 figure is actually an average for 1830–32, and David and Solar (1977, 62) simply assume that money wages did not change between 1830 and 1832. From 1832 to 1840, David and Solar interpolated between their benchmark estimates based on geometric averages of wage rates from the Weeks Report compiled by Abbott (1905) and Smith's (1963) figures for the Erie Canal. From 1840 to 1850, and from 1850 to 1860, David and Solar's interpolations were based entirely on the Weeks data. All interpolations were trend corrected—that is, they adjust for the fact that the trend implied by the benchmark figures may have been (and, in fact, was) different from the trend of the interpolating series.

Like their wage index, David and Solar's price index is spliced together from previously available sources. Its method of construction—trend-corrected interpolation between benchmark dates—is also similar. The benchmark dates for the antebellum period derive from Brady (1966).

Because Brady provided no pre-1850 figures on housing costs, David and Solar calculate their own housing price index by geometrically averaging their common labor nominal wage series and the Warren-Pearson (1933) building price index for New York.[27]

The first steps in the construction of the price deflator were to compute index numbers for benchmark dates from Brady's data and to factor the housing price index into the overall price deflator. Next, David and Solar interpolated between benchmark dates using T. M. Adams's (1939) series of prices paid for various goods by Vermont farmers for the period before 1850. For the 1851–60 portion of the antebellum period, David and Solar linked into Hoover's retail price index, which is based on national prices.[28] Thus, the David-Solar price index is a hybrid between a Northeastern (pre-1850) and national (post-1850) price index. Finally, David and Solar produced their real wage index by dividing the money wage index by their price index, setting the base year (the value of the index is set equal to 100) to 1860.

David and Solar performed several econometric analyses of their wage and price series. Over the two centuries covered by the series, the real wage of common labor rose at about 1.55 percent per year; for the period 1774–1860, the rate of growth was somewhat slower (1.23 percent per year). Visual inspection of the real wage series (David and Solar 1977, 28) suggested a decline in volatility after 1820, which David and Solar attributed to an improvement in the quality of the underlying wage data rather than to any fundamental economic change prior to the Civil War (David and Solar 1977, 30). David and Solar also observed cyclic movements in wages, similar in duration to business cycles and also of longer duration (so-called Kuznets cycles [see David and Solar 1977, 32–33]). Finally, they note a strong coincidence in growth rates of labor productivity and real wages over the long term (David and Solar 1977, 38).

Williamson and Lindert (1980) presented a nominal and real wage series for "urban unskilled labor"—something of a misnomer since the evidence underlying the index does not pertain solely to urban areas. Since their primary interest was in the movement of skill differentials, they also present a skilled wage index.[29] The construction of the Williamson-Lindert index is described in Williamson (1975). Later, I scrutinize the Williamson-Lindert indices when comparing them with my own. My purpose here is simply to describe their general construction and attributes, focusing first on the skilled index and then on the unskilled index.

For the 1820s, Williamson relied on Zabler's (1972) skilled wage estimates. For the 1840s, he used the Aldrich Report, locating wage observations that pertained to occupations covered by Zabler's series. Three variant indices were computed: variant A, pertaining to carpenters and furnace keepers; variant B, which adds smiths; and variant C, which adds millwrights (not found in Zabler's data). Variant A, however, is used in the construction of the final linked series. Lacking suitable data for the 1830s, Williamson interpolated between the 1820s and the 1840s using Smith's (1963) estimates for teamwork even though these refer to an unskilled occupation (teamster). For the 1850s, Williamson constructed his own series from data for six industries from the Aldrich Report, linking it to variant A for the 1840s (the overlap years are 1851–54).

For unskilled labor, Williamson also produced a spliced series of nominal wages. The period 1820–34 was covered by estimates for Vermont farm labor, even though the relevance of the Vermont data to economywide movements in nonfarm common pay may be questioned.[30] For 1835–39, Williamson simply appended Layer's (1955) estimates of operative pay in textiles to the Vermont series.[31] After 1840, the series reverted to Abbott's (1905) compilation of common labor rates from the Aldrich Report, with some minor modifications. Using his nominal wage series, Williamson also computed a real wage index for unskilled labor; the price deflator was constructed from wholesale prices in New York.

A key inference that Williamson and Lindert (1980) derived from the two indices for the antebellum period concerns skill differentials. In particular, their indices suggest that skilled wages grew more rapidly than unskilled wages—the antebellum United States appears to have experienced a surge in wage inequality, assuming that the skilled-unskilled wage gap can serve as a measure of inequality (Williamson and Lindert 1980). Notwithstanding the apparent rise in inequality, common labor gained in real terms before the Civil War, as did, a fortiori, skilled labor.[32] All the growth in real wages occurred in the 1830s and 1840s. The 1850s were a decade of stagnant or declining real wages compared with the 1840s.

2.2 Antebellum Wage Movements: Stylized Facts

In the previous section, I reviewed the principal literature on antebellum wages and prices. In this section, I select three studies and examine their implications for long- and short-run movements, the aim being to establish some stylized facts. For this purpose, I use the studies by Smith (1963), Williamson and Lindert (1980), and David and Solar (1977). For the Erie Canal I report results for common laborers and carpenters, for Williamson and Lindert common laborers and skilled artisans, and for David and Solar common laborers. The time period covered by the Erie Canal regressions is 1828–60, for the other two series 1821–60.

To convert the Erie Canal series into real terms, I divide by Williamson and Lindert's price index (Williamson and Lindert 1980). To convert the Williamson-Lindert and David-Solar nominal wage series into real terms, I use both the Williamson-Lindert and the David-Solar price indices.

Williamson and Lindert's price index is based entirely on wholesale prices in New York City, while, as noted earlier, David and Solar's price index is an attempt to measure retail prices.

Panel A of table 2.1 reports the coefficient of a time trend from regressions of the log of the real wage. All the coefficients are statistically significant at the 1 percent level. For common labor, the growth rates range from 1.2 to 1.9 percent per year, depending on the nominal wage series and the price index. Note that, compared to deflating by the Williamson-Lindert price index, deflating by the David-Solar price index adds 0.24 (in log terms) to the growth rate, or about 0.24 percent per year. Over the forty-year period, this adds about 10 percent to the cumulative growth of real wages—not a trivial sum, but not a substantial one, either.

The trend growth of skilled wages (1.6–2.5 percent per year) exceeded the trend growth of unskilled wages. The difference is not statistically significant in the case of the Erie Canal series but is statistically and economically significant in the case of the Williamson-Lindert series. The difference (0.9 percent per year) forms an important part of the basis for Williamson and Lindert's (1980) contention that a "surge" in skill differentials took place before the Civil War.

The results of the trend regressions suggest that, in the long run, real wages grew from 1820 to 1860 for both skilled and unskilled labor and possibly faster for the former than for the latter. Less consensus is evident, however, on short-run movements. Panel B reports the coefficients of dummy variables for five-year intervals. The left-out dummy variable is 1856–60.

In the case of common labor, the Erie Canal series shows little growth from the late 1820s to the late 1830s. Real wages grow substantially, however, during the early 1840s, an increase that was sustained in the late 1840s. However, little further growth occurred in the 1850s; that is, the 1850s appears to have been a decade of real wage stagnation for common labor, according to the Erie Canal data.

Whether the Williamson-Lindert wage series is deflated by the Williamson-Lindert or the David-Solar price indices, the early 1830s emerges as a period of very rapid real wage growth, in contrast to the Erie Canal series. Growth continued from the early 1830s to the late 1830s; however, the extent of growth is somewhat larger if the David-Solar index is used as the deflator. As in the case of the Erie Canal series, the Williamson-Lindert series suggests that growth occurred in the early 1840s, growth that was then sustained into the late 1840s. The Williamson-Lindert price index implies that real wages of common laborers actually peaked in the late 1840s, while the David-Solar price index suggests that some slight additional growth (about 4 percent) took place during the 1850s. Regardless of the price index, the Williamson-Lindert wage series suggests that

Table 2.1   Growth Rates of Real Wages, 1821–60

	A. Average Annual Rates of Growth, Linear Trend ($\ln w = \alpha + \beta T + \varepsilon$)	
	β	t-Statistic
Erie Canal (1828–60):		
Common labor:		
WL	.0136	7.014
DS	.0140	14.097
Carpenters:		
WL	.0158	6.025
DS	.0162	8.054
Williamson-Lindert:		
Common labor:		
WL	.0161	9.809
DS	.0184	13.950
Skilled labor:		
WL	.0252	14.693
DS	.0276	19.172
David-Solar (unskilled):		
WL	.0119	7.523
DS	.0143	10.965

	B. Real Wage Indices by Five-Year Periods (1856–60 = 100)						
	1821–25	1826–30	1831–35	1836–40	1841–45	1846–50	1851–55
Erie Canal (1828–60):							
Common labor:							
WL		72.0	74.2	76.6	101.1	102.6	100.5
DS		66.4	73.4	82.7	85.7	91.3	102.2
Carpenters:							
WL		69.0	71.9	69.1	98.9	97.6	99.9
DS		63.5	71.1	74.5	83.8	86.9	101.7
Williamson-Lindert:							
Common labor:							
WL	60.2	66.0	78.1	80.3	105.4	107.8	96.8
DS	52.6	59.6	77.3	86.5	89.3	96.0	98.4
Skilled labor:							
WL	45.4	52.8	64.1	69.4	93.8	108.4	100.3
DS	39.7	47.7	63.4	74.9	79.6	96.6	102.0
David-Sollar (unskilled):							
WL	70.2	73.1	68.4	82.6	98.7	98.1	94.6
DS	61.4	66.1	67.6	89.0	83.6	87.4	96.3

Source: See text.

Note: WL = Williamson-Lindert price deflator. DS = David-Solar price deflator. T = linear trend.

real growth was slower after 1840 than before and that the decade of the 1850s saw little or no growth.

The David-Solar series differs considerably from the others; in particular, real wage growth appears much more consistent across decades compared with the other indices. According to the David-Solar index, the late 1830s witnessed a spectacular jump in real wages. However, the path followed by real wages in the early 1840s is influenced by the price deflator: if the David-Solar price index is used, real wages fell, but, if the Williamson-Lindert price index is used, they rose. The choice of a price deflator matters in judgments about the 1850s: reasonably robust growth (about 14 percent) between the periods 1846–50 and 1856–60 if the David-Solar index is used but stagnation if the Williamson-Lindert series is used.

The results for artisanal wages resemble those for common wages (allowing for the trend in the skill differential noted above). The Erie Canal series suggests that artisanal wages experienced little growth in the 1830s, a big jump in the early 1840s that was maintained into the late 1840s, and little growth (about 2.5 percent) in the 1850s. According to the Williamson-Lindert series, skilled wages grew substantially from the early 1820s to the late 1830s and again in the early 1840s and late 1840s but actually fell through the 1850s. Comparing the late 1850s to the early 1820s, the skilled index grew by 0.282 (in logs) relative to the unskilled index; fully 49 percent ($= 0.139/0.282$) of that growth occurred before 1840.

As noted above, the David-Solar real wage index suggests different real wage patterns in certain subperiods than do the other two indices. Although differences in the numerator—nominal wages—play a role (see chap. 3), many of the differences across indices can be traced to certain highly questionable features of the David-Solar price deflator. First, the David-Solar price index shows a much greater decline in the price level from the early 1820s to the early 1830s than do other price indices. This is a consequence of using Vermont prices as the interpolating series; the Vermont series (Adams 1939) shows a much steeper rate of decline than do wholesale prices. Although David and Solar corrected the Adams interpolator for its excessive downward trend relative to Brady's benchmarks, they had no benchmark for the early 1820s. That the Adams interpolator gives too steep a rate of decline is suggested by a regression that David and Solar estimated of their price index against wholesale prices in Philadelphia, which shows a far smaller *predicted* decline in prices from the early 1820s to the early 1830s than the actual David-Solar index.

Second, the David-Solar price index shows a considerably smaller increase in prices from 1834 to 1839 (especially from 1834 to 1836) than do other price indices.[33] Some of this smaller rate of inflation can be traced to Brady's (1966) data and David-Solar's expenditure weights. Brady's data show sharp declines in the prices of coffee and tea (two consumption staples) between 1834 and 1836, declines not present in wholesale price data. Brady's data also show extraordinary short-run declines in the prices of several clothing items, such as hosiery and buttons. In constructing their price index, David and Solar gave a lower weight to food (39.5 percent) than is customary in nineteenth-century price indices, which tends to dampen price increases in the mid-1830s and hence show larger increases in real wages in the late 1830s than are warranted.[34]

Regarding the 1850s, the basic reason why the David-Solar price index produces an increase in real wages turns on the behavior of the subindices making up Hoover's (1960) price index. The Hoover food price index shows a much smaller increase in food prices after 1851 than do other price indices and virtually no change in clothing prices despite very large increases in the wholesale prices of cotton and leather. The Hoover housing price index, as well, shows virtually no increase in housing prices after 1851, but recent research indicates that rents did rise, at least in the urban Northeast (Margo 1996; see also chap. 3 below). The basic problem, noted by Lebergott (1964), is that the price data in the Weeks Report pertained primarily to company stores and company-owned housing in small towns. Price movements from the late 1840s to the Civil War in Hoover's index (and thus David and Solar's) may be artificially dampened, therefore, leading to too rosy a picture of real wage growth.

In sum, my analysis of the three data series reveals two important stylized facts. First, long-run growth rates were positive over the period 1820–60, ranging from a low of 1.2 to a high of 2.5 percent per year, depending on the series. The best current estimate of the growth rate of per capita income between 1820 and 1860 is 1.2 percent per year (Weiss 1992). Thus, the three data series suggest that real wages grew at least at the rate of per capita income and quite possibly faster—and, a fortiori, faster than output per worker because the aggregate labor force participation rate rose between 1820 and 1860.[35] Second, growth was not continuous; real wages grew more rapidly in some subperiods than in others and may even have declined at certain points.

But the evidential basis on which these stylized facts rest is tenuous. There are differences across the series in trend growth rates and, more important, short-run movements. As noted above, the sources of these differences are both the numerators, the nominal wage indices, and the denominators, the price indices.

Even if the discrepancies could be resolved, there is still the fundamental problem that the wage data pertain to the Northeast. This would not be a problem if the vast majority of workers lived in the Northeast throughout the period or if wage series moved in a similar manner at all locations. But, as discussed in detail in chapter 5, the Northeastern share of the labor force declined sharply between 1820 and 1860. The geographic evidence on wages collected in the pre–Civil War national surveys discussed earlier suggests that wage levels varied across regions (Lebergott

1964). Given the redistribution of population, it would be highly prema-
ture to presume that the existing series of real wages are appropriate for
other regions or for the nation as a whole. Without series for other regions,
it is obviously impossible to investigate the effect of population redistribution on regional wage differences—that is, regional labor market integration (see chap. 5).

Perhaps because they are more sensitive to the frailties of historical evidence, labor historians are much more skeptical than economic historians
about the course of real wages before the Civil War. Some of this skepti-
cism concerns issues that I have not directly addressed—such as the "de-
skilling" of artisanal trades attendant to the decline of the artisanal shop,
the use of outwork, the effect of a more intense and regimented workplace
through the use of the factory system, and unemployment, among other
issues—and that, given the limitations of the available evidence, probably
never will be addressed. Still, conventionally defined real wages—such as
those discussed above and those newly developed in chapter 3—are relevant to the historical debate. While basing their arguments on a thick web
of historical evidence—some quantitative, some not—some historians
flatly deny that real wages rose before the Civil War or else emphasize that
growth was slow, erratic, and negative at times (Sullivan 1955, 31; Ware
1924, 32; Wilentz 1984, 117, 363; Licht 1995, 68).

The primary contribution of this book is to improve the measurement
of the numerator of the real wage index, that is, the measurement of nominal wages. I do this by expanding the existing body of wage evidence for
the antebellum period in terms of occupations and location. The loca-
tional component of the evidence, in particular, permits me to study issues
of labor market integration in chapters 4–6 in ways impossible with previously collected series.

Although the emphasis is on wages, I do make minor contributions to
the denominator (prices)—first, by constructing regional price deflators
from primary sources (albeit previously collected wholesale price data)
and, second, by incorporating some new archival evidence on housing
prices (Margo 1996). To expand the body of price evidence for the antebellum period to an analogous degree as I have for nominal wages would
have vastly increased the scope of this research project—and, indeed, may
ultimately prove an impossible undertaking for any economic historian.
Nonetheless, the limitations of the price evidence must always be kept in
mind in using the series developed in this book. Improving the existing
body of price evidence for the antebellum period remains a priority for
future research (see chap. 7).

2.3   New Evidence on Antebellum Wages

Section 2.1 reviewed the existing literature on antebellum wages. Previously constructed series have been based on retrospective data contained in surveys conducted after the Civil War, or in archival records, or in (some combination of) both. The retrospective data are inherently limited in sample size. Archival series, like those for the Erie Canal, are based on large samples but obviously pertain to a single location. The restriction to a single location is not necessarily a limitation—it could be that antebellum labor markets were sufficiently integrated that series for any given location are representative of the entire country. But such an assumption needs to be investigated, not assumed.

In this section, I discuss two new sources of wage evidence developed for this book. The first source consists of payrolls of civilian workers employed at military installations throughout the United States. Compared with other sources of antebellum wage evidence, the payrolls cover a vastly broader array of locations and occupations. The manuscript Census of Social Statistics for 1850 and 1860 is the second source. This source contains even greater detail on wage variations across locations than the payroll sample, albeit for only two points in time; in addition, it contains evidence crucial for constructing location-specific cost-of-living deflators.

2.3.1   *Reports of Persons and Articles Hired*

Civilians were employed at military installations throughout the nineteenth century. The installations most commonly employing civilians were forts, naval yards, and arsenals. Although the original payrolls do not appear to have survived, duplicates were prepared and sent to Washington, where they were used to keep track of expenses and to prepare budgets. These duplicates were eventually filed and stored at the National Archives, in Record Group 92.

By far the most extensive collection of surviving payrolls pertains to civilian employees at forts. As it forged a path for western settlement, and as it sought to protect the coastal seaways, the United States Army built and maintained a large number of posts throughout the United States. The great majority of these posts employed civilians in a wide variety of occupations found in civilian life. Civilians were hired as carpenters, masons, painters, and plasterers and in other building trades; as unskilled laborers; as cooks and teamsters; as inspectors, clerks, and foragemasters; as spies on occasion; and in many other jobs.

The tasks of building, maintaining, and supplying the forts, along with the transportation of troops and supplies, fell to the Quartermaster's Department. At each post, an officer was placed in charge of these tasks. Following the reorganization of the Quartermaster's Department in 1818, post quartermasters were required to maintain payroll records documenting the hiring and pay of the post's civilian employees, the so-called *Report of Persons and Articles Hired.* The individual in charge of maintaining fort supplies and monitoring civilian employees was called the *quartermaster.*[36] Although there were slight variations, the *Reports* are, by and large, standardized, which greatly simplifies collection of the information contained in them.

In general, the following information was reported for each worker (almost all workers were male): the date and place of hire (i.e., the fort); his money wage, daily or monthly; the number of days worked per month; whether he received army rations and, if so, how many; and his occupation or a description of the task performed. Slaves were employed at forts in the South, and there the worker's legal status (slave or free) was commonly notated. At forts hiring only a small number of workers, the name of each worker might be notated, but the recording of names was not consistent across forts or over time.

The civilian payrolls on which this study relies owe their existence largely to the peacetime army's efforts to tame the wilderness (Prucha 1953). It is fortunate that some forts established during and just after the American Revolution in the Northeast and Middle Atlantic colonies remained in operation well after their usefulness as defense posts against British aggression had ceased—otherwise, I would have little to contribute to the literature on the course of wages on the Eastern Seaboard and urban areas like Philadelphia or New York.

The regular army's role in forging a path for western settlement is well known (Prucha 1969). Forts were built in advance of settlement, serving as entrepôts for trade with Native Americans and as "central places" for burgeoning local economies. Many were located near navigable waterways or early settlements that would eventually become major urban areas. For example, forts were located near New Orleans, St. Louis, Baton Rouge, Pittsburgh, Des Moines, Leavenworth, Kansas, and San Francisco. Some installations were located in exceedingly remote areas and remained inaccessible throughout the period (indeed, to this day).

American antipathy toward a standing army and congressional reluctance to provide the necessary revenues meant that army resources were frequently stretched to the limit. Prospective settlers wanted the army to remove the threat of attack from Native Americans by whatever means necessary—unless the settlers benefited from the whiskey trade or other dubious activities. Congress was reluctant to finance its activities, but it expected that the army would serve as a buffer between settlers and Native Americans, all the while expanding the frontier.

Niggardly congressional support meant that the hard work of operating the forts fell squarely on the shoulders of the soldiers and officers. Men who enlisted were frequently unaware that some portion of their time would be spent in the sort of manual labor that they may have been trying to escape in civilian life. "I am deceived," wrote one such enlistee in 1838:

> I enlisted for a soldier because I preferred military duty to hard work; I was never given to understand that the implements of agriculture and the mechanic's tools were to be placed in my hands before I had received a musket or drawn a uniform coat. I was never told that I would be called on to make roads, build bridges, quarry stone, burn brick and lime, carry the hod, cut wood, hew timber, construct it into rafts and float it to the garrisons, make shingles, saw plank, build mills, maul rails, drive teams, make hay, herd cattle, build stables, construct barracks, hospitals, etc., etc. . . . I was never given to understand that such duties were customary in the army, much less that I would be called on to perform them, or I never would have enlisted. I enlisted to avoid work, and here I am, compelled to perform three or four times the amount of labor I did before my enlistment. (quoted in Prucha 1969, 169–70)

Perhaps because of the physical burden imposed on the soldiers, posts were constructed that frequently went beyond the purely functional. On visiting Fort Atkinson in 1823, the duke of Wurttemberg commented favorably on the "good-looking, white washed buildings," the spacious administrative quarters, the ample storehouses, and the numerous artisanal facilities. "The American military establishment," he proclaimed, "must be looked upon as a great industrial center, which provides the post with all its requirements even beyond its needs" (quoted in Prucha 1969, 176–77).

At some locations, the soldier's job extended to growing his own food. A War Department directive in 1818 established a field cultivation program in an attempt to see whether forts could become self-sufficient in foodstuffs (Prucha 1969, 181). Soldiers at Fort Atkinson implemented the directive with a vengeance, harvesting over twenty-six thousand bushels of corn in 1823. The opportunity cost of time spent farming was time spent at military training. When Inspector General George Croghan visited Fort Atkinson in 1826, he noted the "barn yards that would not disgrace a Pennsylvania farmer" and "the herds of cattle that would do credit to a Potomac grazier, yet where is the gain in this, either to the soldiers or to the government?" (quoted in Prucha 1969, 182). Croghan's observations notwithstanding, the farming program lasted until 1833; subsequently, it was revived after the Mexican War for frontier locations that were distant from civilian sources of supply.

Inevitably, however, there were important and recurring labor demands for which soldiers could not be spared or the necessary skills could not be found among the troops. In such instances, post quartermasters turned to the civilian labor market (Risch 1962, 211; Prucha 1953, 165–69; Prucha 1969).[37] At many forts, the demand for civilian labor was sporadic and small, creating many apparent gaps in the records; at others, civilians were routinely hired in large numbers.[38]

A preliminary sampling of the extant payrolls was begun in 1981. This sampling attempted to include every surviving payroll from 1820 to 1844. From 1844, the sampling included every extant payroll where total retrieval was feasible (e.g., forts in large cities in the Northeast) and a selection of reports where total retrieval was too costly. An extract from the preliminary sample formed the basis for earlier estimates of nominal and real daily wages of unskilled laborers, artisans, and clerks by census region from 1820 to 1856 (Margo and Villaflor 1987; Goldin and Margo 1992b). For the purposes of this book, the sampling was carried forward to 1860.

The *Reports* do not exhaust available wage information from military records at the National Archives.[39] Arsenals and naval yards also hired civilians in large numbers, and their payroll records survive. The *Reports,* however, are much easier to collect than these alternative sources, and, except in a few instances, I make no use of arsenal or naval records.[40]

Table 2.2 shows the distribution of the full sample of payrolls drawn from locations in the Northeast, Midwest, and Southern states.[41] Observations are grouped within census region by the state in which the fort was located, decade, and occupational category. The definition of *census region* is the modern one (see, however, below). The full sample is larger than the sample used to produce time series of nominal wage estimates (see chap. 3), but the smaller sample does not differ significantly in its distributional characteristics from the full sample.[42] The unit of observation in table 2.2—and elsewhere when the payroll sample is analyzed—is the "person-month"; that is, each worker appears once for every month he worked. Counting in this manner produces a grand total of 56,190 wage observations.[43] The number of observations per decade is large, except in the 1820s.[44]

It is clear that the geographic coverage of the sample is very wide—far wider than any wage data used in previous studies of the antebellum period. Within the Midwest and South Central states, there is a tendency for frontier locations to be overrepresented compared with the geographic dispersion of population.[45] This is especially true in the Midwest, where locations in the Old Northwest states of Ohio and Michigan are represented by relatively few observations.

For the primary analysis in chapter 3, where I use the payroll sample to generate time series of nominal wages, I rely on the regional categorization of table 2.2. However, a case can be made that Pittsburgh was sufficiently "Midwestern" before the Civil War to include in the Midwest samples (see, e.g., Berry 1943). Chapter 3 also presents wage series for the Northeast and Midwest under this alternative regional definition.

The range of occupations in the sample is exceedingly wide, certainly

Table 2.2   **Distribution of Observations: *Reports* Sample**

	Unskilled		Artisans		White Collar	
	N	Share of Total	N	Share of Total	N	Share of Total
Northeast:						
1820–30	540	.116	147	.053	404	.132
1831–40	1,037	.222	1,203	.435	951	.311
1841–50	1,226	.262	797	.288	983	.321
1851–60	1,872	.400	619	.224	722	.236
New York City	657	.141	166	.060	637	.208
Upstate New York	445	.095	894	.323	136	.044
Philadelphia	2,650	.567	641	.232	1,071	.350
Carlisle, Pa.	361	.077	422	.153	163	.053
Pittsburgh	303	.065	21	.008	355	.116
Southern New England	156	.033	202	.073	630	.206
Northern New England	102	.022	420	.152	68	.022
Total	4,675		2,766		3,060	
Midwest:						
1820–30	127	.013	169	.026	284	.156
1831–40	1,218	.128	1,285	.197	632	.347
1841–50	1,386	.146	2,107	.323	442	.242
1851–60	6,794	.713	2,967	.454	465	.255
Ohio	42	.004	49	.008	127	.070
Michigan	403	.042	388	.059	380	.208
Iowa-Wisconsin-Minnesota	470	.049	1,272	.195	110	.060
Missouri	1,180	.124	592	.091	831	.456
Kansas	7,394	.776	4,227	.648	375	.206
Total	9,525		6,528		1,823	
South Atlantic:						
1820–30	555	.064	910	.182	334	.115
1831–40	5,134	.590	1,889	.376	1,350	.463
1841–50	2,611	.299	1,749	.348	886	.304
1851–60	409	.047	481	.096	342	.117
Maryland, D.C.	369	.042	449	.089	632	.217
Virginia	1,157	.133	582	.116	330	.113
N. Carolina	61	.007	133	.026	N.A.	N.A.
S. Carolina	408	.047	253	.050	349	.120
Georgia	487	.056	650	.129	265	.091
Florida	6,227	.715	2,962	.593	1,336	.459
Total	8,709		5,029		2,912	
South Central:						
1820–30	316	.049	306	.092	167	.118
1831–40	1,103	.172	1,046	.315	466	.329
1841–50	1,732	.270	1,270	.382	418	.295
1851–60	3,271	.509	700	.211	366	.258
Arkansas	3,051	.475	1,408	.424	359	.253
Kentucky	155	.024	254	.076	35	.025
Tennessee	184	.029	122	.037	46	.032
Alabama-Mississippi	160	.025	144	.043	15	.011
Louisiana	2,878	.448	1,394	.420	962	.679
Total	6,422		3,322		1,417	
Grand total	29,331		17,645		9,214	

Source: See the text. Unit of observation is a person-month.

Note: N.A. = no observations. Florida observations from 1835 to 1842 included in South Atlantic totals (see n. 41 in text).

compared to other sources of antebellum wage evidence.[46] Some of the occupations at the posts were unusual or specific to military activities, such as "Indian guide" or "spy," but the majority were not military specific and could readily be classified as unskilled (e.g., common laborer), artisan (e.g., mason), or white collar (e.g., clerk). Typical occupations of civilian employees at the forts were carpenter, clerk, laborer, mason, painter, and teamster, occupations that were also extremely common elsewhere in the antebellum economy.[47]

2.3.2   Censuses of Social Statistics, 1850 and 1860

In 1850, 1860, and—for the final time—1870, the federal government conducted a Census of Social Statistics whose purpose was to supplement the information collected on population, manufacturing, and agriculture. Data were canvased on aggregate wealth, the number and type of churches, the number of libraries, the extent of pauperism, and several other variables, including agricultural yields.[48] In addition, census marshals were instructed to collect information on the average monthly wage of farm laborers, with board; the average daily wage of nonfarm laborers, with board; the average daily wage of nonfarm laborers, without board; the average weekly wage of female domestics, with board; and the average weekly cost of board to "laboring men."

The instructions to the marshals specified that the social statistics were to be collected for civil subdivisions of counties "as far as practicable" and that information was "not to be ascertained entirely by personal inquiry of individuals, but in part from public records and reports, and public offices of towns, counties, states, or other sources of information" (DeBow 1853, xxiv). While "public records" may have been sufficient to determine the number of libraries or the number of individuals receiving poor relief, it is highly doubtful that such records would provide the necessary wage evidence, and it is reasonable to assume that marshals obtained the great bulk of quotations from "personal inquiry of individuals."[49]

State averages of wages from the social statistics were published in the 1850 and 1860 censuses, and these have long been deemed reliable—and relied on—by economic historians (Lebergott 1964). However, microfilms of the census manuscripts for a number of states are available at the National Archives or from various state archives. For the purposes of this study, I retrieved and computerized the information on wages and the cost of board from the census manuscripts for the states shown in table 2.3. The number of observations given for each state indicate the number of minor civil divisions; later, when I analyze the data (e.g., in chap. 4), I aggregate to the county level. While these states do not constitute a random sample of all states, it is clear that coverage is geographically wide.

I use the census manuscript data for two purposes. The first use (see

Table 2.3   **Distribution of Observations: Census of Social Statistics Sample**

	1850		1860	
	MCDs	Counties	MCDs	Counties
Alabama	54	43	63	47
Delaware	20	3	24	3
Florida	23	23	34	32
Georgia	89	88	130	113
Iowa	62	35	375	92
Illinois			540	100
Kentucky	141	97	115	104
Kansas			63	22
Louisiana	52	43	60	46
Massachusetts	311	14	334	14
Michigan	302	33	289	58
North Carolina	98	76	113	84
Pennsylvania	1,137	63	1,465	65
South Carolina	46	29	42	27
Tennessee	157	76	97	74
Texas	65	60	117	108
Virginia	151	130	165	141
Washington			17	17
Total	2,708	813	4,043	1,147

Source: Manuscript census schedules, 1850 and 1860 federal Census of Social Statistics; see the text.

Note: MCD = minor civil division. County = number of counties for which wage observations exist, after aggregating MCD observations to county averages.

below) is as a check on the reliability of the *Reports* sample. This involves matching forts with locations in the census to determine whether the pay of civilian workers in the army systematically deviated from pay in the local labor market.

Second, I use an eight-state sample drawn from the larger sample to study various aspects of labor market integration (see chaps. 4 and 5). In the eight-state sample, there are two states per census region—Northeast (Massachusetts and Pennsylvania), Midwest (Iowa and Michigan), South Atlantic (Virginia and North Carolina), and South Central (Kentucky and Tennessee). I use the eight-state sample for studies of labor market integration because it is more regionally balanced in terms of sample size than the full sample of states listed in table 2.3.

In addition to the data on wages and board, the data on poor relief were also collected. These have been used to study the correlates of the antebellum "welfare explosion" of the 1850s (see Kiesling and Margo 1997; and chap. 7 below).

2.4 Comparing the *Reports* with the Census

By themselves, wages paid to the army's civilian employees are of little inherent interest—except perhaps to a few military historians. What makes the *Reports* sample of such potential value is that the data cover locations and occupations for which little or no wage information was previously available for the antebellum period. But whether the data constitute *information* in this sense depends on whether the wages paid by the army reflected wages paid for comparable work performed for purely civilian employers.

Generally speaking, the tasks the army demanded of its civilian employees do not appear to have been unusual compared with the tasks demanded in the occupation in the civilian economy. Carpenters were hired to build and maintain forts. On the basis of descriptions of the buildings and surviving drawings, it appears that the construction of barracks, supply houses, and so on was not fundamentally different than the construction of similar buildings in the civilian economy. Masonry, painting, and plastering were the same as in civilian life. Army horses required the same amount of attention from teamsters as civilian horses. Clerks and other white-collar workers assisted officers in maintaining records, obtaining provisions, managing stores—just as their counterparts in civilian enterprises did.[50]

Even if the work were comparable, the wages might not have been. Wages at the forts might have deviated from those in the civilian economy by being systematically different in level at some point in time, or they might have deviated over time, either in the short or in the long run.

To investigate biases in the *Reports* sample, I compare wages at a fort with wages paid in the civilian economy surrounding the fort for the same occupation. Such comparisons are necessarily limited in temporal or geographic scope—if they were not, there would have been no need to collect the *Reports* sample in the first place.

One set of comparisons that can be made is between the Erie Canal and forts in upstate New York. These comparisons are shown in panel A of table 2.4. Shown are the sample mean, mode, and range of wages observed, by occupation, at upstate New York forts between 1838 and 1843, along with modal wages at the canal.

The correspondence between the two sets of data is excellent. Although it might be surprising if the modes matched exactly in the comparisons, they do match in five cases. More to the point, the modal wage on the canal falls within the range observed at the forts (except in one case). Clearly, forts in upstate New York were not paying daily wage rates out of line with wages of similar workers hired on the canal.

Additional comparisons can be made using the manuscript Censuses of Social Statistics. These are necessarily limited to 1850 and 1860, but the

Table 2.4   Comparisons with *Reports* Sample

	A. With Erie Canal, Daily Wage Rates, 1838–43				
	New York Forts				Erie Canal
	N	Mean ($)	Mode ($)	Range ($)	Mode ($)
Common laborers and teamsters:					
1838	31	.85	.75	.75–1.00	.90
1839	44	.93	1.00	.75–1.00	1.00
1840	26	.77	.75	.75–.88	.88
1841	71	.86	.90	.50–1.25	.88
1842	71	.81	.88	.75–.88	.88
1843	13	.75	.75	.65–.88	.75
Carpenters:					
1838	299	1.49	1.50	.75–1.75	1.25
1839	89	1.51	1.50	1.25–1.75	1.50
1840	115	1.47	1.50	1.25–1.75	1.50
1841	116	1.45	1.63	.75–2.00	1.50
1842	78	1.34	1.38	1.00–1.75	1.50
1843	23	1.45	1.50	1.00–1.50	1.25
Masons:					
1840	60	1.72	1.75	1.38–1.75	1.75
1841	109	1.41	1.50	1.20–1.81	1.75
1842	4	1.35	1.35	1.35–1.35	1.50
1843	9	1.40	1.38	1.38–1.50	1.25

	B. With Censuses of Social Statistics (CSS), 1850 and 1860					
	Reports			Census		
	N	Mean ($)	Mode ($)	Mean ($)	Mode ($)	Range ($)
Common laborers:						
Philadelphia, 1850	39	1.00	1.00	.98	1.00	.75–1.12
Philadelphia, 1860	190	1.25	1.25	1.16	1.25	.96–1.25
Pittsburgh, 1860	12	.96[a]	.96	.98	1.00	.84–1.00
Norfolk, 1850	10	1.00	1.00	1.00	1.00	.75–1.00
Charleston, 1860	9	1.25	1.25	1.13	[b]	1.00–1.25
New Orleans, 1850	37	1.50	1.50	1.57	1.50	1.50–1.75
New Orleans, 1860	61	2.00	2.00	1.95	[b]	1.50–2.50
Baton Rouge, 1860	15	1.25	1.00	1.00	1.00	1.25–1.25
Fort Atkinson, Kans., 1860	21	1.12	1.25	1.50	1.50	1.50–1.50
Leavenworth, Kans., 1860	165	1.15[a]	1.15	1.25	1.25	1.25–1.25
Carpenters:						
Philadelphia, 1850	1	1.25	1.25	1.39	1.50	1.00–1.75
Philadelphia, 1860	60	1.54[a]	1.54	1.59	1.50	1.25–2.25
Norfolk, 1850	12	1.50	1.50	1.57	[b]	1.38–1.75
New Orleans, 1850	14	2.45	2.50	2.36	2.50	2.00–2.75
Baton Rouge, 1850	36	2.26	2.25	2.75	[b]	2.50–3.00
Baton Rouge, 1860	27	2.19	2.25	3.00	[b]	3.00–3.00
Leavenworth, Kans., 1860	8	1.92[a]	1.92	2.00	2.00	2.00–2.00

(continued)

Table 2.4   (continued)

	C. Wage Growth, 1850–60			
	Northeast	Midwest	South Atlantic	South Central
Common labor:				
Reports	.148	.223	.258	.258
CSS	.135	.221	.211	.320
Artisans:				
Reports	.237	.260	.251	.218
CSS	.160	.222	.225	.235

Note: Figures are log (wage 1860/wage 1850). CSS: computed from published 1850 and 1860 Censuses of Social Statistics; see the text and chap. 3. *Reports:* using 1850 CSS benchmarks (see chap. 3) and 1860 values of nominal wage indices (see the text and chap. 3).
[a]Daily wage estimated by dividing monthly wage by twenty-six days per month of work.
[b]Mode not unique.

geographic scope of the comparisons is wider than that of those in panel A. Comparisons with the census are shown in panel B of table 2.4. In the case of the census, *mean, mode,* and *range* refer to statistics computed for the county in which the fort was located. As in the case of the Erie Canal, the correspondence is extremely close—there is no evidence that the army paid wages (to common laborers or carpenters) that were atypical of the county in which the fort was located.

A final comparison concerns change over time. In chapter 3, I use the census data to compute benchmark estimates of nominal daily wages of common and artisanal labor in 1850, while the *Reports* sample is used to compute annual nominal wage indices. Multiplying the 1850 benchmarks by the 1860 index numbers generates a set of wage estimates for 1860, which can be compared with values from the 1860 Census of Social Statistics. As can be seen in panel C of table 2.4, the *Reports* sample (properly analyzed; see chap. 3) generates wage growth between 1850 and 1860 that generally matches up with that implied by the census data.

In sum, it would appear that, in terms of compensating its civilian employees, the army simply paid the going wage in the local labor market.[51] While this suggests that the army data approximate competitively determined wages, it does not follow that, for example, simple averages accurately measure wage levels or changes in the payrolls. An appropriate analysis of the *Reports* sample requires the estimation of so-called hedonic wage indices, the subject of chapter 3.

2.5   Conclusion

This chapter has summarized the available literature on antebellum wages. While existing bodies of wage evidence suggest that real wages were rising in the long run, there were also periods of stagnation and decline. However, existing data are very limited in terms of geographic and occupational coverage. The chapter concluded with the presentation of two new bodies of archival evidence that provide much scope for further measurement of antebellum wage levels and changes over time.

New Estimates of Nominal
and Real Wages for the
Antebellum Period

This chapter presents annual estimates of nominal and real wages for the antebellum period, making use of the sample from the *Reports of Persons and Articles Hired* discussed in chapter 2. The nominal wage estimates are based on hedonic regressions that control for worker and job characteristics. Nominal wages are converted into real wages by deflating by price indices constructed from regional information on wholesale prices. In general, the indices suggest that real wage growth occurred before the Civil War but that rates of growth varied significantly across occupations, across regions, and cyclically.

3.1 Hedonic Wage Regressions

A major goal of this book is to use the sample of payrolls from the *Reports* discussed in chapter 2 to construct annual time series of nominal and real wages. A key problem in doing so is to adjust for changes in the composition of the sample over time. By *composition,* I mean the characteristics of workers or jobs that potentially influenced wages—for example, the location of the fort.

One way to control for sample composition would be to construct average wage series for homogenous workers and then weight the separate series to produce an aggregate series. In practice, the definition of *homogenous* is data dependent since one can stratify only on the basis of observable characteristics. For example, one might imagine constructing an average wage series at each fort for all individuals reporting the occupation *laborer.* The fort-specific indices could then be aggregated by region, or for the nation as a whole, using an appropriate set of weights.

Unfortunately, the homogenous worker method suffers from a serious practical problem. Although the *Reports* sample is very large by nine-teenth-century standards, it is not sufficiently dense to implement the approach just described. By *dense,* I mean the adequate distribution of wage observations across forts. Few forts were operated continuously between 1820 and 1860, and none hired every type of worker in every year. Simply put, the homogenous worker approach would produce a large number of fort-specific series with too many gaps.

The solution that I propose is the method of *hedonic regression* (Rosen 1972). In a hedonic regression, the dependent variable is a price, and the independent variables are characteristics of the commodity under analysis. The notion is that these characteristics are bundled in the commodity. The price of the bundle is observed but not the prices of the underlying individual characteristics. The regression, however, reveals the prices of the characteristics by identifying them with the regression coefficients. A classic example involves housing—the price of a house can be observed but not the prices of the attributes (e.g., the number of bedrooms, the presence or absence of air conditioning, and so forth) that make up the house. But, with a sample of houses with differing characteristics, the attribute prices can be recovered by the regression—that is, the attribute prices are the regression coefficients. Once the coefficients have been estimated, the price of any type of house can be estimated.

The advantage of the hedonic method is that it provides a straightforward way of controlling for changes in the composition of the *Reports* sample over time. The disadvantage is that a regression specification must be imposed a priori on the data. Tight specifications—those imposing many restrictions—will, in general, produce coefficients with smaller standard errors but at the cost of lost historical detail.[1] By contrast, free specifications—those with few coefficient restrictions—aim at maximizing historical detail but, because of insufficient sample sizes, may produce coefficients whose historical relevance is difficult to distinguish from sampling error.

The specification that I adopt imposes some coefficient restrictions while maintaining the goal of producing annual time series. The regression specification is

$$\ln w_{it} = X_{it}\beta + \Sigma\delta_t D_t + \varepsilon_{it},$$

where $\ln w_{it}$ is the log of the daily wage pertaining to observation i, which is observed in time period t; the X's are worker and job characteristics; β is a vector of regression coefficients; the D's are time-period dummies; and ε is an error term.[2] One of the δ_t's refers to the base period—for example, the final time period, T—and its value is set equal to zero by definition $(\delta_T = 0)$.

This specification divides up the dependent variable, $\ln w$, into two parts. The first part is the value of a given bundle of worker and job characteristics (X_{it}), $X_{it}\beta$. Each component of the vector β is the hedonic price of the associated component of X. By assumption, the specification holds the structure of hedonic prices—that is, the vector β—constant over the sample period. The value of any given bundle $(X\beta)$ is allowed to change from period to period, according to the coefficients of the time-period dummies. However, because β does not depend on t, and because the dependent variable is expressed in logarithmic terms, the value of any given bundle in one period *relative* to another period depends on the coefficients of the time dummies, not on X or on β.[3]

In a less restrictive specification, β would be allowed to vary across time periods—ideally, for each time period. However, allowing β to vary over time greatly increases the number of coefficients to estimate, producing the trade-off noted above between sampling error and historical detail.

While I impose the restriction that β is independent of time, I do allow β to vary across occupation groups, census regions, and—to a limited extent—slave versus free labor. Specifically, I estimate regressions for three occupation groups (unskilled laborers, artisans, and white-collar workers) for four census regions (the Northeast, the Midwest, the South Atlantic, and South Central states). The unit of observation is a person-month—that is, each individual listed on a monthly payroll is treated as a single observation. If the worker was paid monthly, his wage was converted into a daily wage by dividing by twenty-six days per month.[4] The X's are dummy variables for the location of the fort (e.g., upstate New York); occupation (e.g., carpenter); characteristics of the worker or the job associated with especially high or especially low wages (e.g., master or apprentice status); whether the worker was paid monthly; the number of rations, if any, paid to the worker; and the season of the year.[5]

The sample covers slaves employed at Southern forts, so a dummy variable is included for slave status in the artisan and common labor regressions for the South Atlantic and South Central states (no slaves were hired in white-collar occupations). In the case of both South Atlantic regressions and the common labor regression for the South Central region, the coefficient of slave status is permitted to vary across decades (e.g., the 1840s vs. the 1830s and so on).[6]

As far as possible, the time-period dummies—the δ's—refer to specific years. However, in many of the regressions, sample sizes in certain years were judged to be too small to estimate meaningful single-year dummies; instead, observations were categorized by groups of years (e.g., 1851–53). The implications of grouping years for the calculation of nominal and real wage series are addressed later. The regressions are reported in appendix tables 3A.1–3A.4.

Overall, the regressions fit the data reasonably well—the R^2's range from 0.4 to about 0.75. Although the primary goal of this chapter is to convert the coefficients of the time dummies into nominal and real wage series, I briefly discuss the regression coefficients.

3.1.1   Fort Location Effects

There are many reasons to expect variations in wages across forts. Some forts were located in undesirable or dangerous areas; economic theory suggests that quartermasters would have had to pay higher wages to attract civilian workers to such installations. Wages might have been unusually high or low in a given labor market independent of any amenities or dis-amenities associated with the fort's location—however, the evidence presented in chapter 5 suggests that such disequilibria tended to dissipate relatively rapidly during the antebellum period. Finally, the fort location coefficients may also capture unobserved worker or job characteristics—that is, characteristics not reported in the payrolls—that affected wages and also varied across fort locations.

It is clear from the regression coefficients that fort location mattered. Although the results are difficult to summarize succinctly, remote locations seem to have required a wage premium. For example, forts located in northern New England needed to pay higher wages to attract common laborers or artisans. St. Louis, too, was a frontier location, and wages there were generally higher than in Pittsburgh, Cincinnati, or Detroit.

Particularly large was the wage gap between New Orleans and other forts located in the South Central region. For example, compared with Alabama or Mississippi, common laborers in New Orleans commanded a premium of nearly 31 percent. Although some of the wage gap may reflect price effects (New Orleans was a notoriously expensive city during the antebellum period), it might also reflect a risk premium, as morbidity and mortality rates were very high in New Orleans (Rosenberg 1962). Fort effects were generally larger in magnitude for white-collar workers than for common laborers or artisans.

3.1.2   Worker and Job Characteristics

Several variables are included as indicators of worker and job characteristics—the high-low dummies, the dummy for the pay period (monthly vs. daily), the number of rations (certain regressions only), and slave status (South only).

By design, high-low dummies capture differences in pay within occupation categories that reflect differences in skill or—in the case of common labor—differences associated with arduous or undesirable tasks ("cleaning the privies"). Care was taken to assign observations to the high-low statuses in a conservative manner—that is, either there was a clear indication of such status (e.g., master or apprentice status), or the absence of a clear indicator appeared to be an error on the part of the quartermaster preparing a payroll. In doubtful cases, however, no assignment was generally made, so it is likely that the high-low coefficients are biased toward zero.

Relatively little is known about the process by which individuals acquired marketable skills before the Civil War. Sons followed in their father's footsteps, learning a trade while young or learning the skills associated with agriculture. Immigrants came with skills learned in their country of origin, which may or may not have been readily adapted to the New World. In the North, basic literacy was more or less assured for the native-born white population by the time of the Civil War. Scattered evidence for Pennsylvania suggests that the returns to formal education were quite high, perhaps as much as 10 percent per year of school (Soltow and Stevens 1981). The wage evidence presented in this chapter indicates that white-collar workers hired by the army earned higher wages than common laborers.

For young men who could not, or would not, follow in their father's footsteps, apprenticeship was another means for acquiring skills. Apprenticeships began at very early ages and continued at low (or no) pay for several years while the apprentice was learning the basics of the trade. Journeyman status followed the apprenticeship, during which time the individual might strike out on his own or, more commonly, work for a master craftsman in an artisanal shop. Production methods in the artisanal shop were traditional; in the archetypal version, each journeyman worked on an article (e.g., shoes) from start to finish, or else the degree of specialization was very limited. Journeymen owned the means of production—their tools. Although their employers tried to extract monopsony rents by limiting mobility, ultimately they were unsuccessful, and free market competition for journeymen set their pay.

The final step after journeyman status was to become a master artisan. Masters were more than highly skilled members of a craft; they were owners of artisanal shops—a type of capitalist, albeit they worked with their hands—and they were managers of journeymen. Master status was not easily acquired, in terms of either skills or the necessary financial capital. The capital requirements were such that many masters were among the first investors in or owners of the new factories that replaced the artisanal shops as industrialization took hold. But master status was highly desirable because, with it, a journeyman could achieve some measure of economic independence, security, and social and, not infrequently, political status.

In the contemporary United States, wage differentials within labor market groups, such as college or high school graduates, are very large (Goldin and Margo 1992a). My antebellum regressions suggest that large wage differentials existed in the nineteenth century as well. Particularly striking is the difference between master artisans and apprentices; the wage gaps range between 0.83 and 1.14 in log terms, or percentage ranges of 230–313 percent. Significant differentials are also apparent among common laborers, where they have more to do with compensating differentials for specific tasks than pure skill differentials. A wage hierarchy existed among white-collar workers, with the most able commanding wages far above the newly minted.

The coefficient on the monthly dummy is intended to capture the effects of unemployment risk and possibly differences in unobserved nonwage compensation. By *unemployment risk,* I mean differences across occupations in the risk of unemployment. Adam Smith suggested a classic example. In Smith's England, masons typically earned a higher daily wage than carpenters. Smith explained the wage premium by the fact that carpenters could work indoors during the winter while masons could not (masonry was outdoor work). Thus, carpenters were more fully employed during the year than masons and hence earned a lower daily wage.

Implicit in Smith's reasoning was an equilibrium argument: in the long run, the skills required to do masonry work were not much harder to acquire than those required of carpenters. Thus, if masons earned a wage premium in excess of the premium implied by unemployment risk, *and* if the excess premium persisted long enough for the supply of masons to increase, the premium would then be bid back down to its equilibrium level.

Historical evidence on unemployment risk premia in the American case has been analyzed most carefully for the late nineteenth and early twentieth centuries. Various surveys conducted by state bureaus of labor statistics contain information on wages, characteristics of workers, and the number of days annually employed. It is possible to use such information to estimate wage premia associated with less work annually and, in particular, whether any premia compensated fully for the lost work time (Fishback and Kantor 1992). Analysis of several such data sets for the late nineteenth century suggests that workers were less than fully compensated. For example, Kansas laborers in the 1880s received a wage premium of 0.18 percent per day; had they been fully compensated (assuming a workyear of three hundred days), the premium should have been 0.33 percent per day (Fishback and Kantor 1992; see also Hatton and Williamson 1991). In general, workers in the late nineteenth century appear to have received a wage premium sufficient to compensate them for about half the income lost because of involuntary unemployment.[7]

For the antebellum period, unfortunately, there are no data sets available to estimate unemployment risk premia in a manner comparable to Fishback and Kantor's (1992) study (even the *Reports* data cannot be used for this purpose). However, the dummy for monthly pay is arguably a good proxy for unemployment risk. Historians have long recognized that day and monthly wages diverged in a manner suggestive of unemployment risk premia; specifically, workers hired by the month received a daily wage that was below that received by workers hired by the day (Lebergott 1964, 244–50).[8]

Systematic evidence of unemployment risk premia in the *Reports* sample was found in the case of common laborers and teamsters. In all four regressions, the coefficient of the monthly dummy was negative and statistically significant. In the North, the premium for day labor appears to have been larger in the Midwest, suggestive of a somewhat thinner labor market on the frontier than in settled areas.

The magnitudes of the coefficients are also suggestive. Suppose that premia compensated solely for lost income and that common laborers hired monthly were fully employed (as assumed in the regressions) for twenty-six days. Then the coefficient of the monthly dummy can be used to estimate the average number of days of employment per month for workers hired daily. These range from nineteen days per month in the Midwest to twenty-four days per month in the Northeast. Although these are plausible estimates, they should be interpreted cautiously since monthly labor may have received nonwage compensation not indicated in the *Reports,* which would bias the coefficients of the monthly dummies away from zero (and, therefore, bias the estimated days of employment per month downward).

The evidence of a premium for day labor is less systematic among artisans and white-collar workers. Although the monthly coefficient was negative in three of the artisan regressions, it was positive in the South Atlantic regression. Only white-collar workers in the Northeast received significantly lower daily wages if hired on a monthly basis.

Economic theory suggests that nonwage compensation should be associated with lower wages. In particular, workers who received rations should have received lower wages, all other factors held constant. In most cases, the reporting of rations was too uncommon to control for directly in the regressions.[9] When sufficient observations were available to include a dummy variable for the presence of rations, the coefficient was negative, confirming the hypothesis.

The coefficients on slave status were uniformly negative, indicating that slaves earned less per day than free labor. The gaps in wages between free and slave labor were generally larger in the 1850s than in the 1820s, consistent with the views of some scholars that slaves did not share (at least to the same extent as free labor) the benefits of antebellum economic development (Fogel 1989). The percentage difference in pay between slave and free labor was larger among artisans, which suggests that differences in (unobserved) skills between the two types of labor may have existed.[10]

3.1.3   Seasonality

Seasonality in labor demand was a characteristic of economic life in nineteenth-century America (Engerman and Goldin 1993). Agricultural production has always been seasonal, but irregular production was also a characteristic of nonfarm activity, owing to the vagaries of the weather, transportation, and available power sources.

The best example of seasonality is the harvest labor demand in agriculture. The requirements of getting the crop in on time meant that demand for labor spiked around the time of the harvest. Although the supply of labor to the agricultural sector during the harvest was not fixed, it was far from perfectly elastic. There is abundant evidence of a harvest wage premium—that is, farmers were required to pay well above the going wage for temporary help (Schob 1975; Rothenberg 1992).

It is important to note that seasonality need not produce wage premia. What is critical is whether labor can shift between alternative uses of time in a manner that meshes with seasonal fluctuations; if this is the case, then wages could be equalized between the seasons. In addition, labor could be hired on a long-term contract, and, in agriculture at least, there is little evidence of seasonal premia in such contracts (Schob 1975).

Evidence from the *Reports* sample suggests that very modest seasonality in wages was a characteristic of antebellum labor markets, although the fluctuations do not follow any clear pattern. In the Northeast, wages for artisans appear to have been highest in the spring and fall. Wages for common laborers in the Midwest were higher during the fall, which coincides with harvest labor demands. Little evidence is found that wages varied by season at Southern forts, nor is there any evidence of seasonality in white-collar wages.

3.1.4 Occupational Pay Differences

By *occupational pay differences,* I mean the coefficients of the occupation dummies in the hedonic regressions. These coefficients reveal differences in average pay across the various occupations within the broad skill categories and are intended to capture differences in skill, additional aspects of employment risk not captured by the monthly dummy, or, possibly, compensation for capital brought to the job.

In general, masons (and painters and plasterers) were better paid than carpenters. As pointed out above, Adam Smith noted such a difference in England, attributing it to the fact that masons were underemployed during the colder months. If this were true, we would expect to see smaller gaps between masons and carpenters in the South and the North, which is generally what is found.

Some scholars have argued that teamstering was closer to a semiskilled than to an unskilled occupation (Schob 1975). If this were the case, teamsters should have earned somewhat higher wages than common laborers. While teamsters did receive a wage premium in the Northeast and in the South Central states, no such premium was evident in other regions. Finally, persons hired as clerks tended to receive somewhat higher wages than those hired into other white-collar occupations at the forts, such as inspectors.

3.2   Nominal Wage Estimates

This section describes the construction of nominal wage estimates from the coefficients of the time-period dummies. The procedure for white-collar labor is different than that for common labor and for artisanal labor, so I describe both separately.

3.2.1   Common Laborers and Artisans

For common laborers and artisans, I compute annual series of nominal daily wage rates that are benchmarked to 1850 estimates computed from the Census of Social Statistics. The benchmarking is similar to that in Lebergott (1964) in that I compute weighted regional averages of daily wage rates from state-level estimates published in the 1850 census. However, I make two additional adjustments.

First, I adjust the regional estimates to reflect the fact that the state-level figures published in the 1850 census were apparently unweighted averages of figures for minor civil divisions and also contain some arithmetic errors. The adjustment is very crude; using the eight-state sample from the manuscript census, I calculate state averages and then the ratio of the state averages from the manuscripts to the averages published in the 1850 census. Each region has a separate adjustment ratio (computed as an unweighted average of the ratios for the two states in each region in the eight-state sample). I then apply the region-specific adjustment ratios to the initial regional estimates.

Second, in the case of artisans, I further adjust the benchmark to reflect the fact that the census collected data only on the wages of carpenters. I use the hedonic regression coefficients in conjunction with reported occupation totals in the 1850 census to compute this second adjustment factor. In general, this second adjustment raises the benchmark wage because carpenters were paid less than other artisans in the building trades (recall the discussion in the previous section).

3.2.2   White-Collar Workers

It is impossible to benchmark the white-collar series to the 1850 census because the census did not report white-collar wages in that year. In place of such benchmarking, I use the following procedure, to which I refer as a *fixed-worker* series. A fixed value of X is chosen, X^*, and the product $X^*\beta$ is computed.[11] To this product is added the coefficient of the time-period dummy for 1850, δ_{50}. Thus, for 1850, the estimated value of $\ln w$, $\ln w^*$, is

$$\ln w^* = X^*\beta + \delta_{50},$$

and the estimated nominal wage is

$$w^* = \exp(\ln w^*) = \exp(X^*\beta + \delta_{50}).$$

That is, choosing an X^* amounts to choosing a set of weights, which are then multiplied by the hedonic coefficients.

The fort location weights were derived from population figures in U.S. Department of Commerce (1975, ser. A, pp. 195–209) and are averages (of population shares) for 1840, 1850, and 1860.[12] With respect to the other X variables, the weights are as follows. The weight for the "high" and "low" variables is zero, as it is for the "rations" variable; for "spring," "summer," and "fall," the weight is 0.25. The "monthly" dummy is set equal to unity because the vast majority of white-collar workers were hired on a monthly basis.

3.2.3 Benchmark Estimates

The benchmark estimates are shown in table 3.1. Among Northern regions, nominal wages were lower in the Midwest than in the Northeast, with the difference slightly larger in the case of common labor. In the South, the regional contrast was reversed: nominal wages were higher in the South Central states. The ratio of white-collar to artisanal wages was also considerably higher in the North than in the South, suggesting higher returns to educated labor (relative to other skills) in the North.

3.2.4 Calculation of Annual Series

Once the benchmark estimates have been computed, the calculation of annual series is straightforward. Let $w(t)$ be the nominal wage in year t. Then

$$w(t) = w(1850) \times I(t),$$

where

$$I(t) = \exp(\delta_t - \delta_{50}),$$

and δ_t is the coefficient of the dummy for year t.[13]

This procedure must be modified when the time-period dummy refers

Table 3.1   **Benchmark Estimates, 1850: Nominal Wage Rates ($)**

	Common (Daily)	Artisan (Daily)	White Collar (Monthly)
Northeast	.94	1.42	42.17
Midwest	.80	1.35	47.12
South Atlantic	.68	1.44	42.95
South Central	.85	1.81	60.84

Source: See the text.

to a group of years rather than a single year. In general, when the time-period dummy refers to a group of years, the coefficient is assumed to refer to the midpoint of the group. Thus, for example, if the group refers to 1824–25, the coefficient refers to midyear 1824, and the time-period coefficient estimates for adjacent years (1824 and 1825) are linear interpolations based on the midpoint and the preceding (1823) and following (1826) years' estimates.

For common laborers and artisans, the series are average daily wage rates, without board. For white-collar laborers, the series are average monthly wage rates, without board.

3.2.5   Additional Modifications

For the purposes of the calculation of the series, additional modifications were made to the hedonic estimates. On the basis of an extensive analysis of the original data and other evidence, the Northeastern coefficients of the time dummies for 1835–37 for skilled labor and for 1836 for unskilled labor were deemed to be unreliable. To estimate wage changes from 1835 to 1837, data pertaining to workers at the Boston Naval Yard were used.[14] Average wage rates for skilled artisans (carpenters, masons, painters, and plasterers) and common laborers were calculated for each year at the yard, and the resulting percentage changes in wages were used to generate new estimates of the coefficients of the time dummies.[15]

3.2.6   Discussion of Nominal Wage Series

The nominal wage series are shown in appendix tables 3A.5–3A.7. In interpreting (and using) these series, certain limitations should be kept in mind. First, as noted earlier, the series are constructed from regressions that hold constant the structure of wages within occupation-region groups over time, although this structure is allowed to vary across groups. Second, the number of observations underlying certain estimates, particularly in the 1820s, is small. The weighting procedure that produces the benchmark estimates for clerks is crude. Finally, because the regressions do not fit the data perfectly, small fluctuations in wages may not be particularly meaningful. For this latter reason, five-year and decadal averages are also shown in the appendix tables.

Caveats aside, the estimates appear to be reasonable in terms of trends and levels. Wage levels generally increased in the early 1830s, peaking midway to late in the decade. The deflation following the Panic of 1837 is generally visible in every region. Wages generally rose during the renewed price inflation of the late 1840s and into the 1850s.

Unskilled wages in the 1820s were lower in the Midwest than in the Northeast, but the regional difference disappeared in the early 1830s as wages grew faster in the Midwest. Wages in the Midwest fell below levels in the Northeast in the early 1840s, but the gap closed in the 1850s.

The trend in unskilled wages in the South Atlantic region was flat from the 1820s to the 1840s, rising in the early 1850s. Unskilled wages in the South Central states rose from the early 1820s to a peak in 1841, falling sharply from 1841 to 1847. Wages increased from 1847 to 1852, then fell slightly in the middle of the decade. On average, unskilled wages in the South Central states were about 27 percent higher in the late 1850s than on average in the 1820s.

Nominal wages of artisans in the Midwest exceeded levels in the Northeast in the 1820s and 1830s but fell sharply in the 1840s, below levels prevailing in the Northeast. Recovery ensued in the 1850s so that, on average, wages were the same in both regions.

Wages of artisans in the South Atlantic states rose in the 1830s but fell back in the 1840s to the same level prevailing in the 1820s. A similar path was followed by artisanal wages in the South Central states. Outside the South Central states, artisanal wages differed relatively little across regions, on average, by the 1850s.

The wage series for white-collar workers follow different trends than the series for unskilled laborers or artisans. In the Northeast, there was a gentle acceleration in growth rates across decades; for example, white-collar wages grew by 11 percent comparing the 1830s to the 1820s, whereas the growth rate from the 1840s to the 1850s was 22 percent. In the Midwest, white-collar wages also grew more or less continuously, but the growth rate underwent a sharp upward increase in the 1840s, an increase that continued into the 1850s.

In the South Atlantic region, white-collar wages grew briskly in the 1830s and 1840s, but growth was much more modest in the 1850s. White-collar wages in the South Central region grew by 18 percent from the 1820s to the 1830s; the decadal growth rate fell to a more modest 7–9 percent in the 1840s and 1850s.

3.2.7   Alternative Nominal Wage Series: The Northeast and Midwest

The series for the Northeast and Midwest discussed above were constructed from regressions in which Pittsburgh was included in the Northeast. Although the inclusion of Pittsburgh in the Northeast is consistent with census practice (as noted in chap. 2), some might prefer to allocate Pittsburgh to the Midwest. Appendix tables 3A.12 and 3A.13 report nominal wage series for the Northeast and Midwest deriving from regressions in which Pittsburgh observations were included in the Midwestern regression samples. In the case of common laborers and artisans, the decadal averages are about the same regardless of how the Pittsburgh observations are allocated. In the case of white-collar workers, the inclusion of Pittsburgh in the Midwest produces a series that grows somewhat more quickly between the 1820s and the 1850s than when Pittsburgh is included in the Northeast. Correspondingly, white-collar wages in the Northeast grow somewhat more slowly if Pittsburgh is excluded from the Northeastern sample.[16] In general, however, the substantive conclusions are similar regardless of how the Pittsburgh observations are allocated geographically. Analyses in the remainder of the book are based on the nominal wage series reported in appendix tables 3A.5–3A.7.

3.2.8 Comparing Different Nominal Wage Series: Unskilled Labor in the Northeast

Because there are no alternative wage series for the antebellum South or Midwest covering the full sample period, it is difficult to assess the novelty of the insights provided by the new wage estimates for these regions. It is possible, however, to compare the new estimates for the Northeast to previously constructed estimates. I compare my estimates for common labor with those produced by Williamson and Lindert (1980) and David and Solar (1977). I convert my nominal dollar estimates to index numbers because this is the form in which the Williamson-Lindert and the David-Solar series were published.

Table 3.2 provides five-year averages and rates of growth as derived from regressions of the log of the indices on a linear time trend. In several important respects, the three series agree and thus would provide the same substantive insights into real wage growth (as long as the same price deflator were used). All three indices suggest a positive trend rate of growth of nominal wages, between 1.0 and 1.4 percent per year. With regard to trend growth rates, the Margo and the David-Solar indices agree fairly closely (1.0 percent per year), while the Williamson-Lindert index shows a higher growth rate (1.4 percent per year).

However, there are important differences between the indices. Compared with the Margo index, the Williamson-Lindert index shows mark-

Table 3.2   **Comparison of Margo, Williamson-Lindert, and David-Solar Nominal Wage Indices: Common Labor, 1821–60 (1860 = 100)**

	Margo	Williamson-Lindert	David-Solar
1821–25	68.8	65.3	73.6
1826–30	65.1	67.0	71.8
1831–35	69.7	78.3	65.8
1836–40	78.0	93.6	93.6
1841–45	81.7	82.3	74.4
1846–50	84.4	88.3	77.6
1851–55	88.1	92.7	87.4
1856–60	97.2	98.7	95.2
Growth rate (%)	1.09	1.36	.99

Source: Margo, Northeastern common labor, this chapter; Williamson and Lindert (1980); David and Solar (1977).

Note: Growth rate is coefficient (β) in linear regression of the log of the nominal wage index: $\ln w = \alpha + \beta T + \varepsilon$.

edly higher growth from the 1820s to the 1830s and a decline in average wages from the 1830s to the 1840s, while the Margo index shows rising average wages in both decades. The David-Solar index shows a decline between the early 1820s and the early 1830s, while the Margo index is basically flat, and the David-Solar index displays a much steeper increase in the late 1830s than does the Margo index. Agreement between the indices, in terms of levels and the direction of changes, is better after 1840.

It is likely that splicing and other data problems involved in the construction of the Williamson-Lindert and David-Solar indices account for the differences with the Margo index. The Williamson-Lindert index shows an abrupt increase in nominal wages in 1835, an increase not present in the other indices. This abrupt increase occurs because Williamson and Lindert spliced two series together; the 1821–34 portion of their series pertains to Vermont farm labor (from Adams 1939), the 1835–39 portion to manufacturing workers (from Layer 1955). As chapter 4 will demonstrate, while real wages were apparently similar for farm and nonfarm laborers, there was a nominal wage gap (in the aggregate) between the two types of workers. Consequently, the splice in 1835 causes the Williamson-Lindert series to overstate nominal wage growth in the late 1830s.

Likewise, the jump in the David-Solar index in the late 1830s is an artifact of inadvertently mixing data from a high-wage region outside the Northeast with data that otherwise refer to the Northeast and failing to control for the resulting compositional effect. Although David and Solar purport to rely on wage observations strictly from the Northeast for the pre-1840s portion of their nominal wage index, for the period 1836–38 they made use of quotations from the Weeks Report, which actually pertained to St. Louis (see Margo 1992, 188). The hedonic regressions suggest that nominal wages were relatively high in St. Louis—hence the overstatement of nominal wages in the late 1830s by the David-Solar index.

In sum, while the three indices are in broad agreement about long-term trends and important medium-term movements, they differ in their implications for wage growth across decades and over shorter periods. It is not by chance that discrepancies between the indices are more apparent for the 1820s and 1830s than after for these are the decades for which Williamson and Lindert as well as David and Solar were forced to splice together data from disparate sources in order to construct continuous time series. The nominal wage series constructed here, by contrast, relies on consistent data and a method that, by construction, controls for changes in sample composition over time.

3.3   Real Wage Indices

To convert a nominal wage series into an index of real wages, one must deflate by an index of prices. Since my wage series are region specific, so should the price indices be. The only available region-specific price data for the antebellum period are those reported in Cole (1938), which were derived from newspaper and other listings of the so-called *Prices Current,* which pertained to wholesale prices. Using these data, Goldin and Margo (1992b) constructed fixed-weight, region-specific price indices for the period 1820–56 from commodity-specific price indices. For the purposes of this chapter, the Goldin-Margo indices have been updated to 1860, with some modifications.[17]

As deflators for nominal wage series, the new indices are clearly superior to the general purpose indices reported in Cole (1938) because the new indices are based on consumption goods like flour, pork, and coffee and exclude other commodities like iron bars that were not consumed by households (but that were included in previous wholesale price indices).[18]

My procedure assumes that price data for, say, New Orleans provide a usable price deflator for the entire South Central region. If, however, price trends within regions varied from those established in the major wholesale markets, the real wage indices would be biased. However, if changes in wholesale prices were broadly similar within regions, as suggested by Rothenberg's (1992) analysis of farm prices in New England, any such biases would be small.

Because I can measure only prices for commodities included in Cole (1938), the number of goods included in the indices is small, and certain important goods must therefore be omitted. It is necessary, therefore, to proxy certain classes of goods (e.g., meat) by one or two products, which may introduce biases. By far the most important missing commodity is housing. In effect, the indices assume that the relative price of housing did not change over the period, although there is evidence to the contrary (see below; and Margo 1996).

The price indices are shown in appendix table 3A.8. In general, the new indices trace out well-known patterns in antebellum prices. The price level fell from the early 1820s to the early 1830s, rose in the mid-1830s, declined steeply in the early 1840s, and then increased more or less continuously until the Civil War. Overall, the trend in price level was either flat or slightly downward from the 1820s to the 1850s, except in the Midwest, where the trend was upward.

Real wage indices are computed by dividing the nominal wage series by the price indices, after indexing the nominal series at their 1860 values. As defined, these show real wage growth within regions but are *not* adjusted for differences in levels across regions (for this purpose, see chap. 5). Annual values and five-year and decadal averages of the indices' values are reported in appendix tables 3A.9–3A.11.

In the Northeast, real wage growth was relatively sluggish between the 1820s and the 1830s. Growth, however, was much greater comparing the 1840s to the 1830s. Indeed, the average level of real wages was higher in the 1840s than in the 1850s—that is, real wages fell in the Northeast between the 1840s and the 1850s. Overall, however, real wages were higher on the eve of the Civil War than in the 1820s, regardless of occupation group.

Real wage patterns in the Midwest were broadly similar to those in the Northeast, with a few important exceptions. Real wages increased from the 1820s to the 1830s for unskilled laborers, although they fell for white-collar workers. For all three occupation groups, real wages rose significantly from the 1830s to the 1840s, but, as in the Northeast, the 1850s was a decade of falling real wages. Unskilled laborers and white-collar workers ended the antebellum period with higher levels of real wages than in the 1820s, but the real wages of artisans barely increased at all over the four-decade period.

The real wages of common laborers in the South Atlantic states fell from the 1820s to the 1830s, while those of artisans remained constant. The real wages of both groups rose in the 1840s as in other regions and then declined in the 1850s. White-collar wages in the South Atlantic states rose sharply from the 1820s to the 1840s and, like those of the other occupation groups, fell in the 1850s.

Real wages in the South Central region followed patterns similar to those in the Northeast. Real wage growth was sluggish in the 1830s, except for white-collar workers. As in the other regions, the South Central states witnessed substantial real wage growth in the 1840s and saw real wages decline in the 1850s.

Table 3.3 presents long-run growth rates for the new series, as identified with the coefficient of a regression of the log real wage on a linear trend. Several important findings are evident from table 3.3. First, growth rates were generally positive—that is, real wages grew over the antebellum period. Second, growth rates varied across occupations. In general, real wages grew most rapidly for white-collar workers. Third, real wage growth varied across regions, more so for artisans than for unskilled laborers and white-collar workers. In particular, both the South Atlantic and the Midwestern states stand out as regions where artisans experienced relatively little increase in real wages over the period 1820–60.

Table 3.3   **Long-Run Growth Rates of Real Wages, 1821–60 (% per year)**

	Common Laborer	Artisan	White Collar
Northeast	1.28	1.18	1.57
Midwest	.71	−.07	.87
South Atlantic	.97	.24	1.12
South Central	.85	.66	1.44

Source: See the text.

Note: Growth rate is coefficient (β) of time trend in regression of log real wage: $\ln w = \alpha + \beta T + \varepsilon$.

3.3.1   Biases in the Price Deflators: Wholesale versus Retail Prices in the Long Run

The construction of all real wage series is subject to biases. Important potential sources of bias in this case are the price deflators. As described earlier, the price deflators are constructed from regional data on wholesale prices. Regional data are clearly necessary because antebellum price trends varied across regions (Berry 1943). However, from a theoretical perspective, retail prices would be preferable to wholesale prices.

The use of wholesale instead of retail prices could impart biases in short-run movements in real wages if, for example, retail prices were less volatile than wholesale prices. I defer discussion of this issue to chapter 7. Here, my concern is whether any biases are imparted to the long-run growth rates.

Bias would occur if long-run trends in wholesale prices did not match trends in retail prices. A prima facie case can be made that differences in such trends existed. Technical change that caused improvements in the quality and especially the distribution of finished goods, particularly manufactured goods such as shoes and clothing, would not be reflected in my price deflators (Sokoloff 1986a).[19] Fuel prices are generally proxied in my indices by the wholesale price of coal, even though wood was widely used as a fuel and wood and coal prices diverged in the long run (Goldin and Margo 1992b; David and Solar 1977). The wholesale prices pertain to markets in major urban areas. Favorable movements in the retail terms of trade, however, could have been especially significant for the antebellum rural population, owing to improvements in transportation (Taylor 1951).

Because of the paucity of retail price data for the antebellum period, it is difficult to get a precise handle on the magnitude of the bias. Some sense of the magnitude can be gleaned, however, by making use of a retail index constructed by Lebergott (1964). Lebergott's index pertains to five items—textiles, shoes, rum, coffee, and tea—and covers the period 1800–1860. Three of the items—tea, textiles, and shoes—show declines in retail prices over the period 1830–60 relative to wholesale price movements. If Lebergott's prices for these three goods are substituted for the corresponding wholesale prices in my Northeastern index and the real wage index recomputed, real wages grow by about 6 percent more overall than indicated by the original index.[20]

3.3.2   Biases in the Price Deflators: Housing Prices

The price deflators used in this chapter suffer from the omission of housing prices. The implicit assumption is that, over the period 1821–60, the relative price of housing did not change in any region. The omission is necessary because the Cole (1938) collection of wholesale prices contains no information on the price of housing.

Existing housing price indices for the antebellum period are deficient in that they either are not true price indices or do not extend back far enough in the period to be of use. Adams (1975) and David and Solar (1977) constructed indices of new construction costs, but such indices are of limited usefulness because the supply of housing is dominated by the stock, not the flow (of new construction). Hoover (1960; see also Coelho and Shepherd 1974) produced a true price index from rent quotations contained in the Weeks Report, but these indices begin in 1851.[21]

In Margo (1996), I used newspaper advertisements to compute a rental price index for New York City over the period 1830–60. Data on approximately one thousand advertisements were culled from various newspapers. The advertisements were sufficiently rich in detail that it was possible to estimated hedonic regressions controlling for the (reported) characteristics of the unit along with its location in the metropolitan area. Although the papers used (such as the *New York Times*) served a middle-class clientele, a wide variety of housing quality was represented in the sample.

Like the wage regressions in this chapter, the housing price regressions included dummy variables for years or groups of years, making it possible to construct a hedonic price index. Separate indices were computed for units located in Manhattan and other (non-Manhattan) locations (e.g., Brooklyn).

According to the Manhattan index, housing prices rose during the 1830s, then fell sharply during the early 1840s. From 1843 to 1860, rents rose by nearly 57 percent, with most of the increase occurring before the mid-1850s. Except for the early to mid-1850s, when prices advanced more rapidly in the city, the non-Manhattan index mimicked the Manhattan index in terms of price movements.

Decadal averages of the Manhattan index show a 20 percent increase in the rental price of housing from the 1830s to the 1850s. Using the Northeastern price deflator developed in this chapter as the numeraire, the relative price of housing increased by 26.1 percent over the period. My results for New York City, therefore, suggest that the relative price of housing was *not* constant before the Civil War.

To examine the effect of including housing prices in the price deflator, I incorporate the Manhattan index into the Northeastern price index. The revised price deflator (COL) is

$$\ln \text{COL} = \alpha_n \ln p_h + (1 - \alpha_h)p_n,$$

where p_i is the goods-specific price index (h = housing, n = nonhousing), and α_h is the budget share for housing. I assume a budget share of α_h = 0.29 (29 percent [see Margo 1996, 621]).

Decadal averages of the revised Northeastern deflator show a slight rise (1.7 percent) from the 1830s to the 1850s, compared with a decline if hous-

ing costs are ignored. Consequently, allowing for housing costs would re-
duce real wage growth in the Northeast, compared with the series presented in this chapter. However, the upward bias is relatively small, about
7 percent—or about the same order of magnitude as the downward bias
imparted by failing to use retail rather than wholesale prices.

3.4   Conclusion

This chapter has presented new estimates of nominal and real wages for
the antebellum period. The estimates pertain to three occupation groups
and four census regions, a significant expansion of information over previous scholarly attempts, which have pertained to fewer occupations and to
specific locations, mostly in the Northeast. Comparisons with previously
constructed nominal series suggest that the new estimates are superior,
particularly for the pre-1840 period. Newly constructed price deflators are
used to convert the nominal estimates into indices of real wages. These
indices reveal that real wages generally rose over the antebellum period,
but there were significant differences in rates of growth across occupations,
regions, and subperiods.

Appendix 3A

Table 3A.1   **Regressions of Nominal Wages, Northeast**

Variable	Artisan	Common Laborer–Teamster	Clerk
	β	β	β
Constant	.568	.171	1.025
	(20.850)	(4.188)	(11.740)
Fort location:			
Upstate New York	.011	−.071	−.123
	(.642)	(−1.931)	(−2.407)
Philadelphia	−.017	.117	.139
	(−.805)	(4.071)	(5.578)
Carlisle, Pa.	−.157	.026	−.282
	(−8.342)	(.691)	(−4.306)
Pittsburgh	−.042	−.511	−.742
	(−.728)	(14.813)	(−22.795)
Southern New England	.136	−.044	−.394
	(5.791)	(−.743)	(−11.100)
Northern New England	.343	.364	−.702
	(18.530)	(5.751)	(−11.243)
Worker and job characteristics:			
High	.355	.651	.485
	(24.754)	(3.582)	(17.457)
Low	−.479	N.A.	−.370
	(−20.540)		(−7.338)
Paid monthly	−.177	−.079	−.183
	(−10.115)	(4.118)	(−2.815)
Season:			
Spring	.058	−.120	.007
	(3.441)	(−3.862)	(.127)
Summer	.023	−.014	.026
	(1.594)	(−.475)	(.524)
Fall	.041	−.008	.024
	(2.803)	(−.291)	(.491)
Occupation:			
Mason	.111		
	(12.571)		
Painter-plasterer	.047		
	(3.340)		
Blacksmith	.023		
	(1.327)		
Teamster		.078	
		(3.223)	
Foragemaster			−.103
			(−1.785)
Inspector			.013
			(.341)
Year:			
1820	−.166		−.171
	(−3.028)		(−1.739)

(*continued*)

	Artisan	Common Laborer–Teamster	Clerk
1821	−.581	−.334	−.205
	(−7.021)	(−3.325)	(−2.440)
1822	−.353	−.452	−.514
	(−4.730)	(−4.780)	(−5.867)
1823	−.285	−.366	−.445
	(−2.498)	(−3.574)	(−4.995)
1824	−.404	−.368	−.413
	(−3.904)	(−3.724)	(−4.723)
1825			−.389
			(−4.884)
1826			−.496
			(−6.646)
1825–26	−.422	−.306	
	(−5.666)	(−5.379)	
1827	−.308	−.410	−.450
	(−4.304)	(−6.004)	(−5.645)
1828	−.356	−.485	−.481
	(−7.753)	(−7.464)	(−4.817)
1829	−.398	−.442	−.332
	(−12.021)	(−5.385)	(−3.711)
1830	−.446	−.462	−.425
	(−12.662)	(−4.645)	(−3.133)
1831	−.427	−.522	−.419
	(−5.440)	(−7.828)	(−5.010)
1832	−.398	−.407	−.375
	(−7.373)	(−6.382)	(−4.910)
1833	−.377	−.417	−.380
	(−7.716)	(−5.585)	(−4.763)
1834	−.272	−.246	−.380
	(−6.030)	(−2.924)	(−4.763)
1835	−.396	−.248	−.378
	(−7.057)	(−2.849)	(−4.712)
1836	−.461	−.288	−.382
	(−11.549)	(−3.098)	(−5.080)
1837	−.386	−.103	−.208
	(−9.026)	(−1.325)	(−2.834)
1838	−.252	−.214	−.294
	(−11.304)	(−4.283)	(−3.819)
1839	−.198	−.294	−.158
	(−8.356)	(−6.428)	(−2.403)
1840	−.256	−.477	−.176
	(−10.463)	(−10.157)	(−2.575)
1841	−.244	−.292	−.243
	(−10.066)	(−6.157)	(−3.782)
1842	−.344	−.257	−.209
	(−13.900)	(−4.997)	(−2.931)
1843	−.291	−.178	−.090
	(−10.422)	(−3.251)	(−1.200)
1844	−.398		−.196
	(−13.787)		(−2.995)
1844–45		−.112	
		(−2.572)	

	Artisan	Common Laborer–Teamster	Clerk
1845	−.211		−.188
	(−4.882)		(−2.413)
1846	−.268	−.176	−.259
	(−8.471)	(−4.617)	(−4.105)
1847	−.237	−.349	−.126
	(−4.786)	(−5.798)	(−1.954)
1848	−.292	−.054	−.168
	(−8.373)	(.698)	(−1.915)
1849	−.210	−.155	−.173
	(−3.096)	(−1.456)	(−1.261)
1850	−.235	−.146	−.154
	(−6.205)	(−2.799)	(−2.327)
1851	−.286	−.228	−.001
	(−7.682)	(−1.898)	(−.009)
1852		−.127	−.017
		(−1.647)	(−.147)
1852–53	−.210		
	(−3.338)		
1853		−.135	−.052
		(−1.247)	(−.565)
1854		−.081	.014
		(−1.084)	(.176)
1854–55	−.109		
	(−3.370)		
1855		−.042	.057
		(.750)	(.888)
1856	−.006	−.004	.086
	(−.162)	(−.064)	(1.034)
1857	.005	.018	.052
	(.215)	(.512)	(.831)
1858	.034	−.154	.068
	(1.248)	(4.171)	(1.013)
1859	.040	.025	−.052
	(1.433)	(.773)	(−.751)
N	4,335	4,341	2,630
R^2	.606	.569	.812

Note: Artisan: constant term represents an ordinary carpenter, hired on a daily basis without rations in the winter at a fort in or near New York City in 1860. Common laborer–teamster: constant term represents a common laborer hired on a daily basis without rations at a fort in or near New York City in 1860. Clerk: constant term represents an ordinary clerk hired on a daily basis without rations in the winter at a fort in or near New York City in 1860. N.A. = not applicable.

Table 3A.2   **Regressions of Nominal Wages, Midwest**

Variable	Artisan β	Common Laborer–Teamster β	Clerk β
Constant	.911	.297	.760
	(30.400)	(11.900)	(5.209)
Fort location:			
Cincinnati	−.096	−.004	−.140
	(−1.786)	(−.054)	(−2.573)
Detroit	−.335	.036	−.385
	(−10.290)	(1.008)	(−10.811)
Michigan (other than Detroit)	−.198	.136	−.166
	(−8.161)	(1.892)	(−1.130)
Iowa-Wisconsin-Minnesota	−.090	.234	−.418
	(−4.703)	(7.187)	(−7.031)
Fort Leavenworth, Kans.	−.142	.266	−.028
	(−7.709)	(13.188)	(−.631)
Kansas (other than Fort Leavenworth)	−.050	.207	.142
	(−2.187)	(5.735)	(1.411)
Worker or job characteristics:			
High	.441	N.A.	.502
	(20.365)		(8.564)
Low	−.385	N.A.	−.679
	(−21.426)		(−7.505)
Paid monthly	−.117	−.392	.069
	(−7.614)	(−19.614)	(.694)
Season:			
Spring	.005	−.004	.007
	(.259)	(.235)	(.092)
Summer	−.010	−.017	.057
	(−.576)	(−1.023)	(.798)
Fall	−.019	.043	−.012
	(−1.005)	(2.447)	(.162)
Occupation:			
Mason	.026		
	(2.075)		
Painter-plasterer	.028		
	(1.530)		
Blacksmith	.058		
	(4.608)		
Teamster		−.061	
		(−5.933)	
Foragemaster			−.089
			(−1.404)
Year:			
1820	N.A.	N.A.	−.421
			(−3.423)
1821	N.A.	N.A.	−.432
			(−3.207)
1821–22	−.270		
	(−3.345)		
1822		N.A.	−.474
			(−2.933)

	Artisan	Common Laborer–Teamster	Clerk
1823		−.681	−.442
		(−4.684)	(−2.929)
1824		−.430	−.535
		(−5.154)	(−3.703)
1823–26	−.397		
	(−5.789)		
1825		−.612	−.381
		(−6.883)	(−2.399)
1826			−.363
			(−2.538)
1826–27		−.580	
		(−4.994)	
1827			−.443
			(−3.061)
1827–29	−.151		
	(−3.926)		
1828		−.432	−.311
		(−3.583)	(−1.960)
1829		−.432	−.384
		(−3.583)	(−2.718)
1830	−.165	−.433	−.429
	(−2.785)	(−3.448)	(−3.412)
1831	−.047	−.432	−.585
	(−.789)	(−3.583)	(−4.893)
1832	−.068	−.436	−.411
	(−.877)	(−4.021)	(−3.346)
1833	−.161		−.407
	(−4.212)		(−3.442)
1833–34		−.220	
		(−4.465)	
1834	−.170		−.297
	(−3.354)		(−2.464)
1835		−.207	−.434
		(−2.822)	(−3.812)
1835–36	−.228		
	(−3.092)		
1836		−.425	−.468
		(−4.905)	(−4.107)
1837	.108	.040	−.296
	(2.281)	(1.323)	(−2.544)
1838	−.106	−.248	−.233
	(−2.115)	(−2.624)	(−1.944)
1839	−.208	−.038	−.227
	(−7.540)	(−1.583)	(−2.034)
1840	−.208	−.291	−.327
	(−6.603)	(−6.412)	(−2.869)
1841	−.261	−.411	−.348
	(−9.129)	(−11.186)	(−3.111)
1842	−.341	−.273	−.310
	(−9.948)	(−5.442)	(−2.638)
1843	−.511	−.305	−.124
	(−14.808)	(−8.144)	(−.959)

(continued)

Table 3A.2 (continued)

	Artisan	Common Laborer–Teamster	Clerk
1844	−.420		−.156
	(−13.335)		(−1.262)
1844–45		−.384	
		(−11.925)	
1845	−.350		−.133
	(−8.739)		(−.940)
1846	−.535	−.372	−.081
	(−15.398)	(−8.262)	(−.674)
1847	−.402	−.400	−.236
	(−9.843)	(−7.290)	(−2.059)
1848	−.335	−.268	
	(−8.857)	(−5.238)	
1849	−.236		
	(−5.983)		
1848–49			−.111
			(−1.003)
1849–50		−.229	
		(−8.991)	
1850	−.258		−.124
	(−8.922)		(−1.046)
1851	−.127		.101
	(−3.352)		(.794)
1851–52		−.215	
		(−7.316)	
1852	−.150		.060
	(−2.961)		(.465)
1853	−.093	−.218	−.094
	(−3.238)	(−8.504)	(−.783)
1854	−.074	−.095	−.081
	(−2.434)	(−3.833)	(−.734)
1855	−.035	−.090	−.141
	(−1.148)	(−3.250)	(−1.316)
1856	−.032	−.111	−.077
	(−1.307)	(−5.327)	(−.563)
1857	.026	−.021	−.021
	(.909)	(−.925)	(.202)
1858	−.005	−.015	−.033
	(−.190)	(−.708)	(−.334)
1859	−.006	.021	−.212
	(−.216)	(1.062)	(−1.289)
N	4,482	7,691	1,752
R^2	.561	.374	.714

Note: Artisan: constant term represents an ordinary carpenter, hired on a daily basis without rations during the winter at a fort at or near St. Louis in 1860. Common laborer–teamster: constant term represents a common laborer hired on a daily basis without rations in the winter at a fort at or near St. Louis in 1860. Clerk: constant term represents an ordinary clerk hired on a daily basis without rations in the winter at a fort at or near St. Louis in 1860. N.A. = not applicable.

	Artisan	Common Laborer–Teamster	Clerk
	β	β	β
Variable			
Constant	.660	.099	.369
	(5.661)	(1.408)	(2.969)
Fort location:			
Baltimore	−.178	.440	.137
	(−6.767)	(11.763)	(2.313)
Georgia	.038	.419	.129
	(1.334)	(12.874)	(2.095)
North Carolina	−.087	−.008	N.A.
	(−2.723)	(−.125)	
South Carolina	.046	.060	.217
	(1.714)	(1.548)	(3.814)
Florida	.207	.336	.201
	(8.837)	(10.131)	(3.173)
Worker or job characteristics:			
High	.416	.511	.703
	(29.254)	(10.352)	(11.451)
Low	−.720	−.709	N.A.
	(−35.572)	(−9.762)	
Slave	−.135	−.048	N.A.
	(−5.036)	(−.860)	
Paid monthly	.009	−.332	N.A.
	(.317)	(−14.573)	
Season			
Spring	−.009	.016	−.056
	(−.433)	(.479)	(−.533)
Summer	−.008	−.008	.027
	(−.408)	(−.233)	(.288)
Fall	.040	−.086	.036
	(1.701)	(−2.508)	(.397)
Occupation:			
Mason	.027		
	(1.866)		
Painter-plasterer	.033		
	(1.633)		
Blacksmith	.087		
	(3.224)		
Teamster		−.108	
		(−5.290)	
Other white collar			−.228
			(−4.459)
Year:			
1821–23			−.251
			(−1.645)
1822–23	−.210		
	(−1.780)		
1823–26		−.316	
		(−3.529)	
1824	−.373		−.366
	(−3.174)		(−2.516)

(*continued*)

Table 3A.3   (continued)

	Artisan	Common Laborer–Teamster	Clerk
1825			−.123
			(−.757)
1826			−.164
			(−1.041)
1825–26	−.221		
	(−1.794)		
1827	−.140	−.304	−.214
	(−1.162)	(−3.423)	(−1.559)
1828	−.232	−.310	−.247
	(−1.918)	(−3.306)	(−1.615)
1829	−.133		−.275
	(−1.118)		(−1.614)
1829–30		−.417	
		(−4.685)	
1830–31	−.115		
	(−.956)		
1830–32			−.351
			(−2.390)
1831–32		−.433	
		(−5.469)	
1832–34	−.108		
	(−.914)		
1833–34		−.499	−.179
		(−7.046)	(−1.175)
1835	−.062	−.492	−.245
	(−.524)	(−6.604)	(−1.638)
1836	−.020	−.230	−.085
	(−.146)	(−3.021)	(−.610)
1837–39	−.177		
	(−1.358)		
1837		−.137	−.028
		(−1.812)	(−.208)
1838		−.236	.029
		(−3.242)	(.215)
1839		−.215	.087
		(−2.457)	(.665)
1840			.035
			(.274)
1841			−.097
			(−0.756)
1840–41	−.175	−.297	
	(−1.372)	(−3.818)	
1842	−.155	−.496	−.153
	(−1.316)	(−6.103)	(−1.103)
1843	−.194	−.484	
	(−1.650)	(−5.645)	
1844–46	−.201	−.453	
	(−1.699)	(−5.888)	
1843–47			.081
			(.635)
1847	−.309	−.233	
	(−2.288)	(−3.152)	

	Artisan	Common Laborer–Teamster	Clerk
1848–49	−.254 (−2.086)	−.256 (−3.290)	
1848–50			−.054 (−.410)
1850		−.261 (−3.527)	
1850–51	−.248 (−2.077)		
1851			.016 (.113)
1851–53		−.304 (−2.369)	
1852–53			.065 (.277)
1852–55	−.223 (−1.894)		
1854			−.011 (−.079)
1855			−.014 (−0.096)
1854–55		−.200 (−2.319)	
1856	−.194 (−1.554)	−.053 (−.636)	.046 (.337)
1857	−.007 (−.049)		−.001 (−.009)
1858	−.115 (−.960)		−.036 (−.245)
1859	−.060 (−.472)		−.049 (−.185)
1857–59		.035 (.378)	
Slave × 1831–40	−.250 (−5.691)	−.062 (−.996)	
Slave × 1841–50	−.023 (−.339)	−.040 (−.629)	
Slave × 1851–60	−.098 (−1.881)	−.179 (−1.791)	
N	3,319	3,208	1,611
R^2	.788	.588	.490

Note: Artisan: constant term represents an ordinary carpenter hired on a daily basis without rations during the winter at Fort Monroe, Va., in 1860. Common laborer–teamster: constant term represents an ordinary carpenter hired on a daily basis without rations during the winter at Fort Monroe, Va., in 1860. Slave = 1 if the person was a slave, 0 otherwise. Clerk: constant term represents an ordinary clerk hired on a monthly basis without rations during the winter at Fort Monroe, Va., in 1860. N.A. = not applicable. Other white collar = 1 if person held white-collar occupation other than clerk.

Table 3A.4   **Regressions of Nominal Wages, South Central States**

Variable	Artisan β	Common Laborer–Teamster β	Clerk β
Constant	.868	.558	1.135
	(16.499)	(27.521)	(5.327)
Fort location:			
Baton Rouge	.134	−.397	−.369
	(5.834)	(−30.684)	(−8.559)
Arkansas	−.119	−.321	−.256
	(−4.385)	(−27.480)	(−6.380)
Kentucky	−.227	−.255	−.349
	(−7.361)	(−9.917)	(−3.468)
Tennessee	−.568	.036	−.031
	(−8.956)	(1.315)	(−.299)
Alabama-Mississippi	.090	−.268	−.089
	(1.880)	(−8.477)	(.580)
Worker or job characteristics:			
High	.450	.340	.279
	(21.356)	(10.044)	(5.590)
Low	−.568	−.398	−.608
	(−23.909)	(−18.430)	(−9.912)
Slave	−.202	−.043	
	(−4.912)	(−.915)	
Paid monthly	−.136	−.194	−.046
	(−6.884)	(−19.166)	(−.649)
Rations	N.A.	−.046	N.A.
		(−2.404)	
Season:			
Spring	−.047	.004	−.011
	(−1.926)	(.279)	(−.131)
Summer	.001	−.004	.055
	(.062)	(−.315)	(.759)
Fall	−.001	−.016	−.013
	(.049)	(−1.173)	(−.182)
Occupation:			
Mason	−.004		
	(−.233)		
Painter-plasterer	.022		
	(.910)		
Blacksmith	.041		
	(1.945)		
Teamster		.010	
		(1.041)	
Other white collar			−.181
			(−4.101)
Year:			
1820	−.330	−.439	−.343
	(−3.152)	(−10.257)	(−1.543)
1821		−.388	−.443
		(−9.901)	(−1.898)
1821–22	−.279		
	(−3.584)		
1822			−.380
			(−1.578)
1823	−.201		−.502
	(−2.082)		(−2.167)
1824			−.535
			(−2.119)

Table 3A.4 (continued)

	Artisan	Common Laborer– Teamster	Clerk
1822–24		−.353 (−10.972)	
1824–25	−.239 (−3.476)		
1825–26		−.404 (−5.511)	−.364 (−1.615)
1827			−.353 (−1.616)
1826–28	−.018 (−.332)		
1827–29		−.191 (−4.148)	
1828–29			−.232 (−1.150)
1829–30	−.242 (−4.080)		
1830		−.174 (−1.896)	−.129 (−.599)
1831		−.217 (−2.748)	−.436 (−2.073)
1831–32	−.231 (−3.690)		
1832		−.218 (−2.762)	−.451 (−2.154)
1833		−.243 (−3.317)	
1834		−.208 (−4.027)	
1833–34	−.025 (−.511)		−.360 (−1.841)
1835	.021 (.448)	−.267 (−7.902)	−.400 (−2.013)
1836	.014 (.226)	−.138 (−5.872)	−.322 (−1.668)
1837	−.052 (−.658)	−.158 (−3.586)	−.008 (−.039)
1838	−.268 (−5.843)	−.409 (−14.825)	.002 (.012)
1839	−.080 (−1.741)	−.200 (−8.683)	.163 (.872)
1840		−.217 (−2.748)	
1841		−.141 (−5.678)	
1840–41	.094 (1.943)		−.072 (−.391)
1842	−.014 (.295)	−.158 (−6.989)	−.109 (−.548)
1843	−.264 (−6.050)	−.180 (−7.710)	−.224 (−1.196)
1844	−.309 (−5.976)	−.344 (−3.763)	
1844–45			−.172 (−.901)
1845–46	−.242 (−5.644)	−.437 (−18.518)	
1846			−.103 (−.518)

(*continued*)

	Artisan	Common Laborer–Teamster	Clerk
1847	−.139 (−2.247)	−.481 (−13.339)	
1848		−.399 (−11.845)	
1847–48			−.028 (−.139)
1848–49	−.160 (−2.907)		
1849		−.253 (−5.631)	
1849–50			−.139 (−.726)
1850	−.217 (−4.161)	−.254 (−10.154)	
1851		−.142 (−6.446)	−.103 (−.525)
1852		−.036 (−1.083)	−.069 (−.359)
1853		−.070 (−1.094)	
1851–53	−.096 (−2.199)		
1854	−.047 (−.741)	−.122 (−5.670)	
1853–54			−.073 (−.386)
1855	−.027 (−.311)	−.116 (−5.129)	−.099 (−.505)
1856	−.107 (−1.618)	−.129 (−6.918)	−.137 (−.736)
1857	−.015 (−.274)	−.106 (−5.382)	.200 (.945)
1858	.105 (2.137)	−.067 (−3.405)	
1859	.049 (1.181)	−.004 (.092)	
1858–59			−.010 (−.052)
Slave × 1831–40		−.123 (−1.931)	
Slave × 1841–50		.080 (1.469)	
Slave × 1851–60		−.052 (−.908)	
N	3,342	6,263	1,298
R^2	.656	.649	.705

Note: Artisan: the constant term represents an ordinary carpenter hired on a daily basis without rations during the winter in New Orleans in 1860. Common laborer–teamster: the constant term represents a common laborer hired on a daily basis without rations during the winter in New Orleans in 1860. Clerk: the constant term represents an ordinary clerk hired on a daily basis without rations during the winter in New Orleans in 1860. Slave = 1 if slave, 0 otherwise. Other white collar =1 if occupation is other than clerk, 0 if clerk. N.A. = not applicable.

Table 3A.5		Average Nominal Daily Wages, Common Labor: 1821–60 ($)		
	Northeast	Midwest	South Atlantic	South Central
1821	.78	N.A.	N.A.	.74
1822	.69	N.A.	N.A.	.76
1823	.75	.51	N.A.	.77
1824	.75	.65	N.A.	.75
1825	.78	.54	.64	.74
1826	.77	.56	.65	.76
1827	.72	.59	.65	.83
1828	.67	.65	.65	.91
1829	.70	.65	.60	.91
1830	.69	.65	.58	.92
1831	.65	.65	.58	.88
1832	.72	.65	.56	.88
1833	.72	.75	.55	.86
1834	.85	.81	.54	.89
1835	.85	.82	.54	.84
1836	.89	.66	.70	.95
1837	.98	1.04	.77	.94
1838	.88	.78	.70	.73
1839	.81	.96	.71	.90
1840	.67	.75	.67	.88
1841	.81	.66	.61	.95
1842	.84	.76	.54	.94
1843	.91	.74	.54	.92
1844	.95	.71	.55	.78
1845	.95	.69	.56	.73
1846	.91	.69	.63	.70
1847	.77	.67	.70	.68
1848	1.03	.77	.69	.74
1849	.93	.79	.68	.85
1850	.94	.80	.68	.85
1851	.87	.81	.67	.95
1852	.96	.81	.65	1.06
1853	.95	.81	.68	1.02
1854	1.00	.91	.71	.97
1855	1.04	.92	.76	.98
1856	1.08	.90	.84	.96
1857	1.11	.98	.87	.99
1858	.93	.99	.91	1.02
1859	1.11	1.02	.90	1.09
1860	1.09	1.00	.88	1.10
		Five-Year Averages		
1821–25	.75	.57	.64	.75
1826–30	.71	.62	.63	.87
1831–35	.76	.74	.55	.87
1836–40	.85	.84	.71	.88
1841–45	.89	.71	.56	.86
1846–50	.92	.74	.68	.76
1851–55	.96	.85	.69	1.00
1856–60	1.06	.98	.88	1.03
		Decadal Averages		
1821–30	.73	.60	.63	.81
1831–40	.81	.79	.63	.88
1841–50	.91	.73	.62	.81
1851–60	1.01	.92	.78	1.02

Source: See the text.

Note: N.A. = not applicable.

| | | Table 3A.6 | Average Nominal Daily Wages, Artisans: 1821–60 ($) |

Table 3A.6   Average Nominal Daily Wages, Artisans: 1821–60 ($)

	Northeast	Midwest	South Atlantic	South Central
1821	1.00	N.A.	N.A.	1.67
1822	1.26	1.31	N.A.	1.75
1823	1.35	1.25	1.42	1.84
1824	1.20	1.20	1.27	1.79
1825	1.18	1.22	1.41	1.75
1826	1.22	1.40	1.52	2.02
1827	1.32	1.45	1.61	2.21
1828	1.26	1.50	1.47	2.02
1829	1.21	1.49	1.62	1.85
1830	1.15	1.48	1.64	1.77
1831	1.17	1.67	1.65	1.78
1832	1.21	1.63	1.65	1.88
1833	1.23	1.49	1.66	2.08
1834	1.37	1.47	1.70	2.23
1835	1.42	1.42	1.74	2.30
1836	1.52	1.56	1.81	2.28
1837	1.44	1.95	1.67	2.13
1838	1.40	1.57	1.55	1.72
1839	1.47	1.42	1.55	2.08
1840	1.39	1.35	1.55	2.33
1841	1.41	1.24	1.56	2.38
1842	1.27	1.24	1.58	2.22
1843	1.34	1.05	1.52	1.73
1844	1.21	1.15	1.52	1.65
1845	1.45	1.23	1.51	1.73
1846	1.37	1.02	1.43	1.83
1847	1.42	1.17	1.36	1.96
1848	1.34	1.25	1.41	1.93
1849	1.46	1.38	1.44	1.88
1850	1.42	1.35	1.44	1.81
1851	1.35	1.54	1.45	1.92
1852	1.42	1.50	1.46	2.04
1853	1.49	1.59	1.47	2.09
1854	1.57	1.62	1.49	2.14
1855	1.67	1.69	1.50	2.19
1856	1.78	1.69	1.52	2.02
1857	1.80	1.79	1.84	2.22
1858	1.86	1.74	1.65	2.50
1859	1.87	1.74	1.74	2.36
1860	1.80	1.75	1.85	2.25
			Five-Year Averages	
1821–25	1.20	1.25	1.37	1.76
1826–30	1.23	1.46	1.57	1.97
1831–35	1.28	1.54	1.68	2.05
1836–40	1.44	1.57	1.63	2.11
1841–45	1.34	1.18	1.54	1.94
1846–50	1.40	1.23	1.42	1.88
1851–55	1.50	1.59	1.47	2.08
1856–60	1.82	1.74	1.72	2.27
			Decadal Averages	
1821–30	1.22	1.37	1.50	1.87
1831–40	1.36	1.56	1.66	2.08
1841–50	1.37	1.21	1.48	1.91
1851–60	1.66	1.67	1.60	2.18

Source: See the text.

Note: N.A. = not applicable.

Table 3A.7   **Average Nominal Monthly Wages, White-Collar Labor: 1821–60 ($)**

	Northeast	Midwest	South Atlantic	South Central
1821	40.07	34.63	N.A.	44.34
1822	29.42	33.20	34.06	47.20
1823	31.53	34.28	32.15	41.77
1824	32.56	31.24	30.35	40.44
1825	33.34	36.44	38.68	45.32
1826	29.97	37.10	37.14	48.17
1827	31.37	34.25	35.33	48.52
1828	30.43	39.08	34.17	52.63
1829	35.30	36.33	33.25	51.79
1830	32.16	34.73	32.01	60.70
1831	32.35	29.72	30.81	44.62
1832	33.81	35.36	33.00	43.99
1833	33.64	35.51	35.34	46.71
1834	33.64	39.63	35.78	47.47
1835	33.71	34.56	34.24	46.29
1836	33.57	33.40	40.18	50.05
1837	39.95	39.67	42.57	68.50
1838	36.66	42.25	45.03	69.19
1839	42.00	42.51	47.71	81.24
1840	41.25	38.46	45.33	69.47
1841	38.58	37.66	39.73	63.49
1842	39.91	39.12	37.55	61.88
1843	44.96	47.12	40.60	55.20
1844	40.44	45.64	43.90	57.15
1845	40.76	46.70	47.46	59.45
1846	37.97	49.19	45.89	62.23
1847	43.37	42.13	44.37	65.50
1848	41.58	45.48	42.90	61.74
1849	41.38	47.12	41.47	61.33
1850	42.17	47.12	42.95	60.84
1851	49.14	59.01	44.48	62.23
1852	48.36	56.64	45.95	64.46
1853	46.70	48.56	45.54	64.25
1854	49.88	49.19	43.29	63.62
1855	52.08	46.33	43.16	62.51
1856	53.61	49.39	45.80	60.21
1857	51.82	52.23	43.72	84.30
1858	52.65	51.61	42.19	64.18
1859	46.70	43.15	41.65	68.57
1860	49.19	53.34	43.76	69.61
		Five-Year Averages		
1821–25	33.39	33.96	33.81	43.81
1826–30	31.83	36.29	34.38	52.36
1831–35	33.42	34.96	33.83	45.82
1836–40	38.68	39.26	44.16	67.69
1841–45	40.93	43.25	41.85	59.43
1846–50	41.28	46.21	43.52	62.33
1851–55	49.23	51.95	44.48	63.42
1856–60	50.79	49.94	43.42	69.40
		Decadal Averages		
1821–30	32.61	35.13	34.13	48.09
1831–40	36.05	37.11	39.00	56.75
1841–50	41.11	44.73	42.69	60.88
1851–60	50.01	50.95	44.10	66.41

Source: See the text.

Note: N.A. = not applicable.

Table 3A.8　　　　**Price Deflators, 1821–60**

	Northeast	Midwest	South Atlantic	South Central
1821	112.0	87.6	103.2	96.3
1822	120.8	94.1	112.9	109.0
1823	108.5	80.5	104.8	98.1
1824	105.7	78.4	98.4	91.9
1825	108.9	80.8	100.1	99.9
1826	98.3	69.3	89.4	88.1
1827	96.9	68.3	89.2	85.4
1828	94.4	70.2	85.8	88.6
1829	91.8	80.3	84.0	87.0
1830	89.7	74.0	86.1	79.2
1831	92.5	74.8	81.9	81.0
1832	96.6	80.8	86.6	85.2
1833	102.4	84.7	92.4	88.1
1834	96.2	81.4	94.3	85.3
1835	109.6	97.8	105.8	100.0
1836	125.3	115.7	132.1	122.0
1837	117.8	108.9	115.8	111.0
1838	112.1	100.0	109.3	110.0
1839	118.1	105.1	112.1	104.2
1840	96.6	79.4	86.7	86.4
1841	89.5	70.9	83.2	83.4
1842	77.6	55.7	63.5	72.7
1843	70.7	58.2	62.4	59.2
1844	69.5	63.7	65.0	62.0
1845	77.6	66.7	71.3	63.5
1846	78.0	68.9	75.9	65.0
1847	94.1	84.0	88.2	80.8
1848	79.1	64.7	66.7	64.9
1849	82.0	71.0	74.0	71.0
1850	88.5	79.0	83.6	81.0
1851	85.2	79.5	85.7	77.4
1852	90.4	83.8	85.2	76.2
1853	99.7	88.7	88.5	82.7
1854	108.9	92.4	89.9	84.0
1855	113.0	105.4	101.7	99.1
1856	117.4	109.6	100.1	100.0
1857	121.9	120.6	112.5	109.0
1858	103.8	93.0	93.8	95.0
1859	105.3	104.2	97.0	97.6
1860	100.0	100.0	100.0	100.0
	Five-Year Averages (1856–60 = 100)			
1821–25	101.4	79.9	103.3	98.7
1826–30	85.9	68.6	86.4	85.4
1831–35	90.7	79.5	91.7	87.6
1836–40	103.9	96.5	110.5	106.4
1841–45	70.2	59.7	68.7	68.0
1846–50	76.8	69.7	77.2	72.3
1851–55	90.6	84.4	89.7	83.6
1856–60	100.0	100.0	100.0	100.0
	Decadal Averages (1851–60 = 100)			
1821–30	98.2	80.6	100.0	100.3
1831–40	102.1	88.1	106.6	105.6
1841–50	77.2	64.7	76.9	76.4
1851–60	100.0	100.0	100.0	100.0

Table 3A.9	Real Wage Indices, 1821–60: Common Labor, by Region			
	Northeast	Midwest	South Atlantic	South Central
1821	63.9	N.A.	N.A.	69.9
1822	52.4	N.A.	N.A.	63.4
1823	63.4	63.4	N.A.	71.4
1824	65.0	82.9	N.A.	74.2
1825	65.7	66.8	72.6	67.4
1826	71.8	80.8	82.7	78.4
1827	68.2	86.4	82.8	88.4
1828	65.1	92.6	86.1	93.3
1829	69.9	80.9	81.2	95.1
1830	70.6	87.8	76.5	105.6
1831	64.4	86.9	80.5	98.8
1832	68.4	80.4	73.4	93.9
1833	64.6	88.5	67.6	88.8
1834	81.1	99.5	65.1	94.8
1835	71.2	83.8	58.0	76.4
1836	65.2	57.0	60.2	70.8
1837	76.3	95.5	75.6	77.0
1838	72.0	78.0	72.7	60.4
1839	62.9	91.3	72.0	78.5
1840	63.7	94.5	87.8	92.6
1841	83.0	93.1	83.3	103.6
1842	99.4	136.4	96.7	117.6
1843	118.1	127.1	98.4	141.2
1844	125.5	111.5	96.2	114.4
1845	112.4	103.4	89.2	104.6
1846	107.1	101.1	94.3	97.8
1847	75.0	79.8	90.1	76.5
1848	119.5	119.0	117.5	103.7
1849	104.0	111.3	104.5	108.9
1850	97.4	101.3	92.5	95.4
1851	93.7	101.9	88.8	111.6
1852	97.5	96.7	86.7	126.5
1853	87.5	91.3	87.3	112.1
1854	84.2	98.5	89.8	105.0
1855	84.4	87.3	85.0	89.9
1856	84.4	82.1	95.4	87.3
1857	83.5	81.3	87.9	82.6
1858	82.2	106.5	110.2	97.6
1859	96.7	97.9	105.5	101.5
1860	100.0	100.0	100.0	100.0
	Five-Year Averages (1856–60 = 100)			
1821–25	69.4	75.9	72.7	73.8
1826–30	77.4	91.6	82.0	98.3
1831–35	78.3	93.9	69.1	96.5
1836–40	76.1	89.0	73.8	80.9
1841–45	120.5	122.2	92.9	124.0
1846–50	112.6	109.4	100.0	102.8
1851–55	100.1	101.7	87.7	116.2
1856–60	100.0	100.0	100.0	100.0
	Decadal Averages (1851–60 = 100)			
1821–30	73.4	85.0	85.8	79.6
1831–40	77.2	90.7	76.1	82.0
1841–50	116.5	114.8	101.8	104.9
1851–60	100.0	100.0	100.0	100.0

Source: See the text

Note: N.A. = No estimate available.

Table 3A.10   **Real Wage Indices, 1821–60: Artisans, by Region**

	Northeast	Midwest	South Atlantic	South Central
1821	50.1	N.A.	N.A.	77.1
1822	57.9	79.6	N.A.	71.4
1823	69.1	88.7	73.3	83.4
1824	63.1	87.5	69.7	86.6
1825	60.2	86.3	76.1	77.9
1826	69.9	115.4	91.9	101.9
1827	75.6	121.4	97.5	115.0
1828	74.2	122.1	92.7	101.4
1829	73.2	106.0	104.3	94.5
1830	71.2	114.3	102.9	99.4
1831	70.3	127.5	108.9	97.7
1832	69.6	115.2	103.0	98.1
1833	66.7	100.5	97.1	104.9
1834	79.1	103.2	97.5	116.2
1835	72.0	83.0	88.9	102.2
1836	67.4	77.0	74.0	83.0
1837	67.9	102.3	78.0	85.3
1838	69.4	89.7	76.7	69.5
1839	69.2	77.2	74.8	88.7
1840	79.9	97.1	96.7	119.9
1841	87.5	100.0	101.3	126.9
1842	90.0	127.3	134.5	135.8
1843	105.2	103.1	131.7	129.9
1844	96.7	103.1	126.5	118.2
1845	103.9	105.4	114.4	121.1
1846	97.6	84.5	101.8	125.0
1847	83.8	79.6	83.8	107.8
1848	94.1	110.4	114.2	132.2
1849	98.9	111.1	105.1	117.7
1850	89.2	97.6	93.1	99.3
1851	88.0	110.7	91.5	110.2
1852	87.3	102.3	92.6	119.0
1853	83.0	102.5	89.8	112.3
1854	80.1	100.2	89.5	113.2
1855	82.1	91.7	79.7	98.2
1856	84.2	88.1	82.1	89.8
1857	82.0	84.8	88.4	90.6
1858	99.5	106.9	95.1	116.9
1859	98.7	95.4	97.0	107.5
1860	100.0	100.0	100.0	100.0
	Five-Year Averages (1856–60 = 100)			
1821–25	64.7	90.0	78.9	78.5
1826–30	78.2	121.9	105.8	101.5
1831–35	77.0	111.4	107.3	102.8
1836–40	76.2	93.3	86.5	88.4
1841–45	104.3	113.4	131.5	125.2
1846–50	99.8	101.7	107.6	115.3
1851–55	90.5	106.7	95.8	109.5
1856–60	100.0	100.0	100.0	100.0
	Decadal Averages (1851–60 = 100)			
1821–30	75.0	104.2	97.8	85.9
1831–40	80.4	99.0	98.9	91.3
1841–50	107.1	104.0	122.1	114.8
1851–60	100.0	100.0	100.0	100.0

Source: See the text.

Note: N.A. = No estimate available.

Table 3A.11   Real Wage Indices, 1821–60: Clerks, by Region

	Northeast	Midwest	South Atlantic	South Central
1821	72.8	74.1	N.A.	66.1
1822	49.5	66.1	68.9	62.2
1823	59.1	79.9	70.1	61.2
1824	62.6	74.7	70.5	63.2
1825	62.3	84.5	88.3	65.2
1826	62.0	100.4	95.0	78.5
1827	65.8	94.0	90.5	81.6
1828	65.6	104.4	91.0	85.3
1829	78.2	84.8	90.5	85.5
1830	72.9	88.0	84.9	110.1
1831	71.1	74.5	86.0	79.1
1832	71.1	82.1	87.1	74.2
1833	66.8	78.6	87.4	76.2
1834	71.1	91.3	86.7	80.0
1835	62.5	66.3	73.9	66.5
1836	54.5	54.1	69.5	58.9
1837	68.9	68.3	84.0	88.6
1838	66.5	79.2	94.1	90.4
1839	72.3	75.8	97.3	112.0
1840	86.9	90.8	119.5	115.5
1841	87.6	99.6	109.1	109.4
1842	104.5	131.6	135.1	122.3
1843	129.3	151.7	148.7	134.0
1844	118.3	134.4	154.3	132.4
1845	106.8	131.2	152.2	134.5
1846	99.0	133.8	138.2	137.5
1847	93.7	94.0	115.0	116.5
1848	106.8	131.5	146.9	136.7
1849	102.6	124.4	128.1	124.1
1850	96.8	111.8	117.3	107.9
1851	117.3	139.1	118.6	115.5
1852	108.7	126.7	123.2	121.5
1853	95.2	102.6	117.6	111.6
1854	93.1	99.8	110.0	108.8
1855	93.7	82.4	97.0	90.6
1856	92.8	84.5	104.6	86.5
1857	86.4	81.2	88.8	111.1
1858	103.1	104.0	102.8	97.1
1859	90.1	77.6	98.1	100.9
1860	100.0	100.0	100.0	100.0

		Five-Year Averages (1856–60 = 100)		
1821–25	64.8	84.8	75.3	64.1
1826–30	72.9	105.4	91.4	89.0
1831–35	72.5	87.8	85.2	75.9
1836–40	73.9	82.3	93.9	93.9
1841–45	115.7	145.0	141.5	127.6
1846–50	105.6	133.1	130.6	125.6
1851–55	107.5	123.1	114.6	110.6
1856–60	100.0	100.0	100.0	100.0

		Decadal Averages (1851–60 = 100)		
1821–30	66.4	85.3	78.5	72.7
1831–40	70.5	76.3	83.5	80.6
1841–50	106.6	124.7	126.8	120.3
1851–60	100.0	100.0	100.0	100.0

Source: See the text.

Note: N.A. = No estimate available.

Table 3A.12   Alternative Nominal Wage Estimates: Northeast (excludes Pittsburgh) ($)

	Common Laborers (Daily)	Artisans (Daily)	White-Collar Workers (Monthly)
1821	.73	.98	37.12
1822	.72	1.26	29.99
1823	.72	1.35	33.08
1824	.72	1.20	33.08
1825	.78	1.18	34.33
1826	.81	1.22	30.42
1827	.78	1.32	34.33
1828	.71	1.26	35.68
1829	.68	1.21	39.04
1830	.69	1.15	32.63
1831	.66	1.17	36.79
1832	.70	1.21	35.59
1833	.69	1.23	35.40
1834	.84	1.37	35.40
1835	.84	1.42	35.40
1836	.84	1.52	34.50
1837	.98	1.44	42.11
1838	.88	1.40	38.01
1839	.80	1.47	43.71
1840	.66	1.39	43.42
1841	.82	1.41	41.19
1842	.83	1.27	40.88
1843	.90	1.34	45.86
1844	.95	1.21	40.11
1845	.92	1.45	40.50
1846	.90	1.38	37.53
1847	.87	1.42	44.26
1848	.89	1.34	38.98
1849	.91	1.46	41.23
1850	.94	1.42	42.17
1851	.87	1.35	49.37
1852	.96	1.42	48.94
1853	.95	1.49	46.80
1854	1.00	1.57	47.54
1855	1.04	1.72	51.35
1856	1.08	1.77	46.69
1857	1.11	1.80	49.33
1858	.94	1.86	47.45
1859	1.12	1.87	46.88
1860	1.10	1.68	49.59
	Five-Year Averages		
1821–25	.73	1.19	33.52
1826–30	.73	1.23	34.42
1831–35	.75	1.28	35.72
1836–40	.83	1.44	40.35
1841–45	.88	1.34	41.71
1846–50	.90	1.40	40.83
1851–55	.96	1.51	48.80
1856–60	1.07	1.82	47.99
	Decadal Averages		
1821–30	.73	1.21	33.97
1831–40	.79	1.36	38.04
1841–50	.89	1.37	41.27
1851–60	1.02	1.67	48.40

Note: Estimates based on hedonic regressions that exclude observations from Pittsburgh. Estimates for 1835–37 for skilled artisans are adjusted as in table 3A.6 above (see the text).

Table 3A.13   **Alternative Nominal Wage Estimates: Midwest (includes Pittsburgh) ($)**

	Common Laborers (Daily)	Artisans (Daily)	White-Collar Workers (Monthly)
1821	.73	N.A.	36.13
1822	.54	1.20	31.35
1823	.57	1.19	30.49
1824	.63	1.18	29.77
1825	.56	1.22	32.61
1826	.51	1.30	32.73
1827	.50	1.40	29.04
1828	.51	1.50	30.77
1829	.60	1.49	32.38
1830	.62	1.48	32.79
1831	.53	1.66	27.16
1832	.62	1.63	32.44
1833	.71	1.49	32.61
1834	.76	1.47	35.54
1835	.76	1.42	31.80
1836	.63	1.56	30.41
1837	1.02	1.95	36.76
1838	.73	1.57	38.80
1839	.95	1.42	39.44
1840	.73	1.42	36.13
1841	.65	1.35	34.04
1842	.76	1.24	37.27
1843	.73	1.05	48.31
1844	.70	1.15	47.80
1845	.69	1.23	48.44
1846	.70	1.03	47.51
1847	.68	1.17	41.52
1848	.77	1.25	47.73
1849	.80	1.38	49.79
1850	.80	1.35	47.12
1851	.81	1.54	56.83
1852	.81	1.50	55.02
1853	.80	1.59	48.81
1854	.91	1.62	50.36
1855	.91	1.68	50.03
1856	.89	1.69	57.57
1857	.99	1.79	59.26
1858	.99	1.73	59.44
1859	1.03	1.73	46.36
1860	1.00	1.74	57.41
		Five-Year Averages	
1821–25	.61	1.20	32.07
1826–30	.55	1.43	31.54
1831–35	.68	1.53	31.91
1836–40	.81	1.58	36.31
1841–45	.71	1.20	43.17
1846–50	.75	1.24	46.73
1851–55	.85	1.59	52.21
1856–60	.98	1.74	56.01
		Decadal Averages	
1821–30	.58	1.32	31.81
1831–40	.75	1.56	34.11
1841–50	.73	1.22	44.95
1851–60	.92	1.67	54.11

Note: Estimates based on hedonic regressions that include observations from Pittsburgh (see the text).

Intersectoral Efficiency
Farm-Nonfarm Wage Gaps

The next three chapters examine various aspects of the allocative efficiency of antebellum labor markets. This chapter studies so-called wage gaps between farm and nonfarm labor. Although earlier work by Lebergott (1964) showed that labor shifted out of agriculture before the Civil War at an impressive pace, recent revisions to the underlying data suggest both a slower rate of exit and a higher share of the labor force in farming on the eve of the Civil War (Weiss 1992), prompting some scholars to question whether the United States industrialized too slowly (Atack and Bateman 1991). If this were the case, wage gaps in favor of nonfarm labor should be apparent as well as persistent (Williamson 1991, 45). On the other hand, the *absence* of wage gaps could be taken as evidence that the allocation of labor between the farm and the nonfarm sectors was efficient, in which case it would be reasonable to conclude that real wage gains experienced by nonfarm labor "trickled down" to farm labor, the dominant economic activity before the Civil War.

Previous work on antebellum wage gaps has been hampered by sketchy or inappropriately analyzed evidence (see sec. 4.1). This chapter uses samples drawn from the manuscript Censuses of Social Statistics in 1850 and 1860, which permit an investigation of wage gaps in small areas (counties) as well as in the aggregate.

4.1 Theoretical and Historical Background

Modern economic growth is often defined by the shift of labor out of agriculture (Kuznets 1966). Consider a simple, general equilibrium model with two sectors (farm and nonfarm). There is a specific factor in each sector (e.g., land in agriculture) and a single, mobile factor (labor). All labor is assumed to be homogenous in quality.

Efficiency requires that the value of the marginal product (VMP) of labor be the same in both the farm and the nonfarm sectors.[1] Imagine an improvement in technology that raises the value of the marginal product of labor in the nonfarm sector. The nonfarm VMP curve shifts outward, and, to maintain efficiency, labor should be reallocated from the farm to the nonfarm sector.[2]

Labor could also shift out of agriculture if the VMP curve in agriculture shifts inward. In such a case, labor is said to be "pushed" out of agriculture. Because technical regress is unusual, even in less-developed economies, such downward shifts occur primarily because of adverse weather or price shocks. For example, a decline in the farm VMP could easily occur in a single local economy as a consequence of regional specialization. Suppose that improvements in transportation permit local economy X to specialize in agricultural production. It is possible that the delivered price of the agricultural good to local economy Y located in a settled region would be lower than the cost of agricultural production in Y. This causes the VMP of agricultural labor in Y to decline and labor to be pushed out of agriculture.

In the model, efficiency is maintained by a competitive labor market. Labor is a mobile factor, deciding in which sector to be employed on the basis of the wage, which, under competition, equals the value of the marginal product. Thus, when one or the other VMP curves shifts, wages adjust so as to maintain labor market equilibrium.

For various reasons, equalization of marginal value products might not obtain. The adjustment to the new equilibrium might be protracted, in which case the disequilibrium would persist for some time. In developing countries today, wages in the nonfarm sector are artificially boosted by the imposition of minimum wages. A minimum wage set above the equilibrium wage will cause the quantity of labor demanded in the nonfarm sector to decline while simultaneously increasing the quantity of labor supplied in the nonfarm sector. Labor that fails to find a job in the so-called formal sector will be shunted into the informal sector, where wages are free to adjust downward, or will remain unemployed for some time, until a job opens up in the formal sector.[3]

In most historical economies, such as the antebellum United States, the minimum wage is not relevant. However, there can still be short- or medium-run barriers to the reallocation of labor from the farm to the nonfarm sectors. For example, the demand for nonfarm labor may be concentrated geographically at a distance from the supply of farm labor. The costs of adjustment—namely, migration—include not only time and money costs but also the psychic costs of broken ties with family and friends. Farm labor may also need time to adjust to the different pace of life and the intensity of work in nonfarm employment. For these various reasons, much rural-to-urban migration in the past took place in a circular or stages manner. Whatever the cause, the end product will be a wage gap—that is, a difference in the wage between (homogenous) labor employed in the nonfarm and labor employed in the farm sector.

There is much evidence in historical and developing economies of *average* productivity gaps—output per worker in agriculture generally is much less than output per worker in the nonfarm sector (David 1967; Crafts 1985). Indeed, a key aspect of modern economic growth is the eventual convergence of average labor productivity across sectors, all the while labor is shifting out of agriculture (Maddison 1987). Productivity gaps are often said to provide a "free lunch" to an industrializing economy—that is, an extra boost in output if labor shifts from the low-productivity (farm) sector to the high-productivity (nonfarm) sector (David 1967; Crafts 1985; Maddison 1987). The basis of this argument is the following algebraic identity:

$$q = q_f s_f + q_n s_n,$$

where q = aggregate labor productivity; q_i = labor productivity in sector i, $i = f$ (farm), n (nonfarm); and s_i is the share of the labor force in sector i. If $q_f < q_n$, then an increase in s_n mechanically increases aggregate output.

While the algebra of this argument is unassailable, the economics is less clear-cut. As already noted, output will be maximized when the VMP of labor is equalized, not when the average products are equalized. Indeed, there is *no* necessary relation between the two types of gaps. To see this, imagine that the production functions in the two sectors are Cobb-Douglas. Equilibrium in the labor market requires that wages be equalized, or

$$\alpha_f p_f q_f / L_f = \alpha_n p_n q_n / L_n,$$

where the α's are the output elasticities of labor, and the L's are the labor demands in the two sectors. This can be rewritten as

$$\alpha_f \mathrm{AP}_f = \alpha_n \mathrm{AP}_n,$$

where AP = average product. Clearly, the average product of labor could be higher in the nonfarm sector yet wages be equalized—or a wage gap could exist yet average products be the same in the two sectors. Despite this theoretical point, it is widely believed that average productivity gaps are evidence of some type of factor market failure in the allocation of either labor or capital.

4.1.1   Wage Gaps and Antebellum Economic Development

Wage gaps are relevant to three strands of the literature on antebellum economic development. The first, and perhaps most important, concerns the proper interpretation of the so-called sectoral shift in Paul David's (1967) conjectural estimates of antebellum per capita income prior to 1840. David called his estimates *conjectural* because they were derived from the algebraic approach discussed previously rather than from actual data on output. Output per worker in the nonfarm sector exceeded output per worker in the farm sector in 1840, and it is reasonable to assume that the same held true at earlier census dates. According to David's estimates, the shift of labor out of agriculture—the sectoral shift—accounts for approximately one-third of per capita income growth over the period 1800–1860.

Clearly, the sectoral shift was *correlated* with antebellum income growth. However, whether it truly was a cause depends on the existence of a wage gap. If there was a wage gap, then, as discussed earlier, the sectoral shift produced an added boost to per capita income—in effect, a free lunch. If there was no wage gap, however, the sectoral shift was not an independent factor, and growth in antebellum per capita income must be attributed to more fundamental causes—for example, technical progress and factor accumulation.

Related to the controversy over the sectoral shift term in David's calculation is a recent debate over the pace of antebellum industrialization. Traditionally, American economic historians have not questioned whether the pace at which labor shifted out of agriculture was too slow by some metric. Estimates of agriculture's share of the labor force prepared by Stanley Lebergott (1964) are the basis for the belief that few, if any, impediments to intersectoral mobility existed prior to the Civil War. Lebergott's estimates show that 83.3 percent of the labor force was engaged in agriculture in 1800. The rate had declined a scant 4 percentage points by 1820, to about 79 percent. Between 1820 and 1860, however, labor shifted out of agriculture at a rapid pace, with the proportion in farming falling to slightly more than half (53 percent) on the eve of the Civil War. Indeed, as measured by the nonfarm share of the labor force, the pace of industrialization was more rapid in the four decades *before* the Civil War than after. According to Lebergott's (1964, 510) estimates, 40 percent of the labor force was engaged in farming in 1900—a decline of 13 percentage points compared with 1860, whereas the 1860 figure was nearly 26 percentage points lower than the 1820 figure. Given the rapid advances in manufacturing technology after the Civil War compared with the antebellum period, one would be hard-pressed to conclude, on the basis of Lebergott's figures, that antebellum industrialization was a stagnant affair.

New estimates of the antebellum labor force prepared by Thomas Weiss

(1992) have substantially revised the pattern of change in the farm share. For my purposes, the key revisions are to the figures for 1820 and for 1860. According to Weiss (1992, 22), the farm share was 71.4 percent in 1820, compared with 55.8 percent in 1860.

Although most commentary on Weiss's work has focused on its implications for slower per capita income growth before 1800 and for the process by which nonfarm jobs were created (Goldin 1992, 76, 78), his figures also have important implications for understanding the pace of antebellum industrialization. If Weiss's revisions are accepted, industrialization proceeded at about half the pace estimated by Lebergott between 1820 and 1860.[4]

If industrialization proceeded too slowly during the antebellum period, an imprint could have been left in the form of a wage gap in favor of nonfarm labor. In terms of the model, too much labor was employed in agriculture and too little in the nonfarm sector; the farm VMP exceeds the nonfarm VMP, producing a wage gap.

Labor might not have been the only factor misallocated between the farm and the nonfarm sectors. According to Bateman and Weiss (1981), the average return to capital in manufacturing was approximately 20 percent in 1860, compared with 8–12 percent in agriculture (Atack and Bateman 1987). Although there are many possible explanations of the profit gap (e.g., differences in risk), the gap is consistent with the misallocation of capital—too little in the nonfarm sector, too much in the farm sector.

Finally, the existence of a wage gap is relevant to various theories of antebellum industrialization. For example, one interpretation of H. J. Habakkuk's (1962) model of American industrialization is that abundant and fertile land attracted labor into farming, driving up the wage faced by manufacturers, causing them to substitute capital for labor, and perhaps even biasing the direction of technical change toward labor saving (Temin 1971). Although subsequent research has heavily qualified Habakkuk's argument (see, e.g., James and Skinner 1985), all of it is predicated on well-functioning factor markets that respond to shocks to technology or resources by reallocating mobile factors, such as labor.

Alexander Field (1978) developed a labor markets explanation to explain why industrialization first occurred in New England.[5] According to Field, transportation improvements such as the Erie Canal dramatically increased exports of agricultural goods from the Midwest to the Northeast. Increased interregional competition drove down the return to capital in New England agriculture, pushing labor off the farm (recall the theoretical discussion in sec. 4.1). The labor could have migrated to the western frontier but, for various reasons, chose to remain in New England.[6] The supply of labor to the nonfarm sector shifted outward, driving down wages and raising the profitability of further investments in nonfarm capital, such as in the textile industry. Again, while subsequent research has seriously challenged Field's interpretation, all participants in the debate maintain the assumption that labor markets functioned efficiently, with the result that there were no wage gaps (Goldin and Sokoloff 1984; Simkovich 1993).[7]

4.1.2   Previous Research on the Antebellum Wage Gap

Unfortunately, relatively little prior research has been done to measure the size of the antebellum wage gap systematically.[8] Bidwell and Falconer (1925, 274) argued that "farmers could not pay wages equivalent to those paid by manufacturers," but the evidence they cited is of almost no use in determining the size of the wage gap.[9]

More reliable evidence can be found in Adams (1982). As discussed in chapter 2 above, Adams collected archival data on monthly wages of farm and manufacturing labor in the Brandywine area of Pennsylvania (near Philadelphia). The decadal average of the farm-nonfarm wage ratio was 0.92 in the 1850s, with no visible antebellum trend (calculated from Adams 1982). Although Adams's data suggest little or no wage gap, one must keep in mind that they refer to a single area, one long settled with well-developed product and factor markets.

Somewhat broader geographic evidence on the farm-manufacturing wage gap is presented by Sokoloff and Villaflor (1992, 40). Sokoloff and Villaflor compare estimates of the average annual nominal wages of adult males in Northeastern manufacturing for three years (1820, 1832, and 1850) to estimates of average annual nominal wages in Massachusetts agriculture, drawing on Rothenberg (1988). Although differences in sample geographic coverage make comparisons of the two series somewhat problematic, in no year is the wage gap greater than 10 percent, and, moreover, wages in the two sectors clearly moved together over the period.

From a geographic point of view, the most extensive previous analysis of antebellum wage gaps was conducted by Williamson and Lindert (1980, 71–73). Williamson and Lindert examined two pieces of evidence. The first pertained to wage gaps in antebellum Vermont and Massachusetts, drawing on data collected by, respectively, T. M. Adams (1939) and Carroll Wright (1989). In the case of Vermont, Williamson and Lindert compared nominal daily farm wages (from Adams) to an urban nominal daily wage for common labor. The nonfarm wage exceeded the farm wage in Vermont by about 34 percent in the mid-1830s, but the difference fell to 26 percent in the early 1850s and to a mere 8.4 percent during the Civil War (Williamson and Lindert 1980, 313).[10] In the case of Massachusetts, Williamson and Lindert again used nominal daily rates, comparing median farm to urban nonfarm wages. The decadal average of the farm-nonfarm ratio in the 1850s was 0.965, with little or no trend between 1820 and 1860 (Williamson and Lindert 1980, 313).[11]

Williamson and Lindert's second piece of evidence is especially pertinent because it is based on average nominal wages for 1850 that are precisely the published counterpart of the 1850 manuscript census data examined in this chapter (see sec. 4.2). Using the published data, Williamson and Lindert (1980, 73) compute estimates of nominal daily wages of farm and common labor in 1850 by census region and for various states within census regions. The farm-nonfarm wage ratios range from a low of 0.88 in New Hampshire to a high of 1.10 in Connecticut; the unweighted average of the ratios "for the North and for the United States as a whole [was] 0.99" (p. 72). On the basis of both pieces of evidence, Williamson and Lindert argue that farm-nonfarm wage gaps "were trivial in late antebellum America. . . . no region exhibited pronounced . . . wage gaps for labor of comparable skill" (p. 71).[12]

4.2   Wage Gap Estimates

To develop new estimates of the antebellum wage gap, I make use of the samples drawn from the manuscript Censuses of Social Statistics of 1850 and 1860 (for a discussion of these samples, see chap. 2). Recall that the Census of Social Statistics reported wage data for a variety of occupations as well as the weekly cost of board ("to laboring men"). This chapter uses the data on board and that from two wage categories—average monthly wages of farm labor with board and average daily wages of common labor without board.

My use of the wage data from the Censuses of Social Statistics is directed at answering the question, Was the antebellum market for unskilled labor common to both the farm and the nonfarm sectors? Of course, virtually no labor is ever truly unskilled, but that is not the issue. What is meant by *common to both sectors* is whether the tasks to be expected of hired hands on the farm *could* have been performed by the typical nonfarm laborer (and vice versa) and whether the market mechanism worked sufficiently well to equalize the returns to unskilled labor in both sectors.

I focus on common labor as the comparison group with farm labor because qualitative accounts suggest that there were important similarities in skills demanded of unskilled laborers in the farm and nonfarm sectors (Stone 1909; Schob 1975).[13] Contracts for monthly farm labor generally left the tasks demanded unspecified—more or less, whatever the farmer needed done. Although *whatever the farmer needed done* included many tasks specific to agriculture—planting, plowing, weeding, harvesting, taking care of animals, and so on—other tasks were more generic. Farmhands, for example, could expect to chop wood and clear brush, dig cellars and drains and help out with other construction projects, load and unload wagons, and perhaps transport goods to town. With respect to these generic tasks, the necessary skills were minimal and could be learned quickly.

What was valuable were not skills per se but physical dexterity, ruggedness, stamina, reliability, and willingness to follow directions.

The ability to perform these generic tasks was also demanded of common laborers in the nonfarm sector. For example, during the antebellum period, common labor was widely employed in road and canal construction to perform tasks, such as digging and hauling dirt, that were qualitatively similar to tasks occasionally demanded of hired hands on farms (Stone 1909, 143; Lebergott 1964; Schob 1975). Chopping wood was another task common to both unskilled nonfarm laborers and farmhands (Schob 1975, 20).

However, even if some of the tasks demanded of farm and common laborers were sufficiently similar that (from the standpoint of workers and employers) the two types of labor were essentially the same, there could be impediments to the equalization of wages between the two sectors. Labor demand in the farm sector was seasonal. The great bulk of farmhands appeared to have been hired on contracts of six to eight months' duration (Schob 1975; Rothenberg 1992). If a farmhand remained employed on the farm during the winter months, it might be at a reduced money wage or solely for room and board (Schob 1975, 230). Faced with the prospect of seasonal unemployment, some farmhands apparently wintered in nearby towns, consuming their savings in the process. But others attempted to find work in the nonfarm economy, apparently at the very jobs that were common to both, such as chopping wood or hauling (Schob 1975). Further, while there was some complementary meshing of tasks across the seasons, much nonfarm work was done at precisely the same time as farm work. Thus, by itself, seasonality in agricultural labor demand was not necessarily an impediment to wage equalization per unit of time (such as monthly).

Qualitative evidence also suggests that, within local economies, unskilled labor moved more or less freely between farm and nonfarm jobs.[14] Certainly, farm and nonfarm labor was highly mobile geographically (Schob 1975; Sokoloff and Villaflor 1992). Farmhands (and farmers) occasionally hired themselves out as day laborers or were attracted to short-term work on canal or other construction projects (Schob 1975, 8–9, 62). Even literate young men who worked as common school teachers during the winter months sometimes spent summers working as hired hands on local farms, earning roughly similar amounts per month (Schob 1975, 81).

Although wage equalization might occur within local economies, the same might not be true in the aggregate, particularly for money wages. Specifically, farm labor was concentrated geographically in rural areas, where nominal wages might have been low, while nonfarm labor was geographically concentrated in areas—such as towns and cities—where nominal wages might have been relatively high. Within an area, the wage gap could have been nonexistent, but, weighted to reflect the geographic distribution of farm and nonfarm labor across areas, the aggregate wage gap might have been substantial. Factor mobility might still equalize *real* wages, but there would have to have been some economic advantage to nonfarm employers to locate where nominal wages were high, such as higher labor productivity.

4.2.1 Calculation of Wage Gaps

My initial estimate of the wage gap proceeds in three stages. First, I calculate an estimate of the full-time monthly wage for farm (f) and common (n) labor in each county (i), as follows:

$$f_i = w_{fbi} + 4.3 \times b_i,$$

$$n_i = 26 \times w_{ndi},$$

where w_{fbi} = the monthly wage of farm labor with board, b_i = the weekly cost of board, and w_{ndi} = the daily wage of common labor without board. The calculation assumes 4.3 weeks of board per month, on average, for farm labor and twenty-six days of employment per month for common labor.[15]

Next, I compute weighted averages of the f's and n's:

$$f = \Sigma \ \alpha_i f_i,$$

$$n = \Sigma \ \beta_i n_i.$$

Ideally, the weights α and β would reflect the actual distribution of hired hands and common laborers across counties. Such data are not available, however, in 1850 and 1860. In their place, I use county-level data on improved acres in agriculture in conjunction with state-level estimates of the farm labor force to estimate the farm labor force and the nonfarm labor force at the county level (for a discussion of the weighting procedure, see app. 4A). The weighting procedure is extremely crude and should be viewed cautiously, particularly for Southern states, where the weights reflect the use of slave as well as free labor.[16] However, some weighting procedure is clearly preferable to none at all (see below), and, while the weighting procedure could no doubt be refined, sensitivity analysis suggests that the substantive results are robust to plausible alternative weighting schemes.[17]

The *aggregate* wage gap (g) is

$$g = f - n.$$

Note that the aggregate gap can be decomposed into the sum of two components:

$$g = \Sigma\beta_i g_i + \Sigma(\alpha_i - \beta_i)f_i,$$

where $g_i = f_i - n_i$. The first term in the decomposition, $\Sigma\beta_i g_i$, is the average *within-county* gap—that is, the portion of the aggregate wage gap that can be attributed, on average, to the wage gap observed within counties. The second term in the decomposition, $\Sigma(\alpha_i - \beta_i)f_i$, is the portion of the aggregate wage gap attributed to the distribution of farm and common labor across counties.

As written above, the average within-county gap is produced by weighting each county's gap by β_i. However, the average could also be produced by weighting each county's gap by α_i. Although a theoretical case can be made for weighting by β, neither gap is "correct," and I present both calculations.[18]

Decomposing the aggregate gap into *within* and *between* components is motivated by the two fundamental ways in which unskilled labor might be misallocated, as discussed earlier. First, misallocation might occur within a particular local economy: unskilled labor might be priced higher as common labor, for example, than as farm labor. If this sort of misallocation occurred with some frequency, the average within-county gap should have been positive.

Second, farm labor might be concentrated geographically where money wages, on average, were relatively low, compared with the geographic distribution of common labor. If a mismatch of supply and demand of this sort occurred, the *between* component of the decomposition should have been positive in absolute value; that is, the aggregate gap should have exceeded the within-county gap in absolute value.

As noted earlier, the *between* component of the decomposition is relevant to the distinction between nominal and real wage gaps. Within a local economy, it may be reasonable to assume that cost-of-living differences between nonfarm and farm labor were relatively small, at least compared to the differences that might have existed between, say, the urban Northeast and the rural Midwest. Adjusting for such geographic differences in the cost of living (see below) turns the nominal aggregate gap into a real aggregate gap. Also as previously noted, a small real gap (given a large nominal gap) implies that employers of common laborers who located where money wages were high must have had an incentive to do so, a point to which I return later in the chapter.

In mapping the empirical decomposition into the theoretical constructs of *within* and *between* gaps, the use of county-level data is easily criticized. Counties were not necessarily coterminous with local labor markets. In order to calculate the decomposition, however, it is necessary to have some set of weights to apply to each local economy, whatever the definition of *local* happens to be. As noted above, county-level weights can be readily constructed from published census data for 1850 and 1860, which is simply not the case for arbitrarily defined local economies.[19]

Caveats aside, panel A of table 4.1 shows the results of my initial calculations, in the rows labeled *unadjusted*. Results are presented for each state as well as by census region.

Among the Northern states in the sample, the aggregate wage gaps were relatively large, averaging 35 percent ($= 6.38/18.34$) of the mean farm wage in 1850 and 30 percent ($= 6.44/21.55$) of the mean farm wage in 1860. There was also a tendency for the gaps to be smaller, percentage-wise, on the frontier; for example, the Iowa gap was about 20 percent in 1850, compared with 29 percent in Massachusetts.[20] In the Southern sample, the aggregate gaps were somewhat smaller than in the North: on average, the aggregate gap was 26 percent ($= 3.80/14.39$) of the mean farm wage in 1850 and 18 percent ($= 3.78/20.61$) of the mean farm wage in 1860.

As noted above, aggregate wage gaps might be expected if nonfarm labor was concentrated where nominal wages were relatively high, compared with farm labor. The decompositions in panel A of table 4.1 demonstrate that this must have been true in 1850 and 1860 because, in the majority of cases, the aggregate gap exceeded the average within-county gap. But the decompositions also demonstrate that the within-county gaps can account for much of the aggregate gap, especially if the within-county gaps are produced using the β (nonfarm) weights.[21]

It is worth emphasizing that the nominal gaps in panel A are different from those that would obtain if the published averages from the 1850 census were used instead. The published averages were evidently unweighted averages of minor civil division figures. As panel B of table 4.1 shows for 1850 (results for 1860 are similar), in every state the nominal wage gap, as calculated from the published figures, was smaller than that shown in panel A. This is primarily a consequence of the weighting procedure; as noted above, nonfarm labor tended to be concentrated in areas (such as towns or cities) where nominal wages were higher. Because the published figures were unweighted averages, they fail to reflect this geographic distribution of common labor and thus understate the nominal wage gap.

Given that manufacturing activity was concentrated more heavily in the North, particularly the Northeast, the initial calculations suggest that labor market imperfections could have impeded antebellum economic growth. There are several reasons to be suspicious, however, that the within-county wage gaps were truly as large, on average, as my initial estimates imply. First, the evidence presented in chapter 3 suggests that laborers hired on a daily basis received a wage premium to compensate for unemployment risk (Lebergott 1964; Margo and Villaflor 1987). Thus, had the census marshals collected data on the *monthly* wage of common laborers, the gap estimates in panel A might be much smaller.

Table 4.1 **Nominal Farm-Nonfarm Wage Gaps, 1850 and 1860 ($)**

| | A. By State and Region | | | | | | | |
| | 1850 | | | | 1860 | | | |
	w_f	w_c	g	g_c	w_f	w_c	g	g_c
Massachusetts:								
Unadjusted	22.15	28.61	−6.46	−5.27	25.72	30.97	−5.25	−4.01
				(−5.07)				(−4.65)
Adjusted	22.15	25.58	−3.43	−2.24	25.72	27.69	−1.97	−.72
				(−2.18)				(−1.43)
Pennsylvania:								
Unadjusted	17.38	22.42	−5.04	−3.52	20.77	27.03	−6.26	−4.33
				(−3.02)				(−3.58)
Adjusted	17.38	20.05	−2.67	−1.15	20.77	24.16	−3.39	−1.47
				(−.86)				(−1.00)
Michigan:								
Unadjusted	18.17	22.69	−4.52	−4.26	21.36	24.59	−3.23	−2.86
				(−5.88)				(−3.60)
Adjusted	18.17	20.29	−2.12	−1.89	21.36	21.99	−.63	−.25
				(−3.32)				(−.96)
Iowa:								
Unadjusted	18.55	22.19	−3.64	−3.37	21.36	24.30	−2.94	−3.24
				(−4.07)				(−3.28)
Adjusted	18.55	19.84	−1.29	−1.02	21.36	21.72	−.36	−.67
				(−1.67)				(−.67)
Northern sample:								
Unadjusted	18.34	24.72	−6.38	−4.20	21.55	27.99	−6.44	−3.96
				(−3.87)				(−3.64)
Adjusted	18.34	22.10	−3.76	−1.59	21.55	25.02	−3.47	−1.08
				(−1.51)				(−.98)
North Carolina:								
Unadjusted	12.81	16.30	−3.49	−2.83	18.31	22.61	−4.30	−3.02
				(−1.13)				(−1.73)
Adjusted	12.81	14.57	−1.76	−1.10	18.31	20.22	−1.91	−.66
				(.34)				(.40)
Virginia:								
Unadjusted	14.22	18.75	−4.53	−3.51	20.05	23.63	−3.58	−1.81
				(−2.33)				(−1.74)
Adjusted	14.22	16.76	−2.54	−1.53	20.05	21.13	−1.08	.69
				(−.57)				(.57)
Kentucky:								
Unadjusted	15.83	20.10	−4.27	−2.73	22.65	26.56	−3.91	−3.46
				(−2.86)				(−3.84)
Adjusted	15.83	17.97	−2.14	−.59	22.65	23.75	−1.10	−.65
				(−.87)				(−1.04)
Tennessee:								
Unadjusted	14.90	16.69	−1.79	−.11	21.68	25.58	−3.90	−1.97
				(−.83)				(−1.64)
Adjusted	14.90	14.92	−.02	1.66	21.68	22.87	−1.19	.74
				(.84)				(.82)

(continued)

Table 4.1   (continued)

A. By State and Region

	1850				1860			
	w_f	w_c	g	g_c	w_f	w_c	g	g_c
Southern sample:								
Unadjusted	14.39	18.19	−3.80	−2.61	20.61	24.39	−3.78	−2.42
				(−1.86)				(−2.19)
Adjusted	14.39	16.26	−1.87	−.68	20.61	21.81	−1.20	.16
				(−.20)				(.22)

B. Estimates of g, 1850, Using Published Census of Social Statistics

	g	Difference, Panel A − Panel B
Massachusetts	−5.67	−.79
Pennsylvania	−2.58	−2.46
Michigan	−4.04	−.48
Iowa	−2.99	−.65
North Carolina	−1.11	−2.38
Virginia	−2.06	−2.47
Kentucky	−1.88	−2.39
Tennessee	−.73	−1.06

C. Average Weekly Cost of Board

	1850	1860
Massachusetts	2.15	2.63
Pennsylvania	1.81	2.28
Iowa	1.60	1.99
Michigan	1.51	2.06
Northern Sample	1.86	2.31
North Carolina	1.32	1.90
Virginia	1.48	2.04
Kentucky	1.45	2.06
Tennessee	1.47	2.10
Southern Sample	1.44	2.03

Notes: Panel A: w_f = average monthly wage of farm labor (includes imputed value of board). w_c = average monthly wage of common labor, without board. g_c = outside parentheses, weighted average of wage gap within counties, weight is estimated nonfarm share of county labor force; inside parentheses, weighted average of wage gap within counties, weight is estimated farm share of county labor force (see the text for discussion of weighting procedure). $g = w_f - w_c$. Unadjusted = unadjusted for differences in daily pay between monthly and daily labor; adjusted = adjusted for differences in daily pay between monthly and daily labor (see the text for discussion of adjustment procedure).

Panel B: w_f and w_c computed from published 1850 Census of Social Statistics. w_f = (monthly wage of farm labor with board) + 4.3 × average weekly cost of board. w_c = 26 × daily wage of common labor without board. $g = w_f - w_c$.

Panel C: State estimates: average weekly cost of board is a weighted average of county figures; weights are county population shares. Regional estimates: weighted average of state figures, weights are state population shares.

Second, it is quite likely that laborers hired on a monthly basis with board received additional perquisites not paid to daily labor. For example, a hired hand might have received a place to sleep, the washing and mending of clothes, and feed for his horse (Schob 1975; Rothenberg 1992; Hatton and Williamson 1991). Qualitative evidence strongly suggests that the farm labor market functioned well enough that such perquisites would be reflected in a lower wage, although whether they would be fully reflected is another matter (Schob 1975; Rothenberg 1992).

Third, laborers hired on a monthly basis were arguably less skilled than those hired on a daily basis (although whether monthly farm laborers were less skilled than daily nonfarm laborers is unclear). Short-term laborers in agriculture, for example, often specialized in tasks such as prairie breaking or well digging, which required more skills and equipment than general farm labor (Schob 1975). Hired hands were typically younger and more likely to be single than short-term laborers and, for both reasons, might have been less reliable and less productive (Schob 1975; Rothenberg 1992). For all three reasons—unemployment risk, perquisites, and differences in worker characteristics—the within-county wage gaps in panel A are arguably overstated.

Fortunately, some insight into this issue can be gleaned because a few census marshals evidently misunderstood their instructions, reporting the monthly wage of common laborers (instead of the daily wage). I use these misreported observations in the context of a regression of common wages to measure an downward adjustment factor, which is applied to the monthly common wage.[22] While the number of misreported observations is large enough that the estimate of the adjustment factor is reasonably precise, the number of observations is not sufficient to estimate separate adjustment factors at, say, the state level or even for 1850 and 1860.[23] These estimates are shown in the rows labeled *adjusted* in panel A of table 4.1.

The adjusted estimates show dramatically reduced within-county gaps—indeed, in some states, the gaps are now slightly positive, indicating that farm labor was better compensated than common labor. Direct evidence on the cost to workers of switching sectors within counties is nonexistent for the antebellum period. Generically, however, such costs would have included search costs (e.g., trips to town to find work), costs of adjusting personal schedules, and possibly changes in commuting or relocation costs. The adjusted estimates suggest that, if the costs of switching equaled as little as three or four days of labor at the average farm wage, it would not have paid the marginal worker to switch between sectors. But, if the marginal worker was indifferent between sectors (up to the cost of switching), local labor markets were, on average, in equilibrium in 1850 and 1860.

Table 4.2   Real Wage Ratios: w_f/w_c

	1850	1860
Massachusetts	.97	1.01
Pennsylvania	.99	.96
Michigan	.91	1.01
Iowa	.94	.97
North Carolina	.94	.96
Virginia	.90	1.04
Kentucky	.96	1.03
Tennessee	1.08	1.00

Note: Real means adjusted for cross-sectional differences in the weekly cost of board within states (see the text).

4.2.2 Real Wage Gaps

A small within-county gap does not imply a small aggregate gap, and, as the estimates in table 4.1 show, an aggregate gap remains even after adjusting monthly wages in the manner described above. By construction, the adjusted aggregate gap is the true nominal gap because no correction has been made for geographic differences in the cost of living. Thus, a large nominal aggregate gap need not imply a large real wage gap—that is, controlling for the cost of living, wages for farm and nonfarm labor might equalize, on average, across counties.

Ideally, we would need comprehensive, county-level indices of the cost of living in 1850 and 1860 to test for real wage equalization. Data to construct such indices do not exist for 1850 and 1860. In their place, I use the weekly cost of board as a proxy for the cost of living.

Although the limitations of board as a proxy for the cost of living are important (see chap. 5), they should not be overemphasized. Food costs loomed very large in antebellum budgets.[24] Moreover, there was considerable variation in the cost of board across counties; in particular, board was more expensive in the Northeast than in the Midwest or the South (see panel C of table 4.1) as well as in urban than in rural counties.[25]

Table 4.2 shows the ratios of farm to nonfarm wages at the state level, after correcting for differences across counties in the cost of board within states. The correction multiplies nominal wages by the county's relative cost of living, where *relative* means the ratio of the county's weekly cost of board to a weighted average across all counties within the state (for a discussion of the correction procedure, see app. 4B). If nonfarm wages were high on average because nonfarm labor was concentrated in counties where the cost of living was high, the gap between the average farm and the average nonfarm wage should decline and possibly vanish.

In fact, once the cost of board is controlled for, the aggregate nominal gap diminishes substantially. In no case does the farm-nonfarm wage ratio fall more than 10 percent below or above perfect equalization—namely, a ratio of unity. There is also evidence of regression toward the mean—states with ratios below or above unity in 1850 moved closer to wage equalization over the decade. On the basis of table 4.2, there is no reason to suppose that farm and nonfarm laborers were paid a substantially different (monthly) real wage in 1850 or 1860.

4.2.3 Comparison with Williamson and Lindert (1980)

My results suggest that, on average, the antebellum wage gap was small within counties and, adjusted for the cost of living, at the state level. Superficially, these conclusions appear to be the same as those of Williamson and Lindert (1980), as discussed previously. Because of differences in the method of calculation, Williamson and Lindert's gap estimates are not exactly comparable to mine. Conceptually, however, they are closest to the adjusted nominal gaps shown in table 4.1 because Williamson and Lindert use an adjustment factor to convert monthly to daily wages (see below) but do not directly adjust for the cost of living.[26] My results show substantial nominal gaps at the state (or regional) level, contrary to their estimates.

Part of the discrepancy may be attributed to differences in weighting and sample coverage.[27] However, the principal reason for the discrepancy can be traced to a conceptual mistake in Williamson and Lindert's computations.[28] In effect, Williamson and Lindert concluded that aggregate nominal gaps in 1850 were negligible because their computational procedure eliminated them by construction.

4.2.4 The Farm-Manufacturing Wage Gap

My use of the census data is based on the assumption that the day wage of common labor is a reliable summary statistic for the nonfarm sector. Given the importance of wage gaps in models of industrialization, and in the light of the earlier work by Adams (1982) and Sokoloff and Villaflor (1992), an additional test for wage equalization would compare the farm wage to wages in manufacturing (i.e., a specific nonfarm sector). The analysis applies to 1860 because published census data on manufacturing wages at the county level were not reported in 1850. Also, I restrict my attention to the two Northeastern states in the sample (Pennsylvania and Massachusetts) as the Northeast was where the bulk of manufacturing labor was employed.

The estimation of the male manufacturing wage proceeds in two steps. The average monthly manufacturing wage, w_m, is

$$w_m = [(\text{annual wage bill})/(\text{number of employees}) \times 11.5],$$

where 11.5 is the average number of months of operation (for justification of this figure, see Sokoloff [1986a]). Included in the wage bill were wages

Table 4.3   Farm-Manufacturing Wage Gap, 1860: Massachusetts and Pennsylvania

	Massachusetts	Pennsylvania
Estimated monthly manufacturing wage, nominal ($)	26.67	25.48
Ratio, farm wage/manufacturing wage, nominal	.96	.82
Ratio, farm wage/manufacturing wage, real	1.03	.90

Note: See the text for discussion of estimation of manufacturing wage. *Real* = adjusted for across-county differences in the cost of board (see the text).

paid to female manufacturing workers. Since my farm wage data refer to males, it is important to adjust w_m for the gender composition of the manufacturing labor force; as with the average number of months of operation, the adjustment assumes that the female-male ratio of manufacturing wages was a constant.[29] Because the average number of months of operation and the female-male wage ratio no doubt varied across counties, the results should be viewed cautiously.

Table 4.3 shows comparisons between the manufacturing wage and the farm wage in 1860. On average, the estimated manufacturing wages were quite close to the estimated common wages in nominal terms. In Pennsylvania, the manufacturing wage exceeded the common wage by about 5 percent, while, in Massachusetts, the (adjusted) common wage exceeded the manufacturing wage by about 4 percent. Compared with agricultural wages, there was little or no indication of a wage gap in Massachusetts; in Pennsylvania, there was a small gap (about 10 percent in real terms), but this may be within the margin of measurement error, given the crudeness of the adjustments for days of operation and the gender mix. In sum, it would appear that sectoral wage gaps would remain small if manufacturing wage data were substituted for the common labor wage data.

4.3   Conclusion

This chapter has presented new evidence on farm-nonfarm wage gaps in the United States before the Civil War. Strictly speaking, the findings apply to two years and to a sample of counties that covers only a portion of states. It is possible that data for other years, or a geographically broader sample, would reveal different results. However, the data analyzed here suggest that, properly measured, such gaps were small, on average, within local labor markets, at least on an average monthly basis. Adjusted for geographic differences in the cost of living, the real wages of agricultural and nonfarm workers appear to have been about the same in 1850 and 1860, and this conclusion is not altered (for two states in 1860) by substituting manufacturing wages for common labor.

Appendix 4A

Discussion of Weighting Procedures

This appendix describes the weighting procedures used in the construction of tables 4.1–4.3.

Tables 4.1 and 4.2, State-Level Estimates

The first step is to estimate the total labor force and the farm labor force at the county level and derive the nonfarm labor force as a residual. Total labor force at the county level is estimated by multiplying each county's population by the state's aggregate labor force participation rate (computed from Weiss's [1992] labor force estimates and census population figures). The farm labor force in each county is $\tau \times$ Weiss's estimate of total farm labor in state, with $\tau =$ the county's share of total improved acres in the state. The nonfarm labor force is the total labor force less the farm labor force. The weight for the farm wage is the estimated farm labor force; the weight for the common wage is the estimated nonfarm labor force.[30]

Table 4.1, Northern and Southern Sample

Weights are state estimates of farm and nonfarm labor force, as derived from Weiss (1992).

Table 4.3

Weights for farm wage are state estimates of farm labor force, from Weiss (1992); weights for manufacturing wage are reported male employment in manufacturing in the 1860 census.

Appendix 4B

Calculation of Real Wage Estimates

I first compute the average cost of board at the state level, b_s. The state averages are weighted averages of county-level figures on the cost of board; the weights are county population shares: $b_s = \sum p_i b_i$, where p_i is the county population share, and b_i is the weekly cost of board in county i. The state averages are shown in panel C of table 4.1. Let w_{fi} = the nominal monthly farm wage in county i, w_{ci} = the nominal monthly (adjusted, as in table 4.1) common wage in county i. Real wages are

$$rw_{fi} = (w_{fi}/b_i) \times b_s,$$
$$rw_{ci} = (w_{ci}/b_i) \times b_s.$$

State averages are then computed as described in appendix 4A.

For table 4.3, the same procedure as above is followed, except that the sample is restricted to Massachusetts and Pennsylvania.

5

Geographic Aspects of Labor Market Integration before the Civil War

Chapter 4 examined wage gaps between farm and nonfarm labor before the Civil War, a sectoral aspect of labor market integration. This chapter continues the analysis of integration by focusing on geographic wage differentials. Most of the chapter addresses the evolution of regional differences in real wages—for example, whether real wages were initially higher in the Midwest than in the Northeast, whether the gap narrowed over time, and why. Regional wage evolutions have been examined intensively for the post–Civil War period; much less attention, however, has been paid to the antebellum period.

In addition to regional evolution, I also examine patterns of wage convergence at the level of local labor markets—here proxied by counties—using the eight-state sample from the 1850 and 1860 Censuses of Social Statistics. By *wage convergence,* I mean a tendency for high– (low–) real wage counties in 1850 to experience low– (high–) real wage growth between 1850 and 1860.

5.1 Relative Demand and Supply

Throughout the chapter, the interpretation of geographic wage patterns is conducted in terms of the (occupation-specific) relative demand and relative supply of labor. The relative demand for labor is

$$L_{it} = f(X_{it}, \, w/p_{it}),$$

where w/p_{it} is the real wage at location i in year t, f is the demand curve, X is a set of factors that shift the demand curve, and L_{it} is the quantity of labor demanded at location i in year t. By *relative,* I mean comparing location i to another location or to some geographic aggregate, such as a state or a region.

The presumption is that $\partial f/\partial(w/p) < 0$: the demand for labor slopes downward with respect to the real wage, holding X constant. The downward slope reflects both diminishing returns to fixed factors at the location (e.g., land) and substitution possibilities in production across locations. Factors that may shift the relative demand curve include technical progress that enhances the productivity of labor in specific locations, population growth, output prices, and past and current prices of other inputs that may have implications for the spatial pattern of production.

The relative supply of labor is

$$L_{it} = g(Z_{it}, w/p_{it}),$$

where Z is a set of factors that shift the supply curve. Included in Z are amenities or disamenities that make location i relatively attractive or unattractive and, possibly, past values of w/p (see below).

Equilibrium is achieved when the relative demand for labor equals the relative supply ($f = g \ \forall \ i$). The equilibrium values of w/p and L in any period can be stable, in the sense that they would remain unchanged unless X or Z were to change. Or they may be unstable, in the sense that the differences in w/p across locations are large enough to induce shifts in relative supply or demand.

In particular, differences in real wages across locations may be sufficiently large (and persistent) to make it worthwhile for labor to migrate from low–real wage to high–real wage locations. Thus, if location i were a high–real wage location in period t, the relative supply of labor at location i would increase (shift outward) in period $t + 1$. Conversely, if location i were a low–real wage location in period t, the relative supply of labor would decrease (shift outward) in period $t + 1$. In this manner, the relative supply is said to be more elastic in the long run than in the short run— that is, any given increase in w/p elicits a greater supply response over time than in the short run.

If the relative demand for labor remains unchanged while the relative supply curve is shifting outward, the increase in relative supply would cause real wages at location i to decline relative to other locations. Conversely, a decrease in relative supply—again, assuming that the relative demand for labor remained unchanged—would cause real wages at location i to increase relative to those at other locations. Through the process of adjusting labor supplies by migration, real wages are said to converge across locations.

Shifts in relative demand can also affect shifts in relative wages across locations. For example, suppose that technological progress causes labor to be relatively more productive at location i. The increase in productivity raises the relative demand for labor at location i. In the short run, the increase in relative demand will cause real wages to increase at location i, with the magnitude depending on the elasticity of the short-run relative supply curve. In the long run, if labor is mobile across locations, migration will dampen the increase in the real wage by causing the relative supply curve to shift outward. Conversely, a decrease in relative demand will cause real wages to fall in the short run, but the decline will be tempered in the long run by decreases in relative supply through out-migration.

5.2   The Emergence of National Labor Markets

Patterns of real wage convergence across regions speak directly to a central question of American economic history: the emergence of national labor markets. For the most part, the (conventional) story of national labor markets begins after the Civil War (Lebergott 1964; Wright 1986; Rosenbloom 1996). Regional labor markets in the North allegedly became integrated as early as the 1870s or 1880s, as evinced by the absence of economically significant wage differentials between the Midwest and the Northeast (Rosenbloom 1996). Interregional integration was aided by falling interregional transport costs (e.g., the diffusion of railroads), improved information flows (e.g., the telegraph), and falling costs of international transport, which helped integrate Northern labor markets into an Atlantic-based labor market (Wright 1986; Williamson 1995).

The process of regional integration was evidently quite different in the South. According to Gavin Wright (1986, 64), "the defining economic feature of the South prior to World War II was not poor performance or failure" but the "isolation . . . of the southern labor market from national and international flows." The South was left out of the process because of bad timing. After the Civil War, the region was "consumed by the turbulence . . . of Reconstruction" precisely when "mass immigration was becoming an established part of the northern social fabric" (Wright 1986, 74). The "isolation" of Southern labor markets left its imprint in the form of persistently low real wages, particularly in the South Atlantic region, where real wages did not begin to increase appreciably relative to other regions until after World War II (Wright 1986; Rosenbloom 1996).

Finally, labor markets in the West were initially segmented from the rest of the United States by culture, low population densities, and distance. Although the Gold Rush (see chap. 7) led to the earlier than expected settlement of California, only after the closing of the frontier in the 1890s did the Western labor markets join in earnest the process of forming a national market (Rosenbloom 1990).

With the exception of Lebergott (1964; see also Margo 1992, in press), relatively little work has been done on the integration of geographically distinct labor markets before the Civil War.[1] Using state-level data on farm wages, Lebergott made comparisons of coefficients of variation between paired census dates (e.g., between 1830 and 1850 or 1850 and 1860). The implicit assumption was movement toward the "law of one price" as evinced by a decline in the coefficient of variation. This movement might be slow, Lebergott (1964, 134, 136) observed, because "in a dynamic economy relatively short run changes in production and demand forces can readily overlay any longer-run tendency" toward wage equalization. "Regions with lively, growing demands for labor offer rising wage rates," he noted, citing early industrialization in the Northeast and settlement in the Midwest and South Central states in response to growing demands for wheat and cotton. Despite such demand shifts, there was a tendency toward equalization: all pairwise comparisons before the Civil War show a decline in the coefficient of variation of farm wages. Lebergott (1964, 78–85) also showed (graphically) that population growth at the state level between census dates (e.g., between 1850 and 1860) was positively correlated with the initial level of wages in the state, which he interpreted as the response of in-migrants to cross-state wage differentials (i.e., a labor supply response). Despite these findings, he cautioned against the notion that antebellum labor markets were well integrated. Information on wage differentials between markets was often unavailable (or available with a lag), with the result being "occasional marked differentials in wage rates between markets . . . largely explicable in terms of the simple imperfections in the labor market of the time" (pp. 131–32).

5.2.1   The Westward Movement of Population before the Civil War

The United States underwent a massive redistribution of population from East to West before the Civil War. Although this redistribution can be readily traced from census data, its labor force implications have become fully apparent only with the recent publication of Weiss's (1992) state-level labor force estimates. Panel A of table 5.1 shows the regional distribution of the total labor force for the census years from 1800 to 1860 for the Northeast, Midwest, and South Central and South Atlantic regions. In the case of the Midwest and South Central regions, also shown are their labor force shares within, respectively, the North and the South (in parentheses). The data refer to both men and women and include slaves, but none of the fundamental trends revealed by the data would be substantially altered if the figures referred solely to (free) adult males. Panel B shows the change in logs of the labor force shares for the Midwest and South Central regions, both frontiers at the start of the nineteenth century; thus, for example, in log terms, the Midwest's share of the labor force grew by 0.32 (about 37 percent) from 1820 to 1830.

At the beginning of the nineteenth century, virtually the entire labor force—93 percent of it—lived in the Northeast or South Atlantic regions, both long settled. But, following 1800, a process of westward movement began.

Table 5.1	The Regional Distribution of the Labor Force, 1800–1860			

		A. Total Labor Force		
	Northeast	Midwest	South Atlantic	South Central
1800	.431	.008	.503	.059
		(.017)		(.116)
1810	.416	.028	.441	.114
		(.063)		(.205)
1820	.398	.070	.381	.152
		(.149)		(.284)
1830	.388	.096	.339	.177
		(.199)		(.344)
1840	.366	.160	.270	.204
		(.304)		(.431)
1850	.352	.192	.232	.211
		(.349)		(.477)
1860	.321	.230	.197	.214
		(.405)		(.521)

		B. Growth Rates		
1800–10		1.253		.659
1810–20		.916		.288
1820–30		.316		.153
1830–40		.511		.142
1840–50		.182		.034
1850–60		.181		.014

		C. Nonfarm Labor Force		
1800	.506	.004	.450	.040
		(.008)		(.082)
1810	.521	.016	.378	.086
		(.030)		(.185)
1820	.514	.053	.324	.106
		(.093)		(.247)
1830	.546	.061	.270	.123
		(.100)		(.313)
1840	.503	.115	.237	.145
		(.186)		(.380)
1850	.531	.163	.170	.136
		(.235)		(.444)
1860	.531	.177	.154	.138
		(.249)		(.473)

		D. Growth Rates		
1800–10		1.386		.765
1810–20		1.198		.209
1820–30		.141		.149
1830–40		.634		.165
1840–50		.349		−.064
1850–60		.082		.015

Source: Computed from Weiss (1992, 37, 51). *Growth rates* are ln(labor force share in year t/labor force share in year $t - 10$).

Note: Labor force shares of the Midwest within the North and of the South Central region within the South are given in parentheses.

In the case of the Midwest, its labor force share grew very rapidly between 1800 and 1810, but then growth decelerated for the next two decades. During the 1830s, however, the Midwest experienced a 60 percent increase (= 0.51/0.32) in the growth rate of its labor force share. Growth in the share declined in the 1840s but then stabilized in the 1850s. By 1860, the Midwest claimed 41 percent of the Northern labor force, and, while the share continued to increase after the Civil War, the increases were far smaller than those that took place before 1860.

The South followed a broadly similar east-west pattern early in the nineteenth century. Growth in the South Central region's share of the Southern labor force was rapid between 1800 and 1810 but declined monotonically during the 1810s and 1820s. The growth rate during the 1830s (0.14 in logs) was virtually identical to the growth rate for the 1820s (0.15 in logs). However, measured relative to the Southern labor force, growth in the South Central region's share accelerated in the 1830s. The growth rate declined sharply in the 1840s and continued to remain very low in the 1850s. By 1860, 52 percent of the Southern labor force resided in the South Central region.

Panels C and D repeat the calculations for the nonfarm labor force. The westward movement is still evident: the share of the nonfarm labor force in the Northeast and South Atlantic regions declined from 0.956 in 1800 to 0.669 in 1860. The Midwestern share of the nonfarm labor force increased from 0.004 in 1800 to 0.177 in 1860; the South Central share also increased, although not as dramatically (from 0.040 in 1800 to 0.138 in 1860). Growth in both shares decelerated from 1800 to 1830 but then increased in the 1830s, again consistent with a relative demand shock. However, in contrast to the total labor force, only the South Atlantic share underwent a pronounced decline; the Northeastern share fluctuated between 50 and 53 percent over the period 1800–1860. The jump in the Northeastern share between 1820 and 1830 represents the onset of industrialization in the United States, industrialization being concentrated in the Northeast, whereas the jump in the 1840s reflects the first great wave of European immigration (Goldin and Sokoloff 1982; Ferrie 1999).

5.2.2 Why Go West? Explaining the Geographic Redistribution of the Labor Force

Why should labor have moved west before the Civil War? The simplest answer is that, agriculture being a dominant economic activity, locations in the Midwest and South Central regions were perceived to have economic value, provided that the costs of moving factors of production to both regions did not exceed the benefits. The benefit-cost ratio presumably increased, as well, with improvements in transportation, such as canals and railroads, which lowered the cost of shipping Western goods east (and vice versa), raising economic growth through a process of regional specialization (Taylor 1951; North [1961] 1966).

Movement to the frontier generally followed a due-west direction, partly because this minimized transport costs, but also because human capital in farming tended to be latitude specific (Steckel 1983). For slave labor, migration from South to North was obviously impeded by the Peculiar Institution, but slave owners showed no general reluctance to move their chattel from east to west within the South. Immigrants who arrived in the Northeast tended to avoid further migration to the South but otherwise had no reluctance to move to the Midwest (Ferrie 1999).

The simple answer, however, runs into an empirical puzzle. Estimates of per capita income show substantially *lower* values in the Midwest relative to the Northeast in 1840 and 1860, while, in the South, per capita incomes in the East South Central region were virtually identical to those in the South Atlantic (U.S. Department of Commerce 1975, 242).[2] Economic theory suggests that individuals generally move from low- to high-income locations, not the other way around.

One way around the puzzle is to adjust in some manner—or dispute—the per capita income figures. For example, because the dependency ratio (the ratio of children to economically active adults) was higher in the Midwest than in the Northeast, the regional gap in output per worker was smaller than that in per capita income (Fogel 1989). Easterlin (1960) did not correct his income estimates for regional differences in relative prices. Later in the chapter, I show that the cost of living—or at least a key component of it—was lower in the Midwest than in the Northeast.

Aside from questioning Easterlin's original data, the puzzle can be resolved in various ways. Perhaps migration west was selective in an income sense—that is, individuals who moved west came from the lower half of the Eastern income distribution. This is the so-called safety-valve hypothesis of Frederick Jackson Turner (1920)—the idea that the frontier was a respite for the dispossessed and economically downtrodden. Migrants may have had higher incomes on the frontier than back East, but their incomes on the frontier were lower than those of individuals who did not migrate to the frontier. Although historians have not been kind to the safety-valve doctrine, a recent paper by Ferrie (1997), using sophisticated econometric techniques, finds some evidence of selectivity bias in migration that is consistent with the safety-valve hypothesis.

Another explanation is that migration to the frontier was prompted by the possibility of capital gains.[3] It is well established that precedence had economic value on the frontier—early settlers got the best land and emerged (on average) with greater capital gains than latecomers (Galenson and Pope 1992). The capital gains were especially great in the Midwest in the 1850s, with the widespread coming of the railroad (Craig, Palmquist, and Weiss 1998; Coffman and Gregson 1998).

A third explanation, originally suggested by Coelho and Shepherd (1976; see also Margo, in press), is that the marginal product of labor—the real wage—was initially higher on the frontier than in settled areas of the East Coast. In terms of the relative demand-supply model of section 5.1, the existence of a real wage gap provided a potential economic gain to migration. Because much migration involved the self-employed (in agriculture), the relevance of wages to migration decisions might be questioned (Coelho and Shepherd 1976). However, Craig (1991; see also Craig and Field-Hendry 1993) has argued that the value of the marginal product of labor in agriculture generally equalized with farm wages in the Midwest, and there is little reason to suspect that conditions were fundamentally different in the South for free labor. Chapter 4 demonstrated that farm and nonfarm wages equalized in real terms at the state level on an average monthly basis.

5.3   Regional Wage Differentials before the Civil War

Chapter 3 presented real wage series by region. In order to use these series to study the evolution of regional differentials in real wages, it is necessary to adjust the series for cross-regional differences in the cost of living. The procedure I follow has several steps.

The first step is to select a benchmark year. Because the nominal wage series are benchmarked to 1850, 1850 is a natural year to choose. The second step is to compute a regional price deflator for 1850; once this price deflator is calculated, it is straightforward to compute real wage series whose levels can be compared across regions.

To fix ideas, let w_j be the nominal wage in region j in 1850, let p_j be the price level in region j in 1850, and let the base region be the Northeast (region N). For region j, the real wage in 1850 relative to the Northeast is

$$rw_j(1850) = (w_j/w_{\mathrm{N}})/(p_j/p_{\mathrm{N}}).$$

Note that, for the Northeast, $rw_{\mathrm{N}}(1850) = 1$ by definition. The relative real wage can be computed for any year t:

$$rw_j(t) = rw_j(1850) \times [w_{rj}(t)/w_{r\mathrm{N}}(t)],$$

where $w_{rj}(t)$ is the region-specific real wage index number in year $t(w_{rj}$ [1850] $= 100$ for each region).

I also define the aggregate real wage, rw, to be

$$rw(t) = \Sigma\alpha_j(t) \times rw_j(t),$$

where $\Sigma\alpha_i = 1$, and the α_i's are regional occupation-specific labor force shares (see below). Note that the region has lower than average real wages if $rw_j/rw < 1$ and higher than average real wages if $rw_j/rw > 1$.

In computing the 1850 regional price deflators, an ideal solution is to choose a set of identically defined goods that are common to all regions.

Unfortunately, the set of such goods for which price data are available is too small, in my opinion, for the purpose at hand.

To compute the relative price deflators, I use the state averages for the weekly cost of board as published in the 1850 Census of Social Statistics. I calculate regional averages of the weekly cost of board, which are weighted averages of state figures (see app. 5A). Let b_j be the average cost of board in region j, with "N" again indicating the Northeast. The regional relative price deflator is $p_j = b_j/b_N$.

Use of board to compute the benchmark relative price index has advantages and disadvantages. The cost of board is a summary statistic of the cost of living.[4] As discussed in chapter 2, the original data were collected at the minor civil division level and provide far better geographic coverage than other antebellum price data.[5] Similar studies of regional differences in real wages for the postbellum period by Rosenbloom (1990, 1996) also use food prices to construct the price deflator, so there is an element of consistency in doing so for the antebellum period.

The major problem in using the cost of board as the cross-regional deflator is that nonfood items appear to be ignored.[6] However, it is important to keep in mind that the cost of board reflected not only the cost of the raw materials (food) but also other inputs used in producing the final product, including land. Consequently, the cost of board varied widely across geographic areas, in a manner that was consistent with general variations in the cost of living. Coelho and Shepherd's (1974) estimate of the cost of living in the Midwest relative to the Northeast for 1851 was 0.837. My estimate of the relative cost of living in the Midwest for 1851—again, solely using board for the benchmark deflator—is 0.809, very close to Coelho and Shepherd's figure.[7]

The α weights are derived from the 1850 Census of Occupations and Weiss's (1992) regional figures on the total and nonfarm labor force. First, using the 1850 census, I calculate regional totals of individuals in specific occupations. In the case of common labor, the occupations are "farmer" and "laborer," as reported in the census.[8] In the case of artisans, I sum the number of blacksmiths, carpenters, machinists, masons, and painters. In the case of white-collar workers, the occupation is "clerk."

Next, I compute occupation-participation ratios by region, where the numerator is the occupation total and the denominator is the region's labor force. In the case of common laborers, *labor force* means total (i.e., including farm); for artisans and clerks, *labor force* means nonfarm. For example, the participation ratio for clerks in the Northeast is 0.034 (= 57,908 clerks/1,701,400 nonfarm workers). I then assume that the ratios are constant for each of the census years from 1820 to 1860. Using Weiss's figures, it is straightforward to compute, for each census year, estimates of each region's share of the aggregate number of common laborers, artisans, and so on. Finally, I linearly interpolate the weights (the regional occupation shares) between census dates. The weights are shown in appendix tables 5B.1–5B.3.

Panel A of tables 5.2–5.4 shows occupation-specific decadal averages of the log of the ratio of real wages in the Midwest to those in the Northeast and of real wages in the South Central region to those in the South Atlantic. In the North, the dominant long-run pattern was regional equalization. In the 1820s, real wages in the Midwest exceeded real wages in the Northeast by 0.28 in log terms for common laborers and by considerably more for skilled artisans and clerks. By the 1850s, these wage gaps had undergone a pronounced decline; for example, in the case of artisans, the wage gap fell by −0.31 in logs. The declines were not monotonic, however. The regional wage gap for common labor rose slightly in the 1830s and 1850s, as did the gap for clerks in the 1840s and skilled laborers in the 1850s.[9]

The initial real wage advantage of the South Central region over the South Atlantic was smaller than the gap between the Midwest and the Northeast, and, unlike in the North, there was no clear trend in the South toward wage equalization. For common labor, the wage gap between the South Central and the South Atlantic states was about 13 percent in the

Table 5.2   Regional Real Wage Differences: Common Laborers

	A. Within North and South (decadal averages, log of real wage ratio)			
	1821–30	1831–40	1841–50	1851–60
Midwest-Northeast	.281	.308	.140	.153
South Central–South Atlantic	.120	.189	.130	.113
	B. Relative to National Average (decadal averages, log of real wage ratio)			
Northeast	−.084	−.078	−.009	−.052
Midwest	.197	.230	.131	.101
South Atlantic	−.038	−.160	−.192	−.118
South Central	.082	.028	−.062	−.005
Mean absolute deviation[a]	.090	.120	.079	.070

	C. Regression of $\ln(rw_j/rw)_t = \delta + \beta \ln(\alpha_j)_t$	
	β	t-Statistic
Northeast	−.198	−1.385
Midwest	−.149	−3.352
South Atlantic	.057	.686
South Central	−.840	−2.695

[a]Mean absolute deviation is $\sum(\alpha_j |rw_j/rw|)/4$; rw_j is log real wage in region j; rw is log national average; and α_j is decadal average of regional occupation weight.

Table 5.3 **Regional Real Wage Differences: Artisans**

	A. Within North and South (decadal averages, log of real wage ratio)			
	1821–30	1831–40	1841–50	1851–60
Midwest-Northeast	.567	.461	.229	.263
South Central–South Atlantic	.083	.082	.108	.162

	B. Relative to National Average (decadal averages, log of real wage ratio)			
	1821–30	1831–40	1841–50	1851–60
Northeast	−.189	−.189	−.136	−.121
Midwest	.378	.272	.093	.142
South Atlantic	.177	.164	.142	.035
South Central	.260	.246	.250	.197
Mean absolute deviation[a]	.210	.202	.139	.125

	C. Regression of $\ln(rw_j/rw)_t = \delta + \beta \ln(\alpha_j)_t$	
	β	t-Statistic
Northeast	−.765	−4.926
Midwest	−.284	−8.061
South Atlantic	.208	4.826
South Central	−.043	−.179

[a]Mean absolute deviation is $\Sigma(\alpha_j|rw_j/rw|)/4$; rw_j is log real wage in region j; rw is log national average; and α_j is decadal average of regional occupation weight.

Table 5.4 **Regional Real Wage Differences: Clerks**

	A. Within North and South (decadal averages, log of real wage ratio)			
	1821–30	1831–40	1841–50	1851–60
Midwest-Northeast	.562	.359	.448	.273
South Central–South Atlantic	.187	.215	.210	.261

	B. Relative to National Average (decadal averages, log of real wage ratio)			
	1821–30	1831–40	1841–50	1851–60
Northeast	−.161	−.155	−.156	−.117
Midwest	.401	.204	.282	.162
South Atlantic	.086	.076	.082	−.046
South Central	.273	.291	.292	.215
Mean absolute deviation[a]	.171	.163	.186	.130

	C. Regression of $\ln(rw_j/rw)_t = \delta + \beta \ln(\alpha_j)_t$	
	β	t-Statistic
Northeast	−.037	−.127
Midwest	−.179	−4.718
South Atlantic	.132	3.176
South Central	.296	1.508

[a]Mean absolute deviation is $\Sigma(\alpha_j|rw_j/rw|)/4$; rw_j is log real wage in region j; rw is log national average; and α_j is decadal average of regional occupation weight.

1820s. The gap rose in the 1830s but then fell back in the 1840s. The gap declined slightly in the 1850s but was only marginally lower in the 1850s than in the 1820s.

In the case of artisans, the wage gap between the South Central and the South Atlantic regions remained constant at about 8 percent in the 1820s and 1830s, rose slightly in the 1840s, and then increased substantially in the 1850s. The initial regional wage gap was considerably larger for clerks—about 0.19 in log terms—and the gap trended slightly upward over the antebellum period, reaching 0.22 in log terms by the 1850s.

Panel B of tables 5.2–5.4 shows occupation-specific decadal averages of the $\ln(rw_j/rw)$—that is, the log of the region's real wage relative to the national average. Also shown is the weighted mean absolute deviation, which is the weighted average of the absolute values of $\ln(rw_j/rw)$. The mean absolute deviation can be interpreted as a summary statistic of the overall extent of regional wage differentials—if the deviation declines, regional wage differentials, on average, were falling.

Consistent with the findings in panel A, wages of common laborers in the Midwest in the 1820s exceeded the national average but converged from the 1820s to the 1850s. Convergence, however, was not monotonic—common wages in the Midwest rose relative to the national average in the 1830s. Real wages in the Northeast in the 1820s were below average but also converged by the 1850s, although again not monotonically.

The real wages of common laborers in the South Atlantic states were below the national average in the 1820s but slightly above levels in the Northeast. However, by the 1830s, the pattern had reversed itself—the real wages of common laborers were higher in the Northeast than in the South Atlantic states. Real wages in the South Atlantic states fell further behind in the 1840s before recovering partially in the 1850s. The real wages of common laborers in the South Central states were above the national average in the 1820s but by the 1840s had fallen below the national average, as in the South Atlantic region. As in the South Atlantic region, however, some recovery occurred in the 1850s. Overall, the mean absolute deviation declined, but, because of the divergent trends in the 1830s and between the South and the North, the decline was relatively modest in magnitude and not monotonic.

The initial variation across regions in relative real wages of artisans and clerks was much larger than for common laborers. In the case of the North, the pattern of change, however, was similar to that for common labor. Real wages were much higher than average in the Midwest and lower than average in the Northeast; wages in both regions, however, converged on the national average. Again, the convergence was not monotonic; the gap between the Midwest and the national average widened for artisans in the 1850s and for clerks in the 1840s. For both occupations, the mean absolute deviation was lower in the 1850s than in the 1820s; in the case of artisans, the decline took place in the 1840s, while, for clerks, the decline occurred in the 1850s.

Panel C of tables 5.2–5.4 reports the slope coefficients from regressions of $\ln(rw_j/rw)$ on $\ln \alpha_j$. The idea behind the regression is straightforward. If the slope coefficient is negative, then increases in the region's relative share of the (occupation-specific) labor force are associated with declines in the region's relative real wage, which is consistent with shifts in labor supply as the dominant factor behind shifts in relative wages across regions. However, if the coefficient is positive, then increases (decreases) in the region's labor force share were associated with increases (decreases) in the region's relative wage, a signal that demand shifts may have occurred.

The clearest evidence that shifts in supply were dominant appears in the regressions for the Midwest. For all three occupations, the coefficient was negative and statistically significant, with elasticities ranging from −0.15 (common laborers) to −0.28 (artisans). The coefficients were also negative for the Northeast but significant only in the case of artisans. For all three occupations in the South Atlantic states, and for white-collar workers in the South Central region, the coefficients were positive.

5.3.1   Discussion

The findings just presented bear on several important aspects of antebellum economic development. First, and most important, they are broadly supportive of a labor markets explanation of the settlement process, along the lines suggested by Coelho and Shepherd (1976). Real wages were initially higher on the frontier (the Midwest and South Central states) than in the settled East (the Northeast and South Atlantic). The existence of these regional wage gaps provided, at least in principle, an economic incentive to migrate to the frontier and thus help resolve the paradox noted earlier in the chapter—the movement of population from higher per capita income regions, such as the Northeast, to lower per capita income regions, such as the Midwest.

In the North, the shift of labor toward the Midwest coincided with a secular decline in the regional wage gap, especially pronounced in the case of artisans and white-collar laborers. The opposing movement in relative wages and labor force shares in the Midwest is consistent with the view that supply-side factors—migration—explain the secular trend in convergence in wages between the Midwest and the Northeast, although this does not rule out the possibility that other forces played a contributing role.[10]

It is instructive to compare my estimates of regional wage gaps in the North in the 1850s with those for later decades of the nineteenth century. According to Rosenbloom (1991, 427), real hourly wages of common laborers were 10 percent higher in the Midwest than in the Northeast in 1890; for artisans, the gap was somewhat larger (22 percent). Here, *real* means deflated by an index of food prices, similar to my definition of *real*. My estimates imply that real (daily) wages of common laborers were about 16.5 percent higher in the Midwest than in the Northeast in the 1850s; the corresponding gap for artisans was 30 percent. Thus, the process of regional labor market integration in the North began before the Civil War but was not complete on the eve of the conflict.

In the South, the dominant migration pattern was also east-west, but the shift of labor toward the South Central states did not coincide with a narrowing of regional wage gaps—if anything, the gaps were wider on the eve of the Civil War than in the 1820s. The failure of the regional wage gaps to close in the South seems inconsistent with the views of various historians who have argued that the existence of interregional slave markets enhanced the general efficiency of east-west factor mobility in the South (Fleisig 1976; Field 1978; Wright 1978).

In the case of common labor, the absence of regional wage convergence in the South was not the only adverse pattern. Using the regional labor force shares, it is possible to produce an overall estimate of the North-South wage gap for common labor.[11] This gap was slightly *negative* in the 1820s, indicating that real wages were initially higher in the South. But, in the 1830s, the wage gap turned markedly in favor of the North. The gap continued to widen in the 1840s before narrowing somewhat in the 1830s, although still remaining positive.

As noted earlier in the chapter, economic historians have long been aware of the existence of a North-South wage gap after the Civil War, but the origins of the gap—in particular, whether it predated the war—have remained somewhat mysterious (Wright 1986). My results suggest that the origins can be dated to the 1830s, a timing that can hardly be considered random, especially in the light of the evidence presented earlier that shifts in relative demand against the South Atlantic region took place in that decade. Beginning in the late 1820s, and continuing through the 1830s, improvements in internal transportation, rising demand for cotton, and various federal land policies that subsidized frontier development helped fuel a land boom in the Midwest and South Central regions (Temin 1969; Lebergott 1985). This demand shock evidently left its imprint on the labor market in the form of rising real wages for common laborers in both regions relative to their respective regions of settlement (the Northeast and South Atlantic). However, the real wages of common laborers in the South Atlantic region fell relative to wages in the Northeast, a pattern that is difficult to explain except by a shift in relative labor demand in favor of the Northeast. The most plausible candidate for such a demand shift is early industrialization. Manufacturing first took hold in the 1820s and began to grow rapidly in the 1830s. However, the early growth of manufacturing was not distributed uniformly across the antebellum landscape; instead, it was concentrated in the Northeast (Goldin and Sokoloff 1982).

The combination of demand shocks favoring the Midwest and the Northeast can explain why the real wages of common laborers in the South fell below those of common laborers in the North before the Civil War.

In the mid-1840s, the United States became the recipient of large inflows of immigrants. Immigrants generally avoided the South but otherwise dispersed themselves across the Northern landscape (Ferrie 1999).[12] Recent work by Williamson (1995) suggests that the 1840s immigration marked the onset of a global labor market; if so, the infusion of immigrant labor into the North appears to have speeded up somewhat the process of regional wage equalization. By augmenting the Northern labor supply, the influx of immigrants may also help explain why the North-South wage gap for common labor narrowed somewhat in the 1850s.[13]

Finally, it is evident from tables 5.2–5.4 that real wages differed in level across regions and that growth rates of real wages varied across regions (see also chap. 3). It follows, therefore, that the growth rates of the national aggregate series—that is, the weighted average of the regional series—may differ from the region-specific rates of real wage growth.

Appendix table 5B.4 shows annual values of national aggregates of nominal wages, computed by weighting the regional series in chapter 3 by the region-occupation shares (the α's). National aggregates of real wages, constructed in the manner described earlier, are shown in appendix table 5B.5. Long-run growth rates of the aggregate real wage series, calculated as the coefficients on a linear trend, are shown in table 5.5. According to my estimates, between 1821 and 1860, the aggregate real wages of unskilled laborers grew at 1.04 percent per year, those of skilled artisans at 0.73 percent per year, and those of clerks at 1.52 percent per year.

How important was the geographic redistribution of the labor force in influencing aggregate growth rates? One way to answer this question is to recompute the aggregate series under the assumption that α weights are fixed at their 1820 values. Estimates of trend growth derived from these fixed-weight series are shown in table 5.5.

In general, population redistribution had a modest effect on the aggre-

Table 5.5   **Aggregate Growth Rates: Real Wages, 1821–60**

	Common Laborer	Artisan	Clerk
Variable weight	.0104	.0073	.0152
t-Statistic	4.795	4.544	6.432
Fixed weight	.0097	.0064	.0141
t-Statistic	4.603	3.799	6.043

Note: Figures are coefficients (β) of trend in regression of aggregate real wage: ln $rw = \alpha + \beta T + \varepsilon$. Variable weight: allows α_j to vary over time; fixed weight α_j is fixed at initial (1821) value (see the text).

gate real wage growth. The largest effect occurred for white-collar workers, for whom redistribution increased the growth rate from 0.0141 to 0.0152 percent per year. Cumulated over forty years, the real wages of white-collar workers were about 4.5 percent higher in the aggregate than they would have been had no population redistribution occurred.[14]

In the light of the evidently large regional gaps in real wages, it might seem surprising that population redistribution had such a small effect on aggregate growth. While population redistribution from east to west did raise the aggregate growth rate, the convergence of regional wage levels offset these gains.[15] In addition, the South Atlantic states played an important role in dampening aggregate growth; the region did not shed unskilled labor fast enough when its real wages began falling relative to the national average, nor did its share of skilled labor (artisan or white collar) increase when wages in these occupations were above the national average.

5.4 Wage Convergence, 1850–60: Evidence from the Censuses of Social Statistics

Section 5.3 presented evidence that real wages differed in level across regions in the 1820s but that most regions shared in a process of real wage convergence by the 1850s. Can the same be said for real wages measured at the level of smaller geographic areas (local labor markets)?

Differences in real wage levels across local labor markets were, in a quantitative sense, significant during the antebellum period. These differences can be documented at the county level using the eight-state sample from the Censuses of Social Statistics, discussed in chapter 2. Table 5.6 shows the 10-90 spread in the log of the real wage of common labor, for various states in this sample, in 1850 and 1860. (The 10-90 spread is the difference between the log real wage at the tenth percentile and that at the ninetieth percentile, across counties in a given state.) Here, the *real wage* is defined as the nominal wage deflated by the cost of board. On the face of the evidence presented in table 5.6, it would appear that common laborers could potentially increase their living standards by moving from low-

Table 5.6	10-90 Spread: Log of Real Daily Wage of Common Labor, across Counties, 1850			
Massachusetts	.17	North Carolina	.81
Pennsylvania	.31	Virginia	.69
Michigan	.48	Kentucky	.55
Iowa	.46	Tennessee	.63

Source: Sample from 1850 and 1860 manuscript Censuses of Social Statistics.

Note: The 10-90 spread is the difference in log wage at the tenth and ninetieth percentiles of real wage distribution across counties within state. The real wage is the estimated nominal weekly wage ([daily wage × 6]/weekly cost of board).

to high-wage counties within states—typically, a shorter-distance move than one across regions.

To measure the extent of wage convergence at the county level, I use the eight-state sample from the 1850 and 1860 Censuses of Social Statistics. The empirical model that I have in mind is a version of the relative demand-supply model discussed earlier in the chapter:

$$w/p_{it} = -\varepsilon L_{it} + d_{it},$$

$$\Delta L_{it} = L_{it} - L_{it-1} = \Delta s_{it} + \theta(w_{it-1}/p_{it-1}).$$

The first equation is the relative demand curve, i indexes location (county), w/p is the real wage (as above, the nominal wage deflated by the cost of board), d is the demand shift term, ε is the wage elasticity of labor demand (all variables are measured in logs), and t is the time period. The second equation is the relative supply curve: the change in labor supplied to location i between periods $t - 1$ and t is a positive function of the real wage in period $t - 1$ ($\theta > 0$), and Δs is the change in factors that shift supply. Because I am using the census data, $t = 1860$, and, therefore, $t - 1 = 1850$.

Taking first-differences, and solving for $\Delta(w/p)_{it}$,

$$\Delta(w/p)_{it} = \Delta d_{it} - \varepsilon \Delta s_{it} - \beta(w_{it-1}/p_{it-1}),$$

where $\beta = \varepsilon\theta$. At issue is whether $\beta > 0$.

The model of relative supply and demand requires a definition of *relative*. Here, my presumption is that *relative* means "within state," which, in terms of the empirical estimation, is equivalent to including dummy variables for states in the regression given above.[16] Estimation also requires a specification for $\Delta d - \varepsilon\Delta s$. I assume that this expression is approximated by including the growth rate of population in the county as well as the change in urbanization.[17] Because both variables may be proxies for demand as well as supply shifts, the signs of their coefficients are not predetermined (i.e., they could be positive or negative).

Because chapter 4 found essential equivalence in wages of farm and common laborers within counties, I group the data for these two occupations together. Ordinary least-squares regressions are estimated for unskilled laborers (common and farm laborers) and carpenters.

Table 5.7 shows the estimates of β by occupation. The estimates are significantly different from zero and relatively close to unity. Although one might imagine reasons why the coefficients might differ with respect to occupation, little evidence is in fact found of such differences. On average, a county with real wages that were 10 percent higher than average in 1850 experienced real wage growth that was 8 percent below average between 1850 and 1860. This is a substantial degree of wage convergence, especially in the light of the fact that the regressions do not directly control for

Table 5.7   Wage Convergence Regressions, 1850–60: Coefficient Estimates

	A. Common and Farm Labor			
	β	t-Statistic	β	t-Statistic
w/p_{50}	−.854	−28.012	−.859	−28.035
ΔPopulation			−.032	−1.413
ΔUrban			−.051	−1.537
State dummies	Yes		Yes	
R^2	.481		.483	
	B. Carpenters			
w/p_{50}	−.839	−17.731	−.848	−17.719
ΔPopulation			−.041	−.800
ΔUrban			−.113	−1.720
State dummies	Yes		Yes	
R^2	.419		.421	

Source: Eight-state sample from 1850 and 1860 Censuses of Social Statistics (see the text, esp. chap. 2). Observations are county level. Dependent variable is log of weekly real wage in 1860 (= nominal weekly wage/weekly cost of board). Nominal daily wage for farm labor is (monthly wage with board + 4.3 × weekly cost of board)/26. Weekly wage is 7 × daily wage. Nominal weekly wage of common labor and carpenters is 7 × nominal daily wage without board. Δpopulation = log(population 1860/population 1850). Δurban = 1 if county contained at least one urban area of population ten thousand or more in 1860 but not in 1850, 0 otherwise.

location-specific amenities or disamenities, which would tend to bias β toward zero.[18] Population and urban growth were associated with lower rates of real wage growth between 1850 and 1860, which suggests that both variables were associated with outward shifts in relative supply that were greater than those in relative demand.

In sum, the evidence from the census suggests that, given enough time to adjust, local labor markets functioned comparatively well before the Civil War. Counties that were high wage—and, therefore, were more costly locations from a production point of view (cf. chap. 4)—did not remain high wage for very long; the reverse was true for low-wage counties. The pace of wage convergence within states was quicker than the pace of convergence across regions, which is consistent with costs of adjustment (migration) being lower, on average, within states than across regions.[19]

5.5   Conclusion

This chapter has used both the wage series from chapter 3 and the eight-state sample to study geographic aspects of labor market integration. In the North, real wages followed a pattern of convergence: real wages were highest initially on the frontier and tended to decline over time relative to real wages in settled regions. The South Atlantic region was an exception to this pattern: real wages there evidently fell over time relative to other regions, at the same time that the region's share of the national labor force was declining.

I also found evidence of wage convergence at the county level: wage growth between 1850 and 1860 was significantly slower in counties that began the decade with relatively high wage levels. Such wage convergence is consistent with an arbitrage process described by a simple model of (local) labor supply and demand and, therefore, strongly suggests the presence of market forces in the determination of wages at the local level.

Appendix 5A
Computation of Regional Price Deflators, 1850

As noted in the text, the regional price deflators are constructed from the state averages of the weekly cost of board published in the 1850 census. Let b_j be the published state average. Then $b = \sum \gamma_j b_j$ is the regional average, where the weights (γ_j) are computed from Weiss's (1992) labor force.[20] I make a further adjustment to the regional estimates by multiplying each by a regional adjustment factor η.[21] The regional deflators are computed by dividing each region's estimate by the estimate for the Northeast. Multiplying by 100, the results are 100.0 for the Northeast, 74.1 for the Midwest, 85.2 for the South Atlantic region, and 99.4 for the South Central states. Thus, the cost of living was relatively low in the Midwest compared with that in the Northeast, while the reverse was true in the South Central states compared with the South Atlantic. To construct the regional relative real wage indices discussed in the chapter, follow the procedure in the text using these cost-of-living figures, the benchmark wage estimates for 1850 (from chap. 3), and the regional real wage indices from chapter 3.

Appendix 5B

Table 5B.1   **Regional Occupation Weights: Common Laborers**

	Northeast	Midwest	South Atlantic	South Central
1821	.499	.124	.258	.120
1822	.496	.128	.254	.122
1823	.494	.133	.251	.123
1824	.491	.137	.248	.125
1825	.489	.141	.244	.127
1826	.487	.145	.241	.129
1827	.484	.149	.237	.130
1828	.482	.154	.233	.132
1829	.480	.158	.230	.134
1830	.477	.162	.226	.135
1831	.472	.171	.221	.136
1832	.467	.180	.215	.137
1833	.462	.190	.210	.139
1834	.457	.199	.204	.140
1835	.452	.208	.199	.141
1836	.447	.217	.194	.142
1837	.442	.226	.188	.143
1838	.437	.236	.183	.145
1839	.432	.245	.177	.146
1840	.427	.254	.172	.147
1841	.425	.258	.169	.147
1842	.423	.263	.166	.148
1843	.421	.267	.163	.148
1844	.419	.272	.161	.149
1845	.417	.276	.158	.149
1846	.415	.280	.155	.149
1847	.413	.285	.152	.150
1848	.411	.289	.149	.150
1849	.409	.294	.147	.151
1850	.407	.298	.144	.151
1851	.404	.303	.142	.151
1852	.400	.308	.140	.152
1853	.397	.313	.138	.152
1854	.394	.318	.136	.152
1855	.391	.323	.134	.153
1856	.387	.327	.132	.153
1857	.384	.332	.130	.153
1858	.381	.337	.128	.153
1859	.377	.342	.126	.154
1860	.374	.347	.124	.154

Source: See the text.

Table 5B.2   **Regional Occupation Weights: Artisans**

	Northeast	Midwest	South Atlantic	South Central
1821	.608	.087	.224	.079
1822	.610	.088	.220	.081
1823	.613	.090	.215	.082
1824	.615	.091	.210	.083
1825	.617	.092	.206	.085
1826	.619	.093	.201	.086
1827	.621	.094	.196	.087
1828	.624	.096	.191	.088
1829	.626	.097	.187	.090
1830	.628	.098	.182	.091
1831	.621	.106	.179	.092
1832	.615	.115	.177	.093
1833	.608	.123	.174	.093
1834	.601	.131	.171	.096
1835	.595	.140	.169	.097
1836	.588	.148	.166	.098
1837	.581	.156	.163	.100
1838	.574	.164	.160	.101
1839	.568	.173	.158	.102
1840	.561	.181	.155	.103
1841	.561	.187	.150	.102
1842	.561	.193	.145	.101
1843	.561	.199	.140	.100
1844	.561	.205	.135	.099
1845	.561	.212	.131	.098
1846	.560	.218	.126	.097
1847	.560	.224	.121	.095
1848	.560	.230	.116	.094
1849	.560	.236	.111	.093
1850	.560	.242	.106	.092
1851	.559	.244	.105	.092
1852	.559	.245	.104	.092
1853	.558	.247	.103	.092
1854	.557	.249	.102	.092
1855	.557	.251	.101	.093
1856	.556	.252	.099	.093
1857	.555	.254	.098	.093
1858	.554	.256	.097	.093
1859	.554	.257	.096	.093
1860	.553	.259	.095	.093

Source: See the text.

	Northeast	Midwest	South Atlantic	South Central
Table 5B.3	**Regional Occupation Weights: White-Collar Workers**			
1821	.587	.058	.249	.106
1822	.589	.059	.244	.107
1823	.592	.060	.239	.104
1824	.595	.061	.234	.111
1825	.597	.062	.229	.113
1826	.599	.062	.224	.114
1827	.602	.063	.219	.116
1828	.604	.064	.214	.118
1829	.607	.065	.209	.119
1830	.609	.066	.204	.121
1831	.604	.072	.201	.123
1832	.599	.078	.199	.125
1833	.593	.083	.196	.127
1834	.588	.089	.194	.129
1835	.583	.095	.191	.131
1836	.578	.101	.188	.133
1837	.573	.107	.186	.135
1838	.567	.112	.183	.137
1839	.562	.118	.181	.139
1840	.557	.124	.178	.141
1841	.559	.129	.124	.140
1842	.561	.133	.125	.138
1843	.563	.138	.125	.137
1844	.565	.142	.125	.136
1845	.567	.147	.126	.135
1846	.568	.152	.126	.133
1847	.570	.156	.126	.132
1848	.572	.161	.126	.131
1849	.574	.165	.127	.129
1850	.576	.170	.127	.128
1851	.575	.171	.126	.128
1852	.575	.173	.124	.129
1853	.575	.174	.123	.129
1854	.575	.176	.121	.130
1855	.574	.177	.120	.130
1856	.574	.178	.119	.130
1857	.573	.180	.117	.131
1858	.573	.181	.116	.131
1859	.572	.183	.114	.132
1860	.572	.184	.113	.132

Source: See the text.

Table 5B.4   **Aggregate Nominal Wage Estimates ($)**

	Common Laborers (Daily)	Artisans (Daily)	White-Collar Workers (Monthly)
1821	N.A.	N.A.	N.A.
1822	N.A.	N.A.	32.65
1823	N.A.	1.40	32.77
1824	N.A.	1.26	32.89
1825	.71	1.28	36.16
1826	.71	1.37	34.07
1827	.70	1.46	34.43
1828	.69	1.39	34.43
1829	.70	1.37	36.93
1830	.69	1.33	35.76
1831	.67	1.36	33.38
1832	.69	1.40	35.08
1833	.71	1.41	35.77
1834	.78	1.52	36.39
1835	.78	1.56	35.54
1836	.81	1.65	36.98
1837	.95	1.63	44.31
1838	.80	1.48	43.24
1839	.84	1.54	48.56
1840	.72	1.50	45.64
1841	.76	1.50	40.24
1842	.78	1.41	40.83
1843	.81	1.35	44.46
1844	.80	1.28	42.60
1845	.78	1.44	44.00
1846	.77	1.35	43.12
1847	.72	1.41	45.55
1848	.86	1.38	44.59
1849	.84	1.48	44.71
1850	.85	1.44	45.54
1851	.84	1.46	51.93
1852	.89	1.50	51.63
1853	.88	1.57	49.19
1854	.93	1.63	50.86
1855	.96	1.71	51.41
1856	.97	1.75	52.87
1857	1.02	1.84	55.25
1858	.96	1.87	52.81
1859	1.05	1.87	48.41
1860	1.03	1.83	52.10
	Five-Year Averages		
1821–25	.71	1.31	33.62
1826–30	.70	1.39	35.12
1831–35	.73	1.45	35.23
1836–40	.82	1.56	43.75
1841–45	.79	1.40	42.43
1846–50	.81	1.41	44.70
1851–55	.90	1.57	51.00
1856–60	1.01	1.83	52.29
	Decadal Averages		
1821–30	.70	1.36	34.45
1831–40	.78	1.51	39.49
1841–50	.80	1.41	43.57
1851–60	.96	1.70	51.65

Note: Covers Northeast, Midwest, South Atlantic, and South Central regions only. N.A. = not applicable.

Table 5B.5   **Aggregate Real Wage Series (1860 = 100)**

	Common Laborers	Artisans	White-Collar Workers
1821	N.A.	N.A.	N.A.
1822	N.A.	N.A.	54.3
1823	N.A.	72.4	60.3
1824	N.A.	68.2	62.6
1825	65.6	67.1	67.1
1826	74.3	80.6	71.2
1827	74.6	87.4	72.3
1828	75.7	84.4	73.6
1829	75.4	83.9	79.0
1830	77.2	83.6	78.9
1831	74.4	85.9	72.7
1832	73.2	83.6	73.1
1833	71.8	79.8	70.9
1834	82.2	88.8	75.2
1835	71.0	79.3	63.8
1836	61.9	71.2	56.3
1837	79.6	76.9	73.0
1838	71.0	73.8	75.2
1839	73.1	73.5	82.1
1840	78.9	90.2	96.1
1841	87.6	96.3	90.4
1842	110.9	109.9	109.6
1843	119.6	111.1	129.9
1844	114.4	104.5	122.5
1845	104.3	107.5	117.1
1846	100.9	97.8	113.0
1847	78.1	85.0	97.6
1848	115.9	104.3	119.0
1849	106.5	104.5	111.9
1850	97.2	92.7	103.4
1851	97.8	96.5	120.9
1852	99.5	94.9	115.6
1853	91.9	91.8	101.4
1854	92.5	89.8	98.6
1855	86.1	86.2	90.9
1856	85.0	85.6	91.1
1857	82.9	84.3	89.2
1858	96.3	102.8	102.2
1859	98.7	98.4	89.9
1860	100.0	100.0	100.0
	Five-Year Averages (1856–60 = 100)		
1821–25	70.9	73.5	64.6
1826–30	81.5	89.1	79.4
1831–35	80.5	88.6	75.3
1836–40	78.7	81.9	81.0
1841–45	116.0	112.3	120.6
1846–50	107.7	102.8	115.3
1851–55	101.1	97.5	111.6
1856–60	100.0	100.0	100.0
	Decadal Averages (1851–60 = 100)		
1821–30	79.3	84.3	68.8
1831–40	79.2	86.3	73.9
1841–50	111.3	108.9	111.5
1851–60	100.0	100.0	100.0

Source: See the text.

Note: Covers Northeast, Midwest, South Atlantic, and South Central regions only. N.A. = not applicable.

Wages in California during
the Gold Rush

This chapter examines the labor market implications of a specific event—the California Gold Rush of the late 1840s and early 1850s. From the standpoint of studying labor market integration, the Gold Rush is an interesting natural experiment—an unexpected, highly localized demand shock of tremendous size that required the significant and costly reallocation of labor (and other mobile factors) from distant locations to a very sparsely populated region. Although it is abundantly obvious from the historical record that labor migrated to California in response to the discovery of gold, the time path of wages and labor supply has remained unclear.

Following a recounting of the history of the California Gold Rush, the chapter develops a simple model of wage determination in a gold rush economy. I argue that the most likely path was an initial rise in wages, followed by a steep decline.

Similar to that in chapter 3, the analysis here uses a sample of California forts drawn from the *Reports of Persons and Articles Hired* to estimate nominal wage series for common laborers–teamsters, artisans, and clerks. A price deflator is constructed from Berry's (1984) compilation of wholesale prices.

The time path of real wages revealed by the *Reports* is consistent with the stylized model of wage determination. Real wages rose very sharply during the initial phase of the rush, fell abruptly in 1852, and then remained roughly constant for the remainder of the decade. Although it was, by definition, a purely transitory shock, the Gold Rush appears to have left a permanent imprint on California wage levels. I argue that the permanent effect occurred because, as a result of the Gold Rush, California became integrated into the economy of the Northern United States, where wages were relatively high.

The chapter concludes by examining the wage elasticity of labor supply into Gold Rush California over various periods of years (e.g., 1848–52), using labor quantities computed from the federal censuses and the state census of 1852. The estimates range between 2 and 3, suggesting a relatively elastic response. However, labor supply into Gold Rush California was less elastic than it was into Alaska during the Pipeline era (1973–76).

6.1   The California Gold Rush

Other than the Civil War, few events in nineteenth-century American history capture the imagination like the California Gold Rush.[1] The initial discovery of gold in 1848 and the subsequent rush of people into the state were the subject of innumerable newspaper articles, diaries, and related contemporary accounts. The Gold Rush was an epic adventure for the "argonauts" and "forty-niners" who took part in it. It has also been a lightning rod for historians seeking metaphors for the grand issues of frontier development—the callous exploitation of native peoples and natural resources, the slow and uncertain development of orderly government from chaos, the haphazard taming of the American West (Goodman 1994).

Although the coastal regions of California had been explored in the sixteenth century, the true origins of California settlement lie in Spain's acquisition of French claims to the vast Louisiana territory following the end of the Seven Years' War in Europe in 1763. Charles III of Spain subsequently sent the adventurer Jose de Galvez to push Spanish settlement north of Mexico, in the hope of preventing English encroachment into Mexico and its rich mining region. Galvez invented the mission—in reality, a colonizing institution whose purpose was to Christianize native populations, settle them into agriculture, and ultimately create an interlinked set of local economies (Coman 1912, vol. 1; Lavender 1976, 18).

The mission approach was largely successful in Baja California and southern Arizona, but rebellious Indians blocked its extension into Alta (Upper) California. Galvez appointed Fray Junipero Serra to head an expedition to Alta California, along with the governor of Baja, Gaspar de Portola. After great hardship, they established a *presidio* (fort) at San Diego and later one at Monterey (Lavender 1976, 19–22). By 1772, there were five missions and two *presidios.* The number of missions grew slowly but steadily. San Francisco was added in 1776, Santa Barbara in 1782 (Coman 1912, vol. 1; Lotchin 1974).

Life at the missions was hard. Mortality was extremely high, agricultural productivity was frequently low, and there were periodic skirmishes with Indians. Nonetheless, by the early nineteenth century, missions were taking root, particularly in the south, where ranching and some wheat farming flourished (Coman 1912, 1:145–55; Lavender 1976, 24–27).

The missions began to fall somewhat out of favor in the early nineteenth century. Conflict arose over access to land in California, and anticlerical sentiment erupted in Mexico. By the mid-1830s, mission land was placed under secular control, and a series of private land grants was initiated. Fueled by cheap labor, primarily Native American, southern California ranches had become highly profitable through cattle production, yet the standard of living of the "working class" was miserable (Coman 1912, 1: 172–89; Lavender 1976, 29–31).

Throughout its colonization of California, Mexico faced serious difficulties keeping out interlopers. American trappers and fur traders appeared in Alta California as early as 1800 (Coman 1912, 1:160). Furs were traded for manufactured goods brought by Boston shippers who stopped in Monterey and San Francisco on the way to China (Coman 1912, 1:163–64). Russia established Fort Ross in Alta California in 1812 (illegally, but with the full knowledge of the Mexican government) and kept it in operation until 1841. By 1832, there was a well-traveled trade route between Sante Fe and Mission San Gabriel (Coman 1912, 2:214). In addition, there was a steady stream of Americans who became Mexican citizens and practiced (or promised to practice) Catholicism in exchange for land grants. By the early 1840s, they were joined by small bands of settlers (Coman 1912, 2:228–41; Lavender 1976, 34, 37–40).

Slowly, but inexorably, disputes occurred between the settlers and the Mexican government. In June 1846, a group of settlers staged the so-called Bear Flag Revolt (near present-day Sonoma) with the aid of Charles Fremont of the U.S. Corps of Topographical Engineers and sixty troops under his command (Coman 1912, 2:246; Caughey 1948, 4–5). Word soon came that the United States was at war with Mexico. The mission at Monterey was seized by Commodore John D. Sloat. Additional troops and naval units were despatched from the Army of the West, the Mormon Battalion, and a contingent of poor artisan volunteers from New York who had been promised free passage for themselves (and their tools) if they stayed in California at the end of their tour of duty (Caughey 1948, 4–5; Lavender 1976, 49). By mid-1846, the United States Navy had occupied all usable ports in California (Lavender 1976, 46).

The Mexican War came to a formal end with the signing of the Treaty of Guadalupe Hidalgo on 2 February 1848. In exchange for $15 million and the forgiveness of $3.3 million in American claims against the Mexican government, Mexico ceded California, New Mexico, Utah, Nevada, Arizona, and disputed parts of Texas to the United States (Lavender 1976, 4).

Ironically, the treaty was signed two weeks after—and, apparently, without knowledge of—the discovery of gold that marked the formal beginning of the Gold Rush.[2] James Marshall, a carpenter working for John Sutter (a recipient of a land grant from Mexico), happened on a pea-sized pellet of gold near the American River. At first, Marshall and Sutter attempted to keep knowledge of the discovery a secret, but they were unable to prevent the information from leaking. Teamsters and other travelers delivered the news to various settlements on the way to San Francisco (Coman 1912, 2:256; Lavender 1976, 50–51).

The local response was rapid and extreme. According to an eyewitness, when the news reached Monterey in early May, "The blacksmith dropped his hammer, the carpenter his plane, the mason his trowel, the farmer his sickle, the baker his loaf, and the tapster his bottle. All were off for the mines. . . . [there is] only a community of women left, and a gang of prisoners" (quoted in Lavender 1976, 51). According to a 1 June report, half San Francisco's population (at that time, between eight hundred and one thousand) had left for the mines, and fully three-quarters were gone by the middle of the month (Coman 1912, 2:257; Caughey 1948, 21).

The local labor supply was supplemented by in-migration. The schooner *Louisa* relayed the news to Honolulu, and other ships, bound for points north and south, did the same (Caughey 1948, 23). Migrants poured in from Oregon (according to some reports, *half* the male population) and from Hawaii, Mexico, Chile, Peru, China, and Australia (Lavender 1976, 53; Caughey 1948, 23–24; Marks 1994, 24).

The news took somewhat longer to reach the East. The first report, a letter in the *New York Times,* appeared in mid-August, and the *New Orleans Daily Picayune* reported the discovery in mid-September (Caughey 1948, 34–35). The early newspaper reports prompted disbelief, but official army accounts led President Polk to make a formal announcement in December (Lavender 1976, 55). Transportation companies quickly formed; handbooks for argonauts, such as George G. Foster's *The Gold Regions of California* (1848), were hastily written; and an avalanche of migrants followed (Caughey 1948, 51–55).

Although the specific routes varied enormously, there were three general ways to get to California. One way was by ship around Cape Horn, the chief disadvantages being the time cost (from three to eight months) and the hazards of shipwreck and onboard disease. A theoretically quicker route (six to eight weeks) was to take a ship to the Isthmus of Panama, travel overland to the Pacific, and then board another ship for San Francisco. Until Cornelius Vanderbilt built a railroad across the Isthmus (for which the fare was $25.00), the trip through Panama was extremely arduous (Coman 1912, 2:261).

Another popular route was overland (Caughey 1948, 95). Migrants banded together in groups leaving from various points in the Midwest, such as St. Louis. Because travel during winter was next to impossible, most tried to leave in April or May at the latest, the goal being to arrive in the gold fields by September. Overland migrants battled impassable terrain, bad weather, wagon damage, hunger, thirst, disease (cholera epidemics were frequent), and the occasional Indian attack (Caughey 1948, 58–60; Parke 1989).

Aside from the time costs, the money costs of migration were very high by the standards of the time. Depending on the port, fares on the Panama Route ranged from $100 to $300, for example, and the money costs of equipping an overland trip were in a similar range (Caughey 1948, 66; Parke 1989, 137). Despite the high time and money costs of transport, the numbers of migrants are impressive—an estimated eighty to ninety thousand annually in 1849 and 1850 (Wright 1940, 341–42; Lavender 1976).[3]

Although all surely had gold on their minds, not everyone became a miner (or remained one for long). Many migrants realized that profits could be made transporting consumer goods to the mines and set up makeshift stores under tents at mining camps (Coman 1912, 2:274–76; Lavender 1976, 75). Others sought to make their fortune in commerce, real estate, banking, or other services in rapidly growing San Francisco (see below). By 1860, there were 217 miners for every 1,000 people in the state, compared with 624 per 1,000 in 1850 (DeBow 1853, 976; Kennedy 1864, 35).[4]

The immediate consequence of the in-migration was rapid population growth. Estimates of the population on the eve of the Gold Rush, excluding non-Christianized Indians, range from three to eight thousand (Coman 1912, 2:217; Caughey 1948, 2; Lavender 1976, 15). The 1850 federal census put the population at ninety-three thousand, 77 percent of whom were males between the ages of fifteen and forty (DeBow 1853, 966–68; Kennedy 1862, 130).[5] By 1852, the population had grown to approximately 264,000 (DeBow 1853, 982).

Although most scholars date the end of the rush sometime in the early 1850s (some as late as 1857 [see Marks 1994, 31]), population growth fueled by in-migration continued through the rest of the decade, albeit at a slower pace. By 1860, the population had risen to 380,000, but the adult male (ages fifteen to forty) share had fallen to 49 percent, indicating a substantial shift in the demographic composition of the in-migrants toward more permanent settlers (Kennedy 1862, 131; Kennedy 1864, 26–27).

Some of the most spectacular growth occurred in San Francisco. In 1844, the population of Yeuba Buena (the Mexican name for San Francisco) was about fifty. A town census in 1847 showed that the hamlet had grown to 459 souls over the preceding three years, and the population doubled again the next year, presumably because of the establishment of the quartermaster's depot and the military presence left over from the Mexican War (Lotchin 1974, 8). Then, as a consequence of the Gold Rush the population exploded. By 1852, San Francisco housed thirty-four thousand inhabitants and, by 1860, fifty-six thousand (Lotchin 1974, 102). External trade expanded swiftly, being surpassed during the decade only by that in New York, Boston, and New Orleans (Lotchin 1974, 45).

San Francisco's extraordinary growth can be attributed to two factors— direct access to the Pacific (i.e., its port facilities) and proximity to the gold fields (Coman 1912, 2:277; Lotchin 1974, 5–6). Prospective forty-niners who took the sea route arrived at San Francisco, where they sought to buy supplies for the final leg of their journey and equipment for the mines, thereby creating a booming market in pans, shovels, and Indian baskets (Coman 1912, 2:279; Caughey 1948, 32). Miners journeyed back to the city with their treasure, where they attempted to purchase goods and services. During the early years, most goods, including food, were imported into San Francisco—including, evidently, turtle meat from the Galapagos Islands. Eventually, the imports gave way to locally produced agricultural and manufactured goods, most of which were marketed in San Francisco (Lotchin 1974, 10, 47; Caughey 1948, 210–13).

In the case of certain locally produced services, the shock to demand was sometimes so great that the line between traded and nontraded goods blurred. The cost of washing, it is said, rose so rapidly after 1848 that clothes and restaurant linens were sent by clipper ship to Hawaii or even China for cleaning (Marks 1994, 197–99).[6]

After the initial deposits near Sutter's Mill were exhausted, miners spread out over a thirty-five-thousand-square-mile area looking for more gold (Coman 1912, 2:266–68; Caughey 1948, 52–54). Some of the gold— so-called placer deposits—was so easy to find that it could be literally scooped out of streams, but other deposits were harder to locate and re-trieve.

By the second half of 1849, the easy gold nearby the mother lode was gone, and more complex methods—using cradles, "long toms," and sluice boxes—had to be employed. Miners discovered that mercury ("quick-silver") bonded with gold in an amalgam, which could then be cleaned. Quicksilver was readily available owing to the discovery of rich deposits near San Jose (Lavender 1976, 62).

Although placer mining remained the most significant method of min-ing until late in the 1850s, alternatives soon appeared. Quartz mining grew after extensive deposits were discovered near Mariposa in 1849. Stamp mills, the use of hydraulics, and tunneling were other important innova-tions. By comparison with placer mining, however, the required capital investments (and associated risks) of these alternative methods were sub-stantial, beyond the means of ordinary miners. Mining companies formed, and entrepreneurs competed with placer mining to hire laborers (Caughey 1948, 249–66).

Wherever significant deposits were found, mining camps soon followed. By the standards of the day—and certainly by those of the twentieth century—living conditions in the camps were extraordinarily bad. Aside from mining, there was little to do, and alcoholism was rampant. So, too, was disease and malnutrition, as sanitary conditions were horrible, in part owing to the environmental damage caused by the mining operations and the close (and crude) living quarters. Nonetheless, the camps thrived as miners fashioned crude local government and rudimentary procedures for enforcing their stakes (Caughey 1948; Lavender 1976, 65–66; Marks 1994).

Once the gold ran out, the camps were abandoned as quickly as they had been established (Caughey 1948, 267). Those still bitten by the gold bug moved on to the next strike or, sometimes, gold rushes elsewhere (e.g., Australia [see Caughey 1948, 293]). The less successful sought to return home but, hampered by high migration costs, frequently settled for employment in agriculture or in the burgeoning nonfarm sector in and around San Francisco (Caughey 1948; Lotchin 1974; Lavender 1976).

The Gold Rush had important political consequences. By far the most important was California's early admittance into the Union in 1850, thereby bypassing territorial status. A constitutional convention was called in 1849, and the constitution was overwhelmingly ratified by popular vote on 13 November. From the standpoint of statehood, the critical issue was slavery: Californians desired admittance as a free state, which upset the delicate political balance in Washington. The furor was abated by the Compromise of 1850, by which California was admitted as a free state while New Mexico and Utah were organized as territories that could then decide for themselves whether to be slave or free (Lavender 1976, 69–71).

6.2   Wage Determination in a Gold Rush Economy

This section presents a simple model of wage determination in a gold rush economy. The model is not novel—it is a standard Dutch disease framework, and a similar version of it has been used to analyze another historical gold rush, that of Australia in the early 1850s (Maddock and McLean 1984).[7] The prediction for nominal wages in the model economy is straightforward: nominal wages rise after the discovery of gold, then decline once labor supply fully adjusts to the spatial shock to labor demand. The comparative static path followed by real wages may be more complex, but it is likely, too, that real wages rise initially and then fall.

As a point of departure, imagine a pre–gold rush economy, by definition one in which population is small and perhaps highly scattered. There are N individuals, each of whom is endowed with equal shares ($1/N$) of the economy's known stocks of gold. N is fixed in the short run but may vary in the long run. Initially, I assume that known stocks of gold are very small; however, as the number of individuals changes, I maintain the assumption that each is endowed with $1/N$ of the stock of gold.[8] The total capital stock, K, is fixed in the short run, and each individual has an equal share $(1/N)$ of it.

Individuals maximize utility, which is defined over the consumption of a locally produced good, X, whose price is p_x, and an imported good, Z. The traded good is supplied from a settled economy removed by distance from the gold rush economy. The supply of the traded good is assumed to be perfectly elastic at price p_z.

Individuals allocate their available labor supply (L) between the production of the local good and gold production. The production function of the local good is $X = F(L_x, K)$, where K is capital. Once produced, the local good can be either consumed or sold at the price p_x. Gold, as well, can be used to purchase either X or Z, but it cannot be consumed. Gold is the numeraire commodity.[9]

The function g is a *harvesting* function, which converts the stock of ore (O) into a flow (g) available for export or for purchase of X. I assume that both F and g are concave; $g(0)S = 0$ (if no labor is allocated toward gold harvesting, gold output is zero); and $g \leq 1$ for any value of $L_g = L - L_x$.

The first-order conditions are straightforward.[10] Consumption of X and Z should be efficient, as should the allocation of labor between the production of the local good and the harvesting of gold: that is, labor is allocated to equalize the value of the marginal product in both production activities.

I model a gold rush as an increase in the economy's known stock of ore (S). An increase in S shifts the harvesting function outward, but, because $g(0)S = 0$, the shift is not a parallel one. At a fixed level of $p_x F_L$ ($= w$, the nominal wage), individuals will want to allocate more labor to gold harvesting than in the initial equilibrium. In the aggregate, the increase in L_g produces an inward shift in the supply of labor to the production of the local good, causing w to rise.

Gold has value in exchange, however, so the aggregate demands for X and Z may change. As long as X is a normal good, the demand for X will increase, leading to an increase in the demand for labor in the local goods sector. The increase in the demand for labor in the local sector further drives up w and also p_x. Define the real wage to be $w/h(p_x, p_z)$, where h is a cost-of-living function.[11] Because p_z is exogenous (the supply of Z is perfectly elastic), whether the real wage rises or falls depends on w/p_x. However, $w/p_x = F_L$. If, in the new (short-run) equilibrium, the quantity of labor demanded in the local sector declines, F_L will increase, and so will the real wage.[12]

In the long run, mobile factors (labor and capital) may flow in (or out) of the gold rush economy, provided that, in the new equilibrium, factor returns are sufficiently high to justify costs of adjustment (see below). Labor may be attracted into the gold rush economy because real income is higher after the discovery of gold. Capital may be attracted, especially because in-migration of labor will increase the aggregate demand for X.[13] For modeling purposes, I assume that any new labor shares in the endowment of gold equally with the initial residents. Consequently, from the standpoint of individuals, S falls, and the harvesting function shifts inward. The inward shift reduces the incentive to mine gold, thereby increasing the incentive to supply labor to the local goods sector. If the labor supply effect dominates relative to any shift in product demand, w will fall, as will w/p_x (and, thus, so will the real wage).

The model captures certain essential features of wage determination in a gold rush economy, but there is no question that it is highly stylized in several respects. For example, the model presumes that a representative individual allocates time to gold production and to production of the local good. While miners often did just that over the course of the year (because mining was seasonal [see below; and Lotchin 1974]), others clearly specialized their labor supply. Specialization does not alter the basic thrust of the model as long as some individuals were at the margin of shifting into gold production just prior to the gold discovery.[14]

Second, it was necessary to prospect for gold and establish a claim before harvesting it. Both activities had uncertain returns. Uncertainty can be incorporated in the model in the following manner. Assume that time spent harvesting gold is divided into two activities: prospecting (which includes establishing claims) and harvesting. By allocating L_p to prospecting, each individual can increase the probability $p(L_p)$ that he will find gold (I assume that $p'' < 0$). Expected income from gold harvesting is now

$$p(L_p)g(L - L_x - L_p)S.$$

There are now two ways to model a gold rush—either an increase in S or an upward shift in p for any given level of L_p. Either way, the gold rush increases the expected marginal product of labor in gold harvesting, and the remainder of the static analysis is unchanged.

6.2.1 Wage Dynamics

The model developed above does not directly address the dynamics of wage adjustment in the gold rush economy. To describe the dynamics of wage adjustment, it is necessary to specify expectations about the occurrence and duration of the shock and about adjustment costs. In what follows, I assume that the gold rush is a transitory shock—that is, the probability that its duration will continue indefinitely is known, in advance, to be zero.[15] For the moment, I assume that labor is the mobile factor and, therefore, ignore capital in- (or out-) migration.

Suppose that individuals had perfect foresight that the gold rush would begin at date t and last until date t' and that adjustment costs were convex.[16] By *adjustment costs,* I mean all costs associated with changing the allocation of labor from its initial pre–gold rush equilibrium and changing it back again once the gold rush has ended.

With perfect foresight and convex adjustment costs, it would be rational for labor to begin migrating into the economy *before* the gold rush, in order to avoid incurring high marginal adjustment costs at date t. Similarly, it would make sense for labor supply to decline just before the end of the rush, again to avoid high marginal adjustment costs. Therefore, w falls somewhat before date t, but the influx of labor before t will generally not be sufficient to prevent w from rising above its long-run equilibrium value for a while after t (Carrington 1996).[17] Analogously, some excess labor will remain after t', causing a temporary slump in wages.

What if dates t and t' are uncertain but adjustment costs are zero? By *uncertain,* I mean that no individual knows exactly when (or even if) a gold rush will occur. Once the shock occurs, however, information that a rush has begun is instantaneously available to all individuals. Similarly, the end of the rush is uncertain, but, once it has occurred, this information is immediately transmitted.

If adjustment costs were zero, then uncertainty over t and t' has no economic consequence. Labor simply adjusts once the shock occurs, and wages move immediately to their new equilibrium value, returning to their original level when the rush is over.

Of course, individuals did not have perfect foresight about the discovery of gold or the duration of the rush, and, on the basis of the discussion in section 6.1, adjustment costs were obviously nonzero. Further, as section 6.1 argued, the discovery of gold took place in stages—that is, the shock was spread through time.

If the gold discoveries were unanticipated but sequential and adjustment costs were convex, then wages would rise steeply during the period of discovery, followed by an abrupt decline when the rush ended (because all the labor would be surplus at that point). If, as assumed above, the rush were a transitory phenomenon, wages would then eventually return to their prerush level after the rush's end. The precise pattern followed by wages during the period of discovery would depend on the size of the shocks to labor demand, their precise timing, and how quickly labor responds.

Up to this point, I have ignored capital mobility. Allowing for capital mobility (with adjustment costs) might alter dramatically the wage adjustment path (Taylor 1996). For example, if adjustment costs for capital were uniformly lower than for labor, the initial jumps in wages would be greater. If the capital were of the "putty-clay" variety—capital costs are mostly sunk once the capital is in place—relatively high wages might be sustained a while after the rush is over. However, wages would still eventually return to their initial equilibrium, unless it was profitable for some other reason to continue to invest in the gold rush economy after the rush was over.

More complex dynamic models could also be fashioned by considering exactly how factor supply, particularly labor, would change in the short as opposed to the long run and by incorporating inflationary feedback. For example, individuals in the gold rush economy have strong incentives to substitute leisure intertemporally. They expand effort in the short run following the discovery of gold, believing that the additional work will be temporary, and, having accumulated gold (a store of value), they will enjoy more leisure and possibly consumption in the future. However, given that daily and weekly hours of work in the late 1840s and early 1850s were already quite high—for example, a ten-hour day and sixty-hour workweek were not uncommon—it is unclear that increases in hours at either intensive margin offered much scope for substitution (Lotchin 1974, 86). But the same may not have been true of annual hours, in the light of the widespread seasonality of labor demand during the antebellum period (Engerman and Goldin 1993).

The particular timing of migration could also be analyzed in a more complex model. Because gold harvesting was uncertain, individuals in the settled economy might prefer to wait rather than migrate immediately because the majority of the costs of migration were sunk once incurred.[18] However, the very concept of a *rush* suggests that prospective migrants believed that the easy gold would be gone unless they got there first.[19] Given high migration costs, if the first effect dominates, labor supply will be inelastic in the short run but might become abruptly elastic. If the second effect dominates, however, labor will rush in, but migration will eventually tail off.

By *inflationary feedback,* I mean a nonneutral effect of changes in the stock of gold on wages and prices. Because the country was on a metal standard, there is little doubt that the California Gold Rush raised the general price level. But the issue here is not the general price level; it is whether increases in the stock of gold affected local prices more quickly than wages—that is, whether nominal wages in California were sticky in the short run (for an analysis of nominal wage rigidity, see chap. 8). Certainly, the anecdotal evidence on prices during the Gold Rush is suggestive of the possibility of inflationary feedback (Caughey 1948, 203; Marks 1994, 177).[20] Unfortunately, the wage and price data at hand are not sufficient to determine whether inflationary feedback occurred, and I ignore the possibility in my empirical analysis.[21]

6.3 Data and Estimation of Wage Indices

Traditional accounts of the California Gold Rush provide anecdotal evidence on wages and prices but not the sort of quantitative basis to construct a continuous nominal or real wage index comparable in quality to those presented in chapter 3.[22] To construct wage indices, I make use of a sample of wages paid to civilians hired at United States Army installations in California drawn from the *Reports of Persons and Articles Hired,* the same source used in chapter 3. As indicated in the discussion in section 6.1, the army was present in California before the Gold Rush, and its installations continued to operate during and after the discovery of gold. California forts appear to have functioned like their counterparts elsewhere in the country, civilians being hired to perform various tasks. The occupations of civilians at California forts were also similar to those at forts elsewhere in the country (e.g., laborer, teamster, artisan, clerk).

Table 6.1 shows the distribution of wage observations in the sample of California forts, by occupation, fort location, and time period. The sample covers the period 1847–60 and, as in chapter 3, is restricted to common laborers (including teamsters), skilled artisans, and white-collar workers. Approximately 45 percent of the wage observations for common laborers and artisans pertain to forts located in modern-day northern or central California (i.e., in direct proximity to the gold), the remainder to forts in southern California or scattered field locations. About 90 percent of the observations pertain to common laborers–teamsters or to artisans. Overall, there are 5,753 wage observations.

Chapter 2 demonstrated that quartermasters appear to have paid the going wage in the local labor market. Can the same be said for forts in

Table 6.1   Distribution of Wage Observations: California Forts, 1847–60

	Unskilled	Artisan	White Collar
By year:			
1847–50	.202	.109	.103
1851–55	.649	.613	.654
1856–60	.149	.278	.243
By occupation:			
Laborer	.409		
Teamster	.591		
Mason		.134	
Painter		.021	
Blacksmith		.240	
Carpenter		.605	
By location in California:			
San Francisco	.167	.197	.496
Northern	.067	.131	.096
Central	.176	.121	.132
Southern	.568	.542	.269
"Field"	.022	.004	.007
Number of observations	3,879	1,261	613

Source: Sample of California forts from *Reports of Persons and Articles Hired,* Record Group 92, National Archives (see the text).

California? Unfortunately, the paucity of wage data for the state makes comparisons difficult. However, it is clear from inspection of the original data that the wages paid at California forts were far in excess of those paid elsewhere in the United States—and, as will be demonstrated shortly, the army data imply that wages rose very sharply in the aftermath of the discovery of gold.[23]

6.3.1 Hedonic Wage Regressions

Like the sample analyzed in chapter 3, the California sample is not large enough to construct occupation-specific wage series for each fort. Few forts hired the same type of labor every year, and the numbers of observations across forts varies over time. As pointed out in chapter 3, analysis of the data that ignored such composition effects would be misleading. Thus, following chapter 3, I estimate hedonic wage regressions of the form

$$\ln w = X\beta + \varepsilon,$$

where $\ln w$ is the log of the nominal daily wage, X is a vector of independent variables, the β's are the hedonic coefficients, and ε is the error term. Monthly wages are converted to daily wages by dividing by twenty-six days per month. As in chapter 3, the independent variables are dummy variables for fort location, characteristics of the worker or job associated with especially high or low wages, whether the worker was hired on a monthly basis, season of year, and time period. Separate regressions are estimated for the three occupation groups (common laborers–teamsters, artisans, and white-collar workers). The regressions are reported in appendix table 6C.1.

The cross-sectional patterns revealed by the regression coefficients are informative about the antebellum labor market in California. Seasonal variation in wages, for example, is broadly consistent with what is known about seasonal fluctuations in labor demand. Summer was the slack season in gold production, and miners flocked to San Francisco to find alternative employment (Lotchin 1974, 49), while "every spring [the miners] drifted back to the diffings, leaving a shortage of labor" (Coman 1912, 2:316). The seasonal lull in gold production may explain why the wages of common laborers were relatively low in the summer. Artisanal wages were temporarily higher during the summer, a prime season for construction activity. Rapid growth in population placed enormous strains on the construction sector, which needed to bid skilled labor away from the mines (Lotchin 1974, 50). This may also explain why carpenters were highly paid in California relative to other artisans, at least compared with elsewhere in the United States (see chap. 3 above; and Coman 1912, 2:317). The choice to enter the white-collar market was not a seasonal one, and, therefore, it is not surprising to find an absence of seasonality in clerical wages.

Despite generally high labor demand during the period, there is still evidence of a premium for unemployment risk, as artisans hired on a monthly basis generally earned a lower average daily wage than those hired daily. There is no evidence of a daily wage premium for clerks—indeed, the positive coefficient of the "monthly" dummy suggests that the few clerks hired on a daily basis were of a lower level of skill than indicated by their occupation designation in the payrolls.

Regional patterns in money wages in California bear resemblance to those occurring elsewhere. Skill differentials were generally lower in northern California than in southern California. However, the negative effect of a southern California location may also be proxying for unobserved ethnic or racial (Native American) background. Hispanics, who were concentrated in southern California, earned much less than other workers, and Hispanic status may very well be underreported in the data.[24]

6.3.2   Time-Series Patterns

As in chapter 3, I use the hedonic coefficients to estimate annual series of nominal daily wages for the three occupation categories. The procedure used to calculate the series is discussed in appendix 6A. In brief, the procedure is similar to that used in chapter 3 in that the wage series are derived from hedonic indices applied to benchmark wage estimates. However, additional adjustments were deemed necessary to produce estimates for the initial rush years of 1847–49 (for further details, see app. 6A). The nominal wage estimates are shown in appendix table 6C.2.

Consistent with the theoretical model, nominal wages rose sharply for all three groups from 1847 to 1850 (or 1851 in the case of artisans). Wages then declined sharply for all three occupation groups, fluctuating for the remainder of the 1850s.

The annual movements are broadly consistent with qualitative accounts of the rush. Scattered estimates of wages in newspaper articles suggest that wages rose after the gold discoveries and remained roughly stable until 1853 (Lotchin 1974, 86; Gerber 1997). My series clearly capture the steep initial rise and subsequent decline.[25] A business-cycle downturn is known to have occurred in 1855 following a local banking panic, and this, too, apparently left its imprint in wage levels (Coman 1912, 2:285–87; Lotchin 1974, 51, 59).

To convert the nominal wage series into real wage indices, it is necessary to deflate by a price index, as in chapter 3. Data to construct a price deflator for antebellum California are extremely scanty, but it is possible to use Berry's (1984) compilation of prices from newspapers to construct a rough price deflator.[26]

The price deflator is given in appendix table 6C.3. Although there are severe fluctuations at annual frequencies, the general pattern is of a rise in prices during the early years of the rush, followed by an abrupt (and apparently persistent) decline. The short-run increase in prices is consistent with anecdotal evidence of goods shortages during the initial phase of the rush, while the subsequent decline in prices presumably reflects the dramatic growth of the commercial sector in and around San Francisco (Caughey 1948; Lotchin 1974).[27]

The real wage series, formed by dividing the nominal wage estimates (indexed at 100 in 1860) by the price deflator, are shown in appendix table 6C.3. The series should be viewed with caution for three reasons. The price data refer solely to wholesale prices, and no provision is made for housing prices. It is entirely possible that including housing prices would dampen the short- and long-run increases in real wages evident in the indices. The range of goods included in the price deflator is limited, even compared with the price deflators used in chapter 3. Berry's price data refer exclusively to non–southern California locations.[28] However, it can be shown that the substantive findings are similar if the wage sample is restricted to non–southern California forts.

Despite these problems, the real wage indices essentially mimic the patterns evinced in the nominal wage series. Real wages of common laborers increased by approximately 615 percent from late 1847 and early 1848 to their peak in 1849. Because of the timing of the observations, the overall rate of increase over the same period cannot be determined for artisans and clerks, but it is clear that their real wages also grew rapidly. For example, the real wages of artisans rose by nearly 259 percent from the spring of 1848 (March–May 1848) to 1849; those of clerks rose by 189 percent over the same period.

Following the very steep rise, real wages fell, except for a spike in 1851 caused by a sudden drop in prices that was reversed in 1852. The real wages of common laborers fell sharply in 1855 but recovered by the end of the decade to the level reached in 1852 and 1853. Similarly, the real wages of artisans and clerks in the remainder of the 1850s hovered close to the 1860 index value of 100.

The real wage series suggest several findings. Real (and, for that matter, nominal) wages were clearly flexible during the Gold Rush; accepting the indices at face value, there can be no question that the discovery of gold markedly affected wages.

However, what is *not* consistent with the model is the finding for all three occupations that real wages were far higher in 1860 than in 1847. The Gold Rush was a transitory shock, yet the rush appears to have left wages permanently higher in California.

Implicit in the model was an assumption that real wages in the settled economy were constant over the period of the Gold Rush. The real wage indices in chapter 3 indicate that, elsewhere in the United States, real wages were higher in 1860 than in 1847. Thus, real wages could have trended upward in California simply because they were trending upward elsewhere.

However, while rates of growth of real wages elsewhere were positive over the period 1847–60, they were far lower than in California.[29] In addition, wage data from the 1860 Census of Social Statistics suggest that real wages in California on the eve of the Civil War were similar to average levels elsewhere in the country.[30] If so, the clear implication is that real wages in California just before the rush were well below real wages elsewhere in the United States.

That real wages in California circa 1847 may have been low by Northern standards is less paradoxical than it seems. To the extent that pre–Gold Rush California was part of any regional economy at all, it was part of the Mexican economy, the economy of coastal points north, and, to a much lesser extent, that of Central and South America (Wright 1940, 323).[31] As pointed out in section 6.1, initial in-migrants came from these locations, and, for them, the returns to migration, on average, were surely positive. By the time labor flows had begun to arrive from the Eastern and Midwestern United States (1849), real wages in California substantially exceeded those elsewhere in the United States.[32]

But the Gold Rush could not have left a permanent imprint on real wages unless there had been a substantial inflow of factors complementary to labor *and* continued incentive to invest capital. The Yukon Gold Rush of the late 1890s did not transform southern Alaska into the equivalent of California. What became clear to the migrants (and to many miners who struck gold early in the rush) was that California was rich in many ways, specifically in agricultural resources. As noted in section 6.1, California bypassed territorial status, and statehood presumably reduced the risk of permanent settlement. The rapid, sustained growth of San Francisco is prima facie evidence of agglomeration effects and a widening of the market for locally produced agricultural (and manufacturing) goods (Coman 1912, 2:291–314; Caughey 1948; Lotchin 1974).

Evidence of an inflow of complementary factors is both indirect and direct. Indirect evidence of an inflow of complementary factors can be gleaned from Berry (1984), who, in addition to wholesale prices, collected a series of monthly interest rates in San Francisco. The wage-rental ratio in 1850 was less than half its value in 1860, suggesting extreme initial scarcity of capital (Coman 1912, 2:307). Translating the trend in the ratio during the 1850s into equivalent movements along a factor price frontier, the implication is that the capital-labor ratio must have been rising.

While the extraordinarily high relative price of capital that prevailed in San Francisco in the early 1850s may have been partly due to unusually high risk, direct evidence of capital accumulation can be found in the city's (and state's) active participation in issuing bonds in the New York and London financial markets (Lotchin 1974, 60–61, 77). Additional direct evidence comes from the 1850 and 1860 censuses. In 1850, per capita investment in manufacturing capital was negligible but, by 1860, had grown in real terms over the decade by 1,204 percent. Investments in land clearing and complementary factors raised wheat output per acre by 463 percent over the decade.[33] Capital inflows sustained the transitory wage effects of the Gold Rush, initializing the long process by which California became an integral part of the American economy.

6.4   The Elasticity of Labor Supply into Gold Rush California

In this section, I present estimates of the elasticity of labor supply into Gold Rush California. I compare my elasticity estimates to Carrington's (1996) estimates for labor supply into Alaska during the building of the Alaska Pipeline in the mid-1970s.

The elasticity of labor supply is

$$\varepsilon_{Lw} = d(\ln L)/d(\ln w),$$

where d indicates the difference operator. I identify $d(\ln L)$ with estimates of the logarithm of the change in the ratio of the number of adult men between the ages of fifteen and forty in California relative to the aggregate population in this age (and sex) group. For the purposes of the calculation, I use the real wage series for common labor in California, expressed relative to the national aggregate series for common labor constructed in chapter 5. The calculation of the elasticity estimates is described in appendix 6B, and the estimates are shown in table 6.2.

The estimates suggest that, in the immediate short run of the discovery of gold, labor supply into California was highly inelastic ($\varepsilon = 0.24$). However, as labor made its way to the state, supply became much more elastic. By the early 1850s, the supply elasticity fell between 1.7 and 2.6, where it remained on the eve of the Civil War.[34]

Measured against the experience of the Alaska Pipeline, labor supply into Gold Rush California was considerably less elastic. For various reasons,

Table 6.2   **The Elasticity of Labor Supply**

	Elasticity		Elasticity
Gold Rush California:		Gold Rush California:	
From 1847–February 1848 to:		From 1847–February 1848 to:	
March 1848–December		1850–52 average	2.03
1848	.24	1860	2.24
1849	1.01	Alaska Pipeline (March	
1850	1.65	1973–June 1976):	
1851	1.75	Construction, hourly earnings	
1852	2.61	versus employment	5.88

Source: California, see app. 6B. Alaska Pipeline, computed from Carrington (1996, 196, 206, 208).

Note: Elasticity = $\Delta\ln L/\Delta\ln w$; Δ = change between successive dates.

direct comparisons between the Gold Rush and the Pipeline labor supply are difficult to make, but, on the assumption that daily hours were not the primary intensive margin during the rush, the relevant comparison is Carrington's (1996) estimate for Pipeline construction workers, as computed from changes in total employment and hourly wages, $\varepsilon_{Lw} = 5.88$ (see table 6.2).[35] In the case of the Pipeline, the period covered is March 1973–June 1976, or three and a half years. By this standard, labor supply into Alaska during the Pipeline era was roughly three times as elastic as labor supply into California during the Gold Rush.

That labor was more elastically supplied during the Pipeline era is not too difficult to rationalize. The Alaska Pipeline was a project of known duration, in which the shock to local labor demand was fully anticipated and the returns to migration were essentially known ex ante. By contrast, the discovery of gold was unanticipated, the duration of the Gold Rush was unknown ex ante, and the returns to migration were highly uncertain.[36] More fundamentally, vast improvements in internal transportation and in access to economic information across regions in the 125 years between the Gold Rush and the Pipeline era dramatically reduced migration costs for the prospective worker on the Alaska Pipeline, compared with the costs faced by the prospective argonaut.[37]

6.5   Conclusion

This chapter has examined how the antebellum economy coped with a very large, highly localized shock to the demand for labor—the California Gold Rush. A simple model of wage determination, in which real wages rose sharply during the initial stages of the rush and subsequently declined, fit the data reasonably well. However, the rush was far more than a transitory phenomenon for it left California wage levels permanently higher. Americans became convinced that the Golden State held riches far beyond the nuggets found at Sutter's Mill. Capital poured into California, sustaining wages after the rush ended. Newly minted as a state, California left behind its Hispanic economic heritage to become part of the high-wage American economy.

Appendix 6A
Construction of Nominal Wage Estimates

Estimates for 1847–60

This appendix describes the construction of the nominal wage estimates for California from 1847 to 1860.

Common Laborers

The 1860 estimate ($2.62) is the value reported for California in the 1860 Census of Social Statistics. I use 1860 rather than 1850 as the benchmark date (recall that 1850 was used as the benchmark in chap. 3) because the incompleteness of the 1850 manuscripts for California suggests that 1860 would be preferable.[38] For 1847 and 1849–60 annually, I use the coefficients to generate a nominal wage index (1860 = 100) in the same manner as in chapter 3. The nominal wage estimates for each year are $[I(t)/100] \times \$2.62$, where $I(t)$ is the index number for year t.

Artisans

I benchmark the daily wage of carpenters at the 1860 census estimate ($4.43), which is then adjusted to reflect the distribution of masons, painters, and blacksmiths in the state. The adjustment multiplies the coefficients of the dummy variables for these occupations from the hedonic regressions by an assumed set of weights (masons, 0.056; blacksmiths, 0.371; painters, 0.102; the occupation weights are based on averages of counts reported in the 1850 and 1860 censuses). The adjustment in log terms to the 1860 benchmark for carpenters is −0.081, which produces an adjusted benchmark wage of $4.08. For 1848 and 1849–60, the procedure to compute the artisanal series is the same as that for common laborers (see above).

White-Collar Workers

It is not possible to benchmark the wage series for white-collar workers. To derive an 1860 benchmark for white-collar workers, I follow the same procedure as in chapter 3 by multiplying the regression coefficients by an assumed set of weights. The seasonal weights are 0.25 each for fall, winter, and spring; and the high-low dummies are set equal to zero. Because the vast majority of white-collar workers were hired on a monthly basis, I set the monthly dummy = 1. The fort location weights are as follows: San Francisco, 0.215; southern California, 0.058; central California, 0.639; and field, 0.

The fort weights are averages of population counts in the 1852 state census (DeBow 1853) and 1860 federal census (Kennedy 1864). For the purpose of calculating the fort weights, it was necessary to allocate county populations to the forts. The allocation of counties is as follows: San Francisco: San Francisco, Marin, San Mateo, Alameda, Sulano, Napa, and Sonoma; southern California: San Luis Obispo, San Bernardino, Santa Barbara, Los Angeles, and San Diego; and northern California: Del Norte, Siskiyou, Humboldt, Trinity, Shasta, Mendocino, Colusi, Butte, and Plumas. All other counties are allocated to central California.

To construct the estimates for white-collar labor, multiply each regression coefficient by its relevant weight, sum, and add the coefficient of the appropriate year dummy; call the result β. The nominal wage estimate, therefore, is $w = \exp(\beta)$. Also, as in chapter 3, I linearly interpolate when the year dummies refer to two or more years grouped together.

Adjustment of 1847–48 Estimates

I divide this period into three subperiods: 1847–February 1848; March–May 1848; and June–December 1848.

Common Laborers

The 1847 estimate for common laborers described above is assigned to 1847–February 1848. For 1848, I use a direct observation on a common laborer hired at the San Francisco fort, who experienced a 400 percent increase in his nominal wage between early 1848 and fall 1848; applying this ratio to the 1847 estimate yields a daily wage of $4.00, which I assign to the June–December 1848 group.

Artisans

The 1848 estimate is assigned to the period March–May 1848 on the basis of the dating of the payrolls.

White-Collar Workers

The 1848 estimate computed from the coefficients of the 1848 year dummy, in the manner described above, is $113.62. However, on the basis of direct inspection of the payrolls, it is clear that this estimate overstates white-collar wages during the first half of 1848 and understates them during the second half. To compute new estimates, I used, as in the case of common laborers above, wage data for specific workers employed in San Francisco. These yielded monthly wage estimates, respectively, of $83.33 for the period up to May 1848 and $125.00 for the period June–December 1848.

Appendix 6B

Construction of Labor Supply Elasticities

This appendix describes the construction of the labor supply elasticities reported in table 6.2. As noted in the text, I identify $\Delta(\ln w)$ with the change in the real wage of common labor in California relative to the national average real wage of common labor, from chapter 5. I identify $\Delta(\ln L)$ from estimates of the number of adult men between the ages of fifteen and forty in California relative to the nation as a whole. I first estimate total population in the state in various time periods, then multiply the total population by assumed ratios of adult men to population.

For the first time period (1847–February 1848), I assume that the population equaled 15,000, which is Wright's (1940, 323) estimate. I also assume that the population totals in 1850 and 1860 were as given by the federal census (93,000 and 380,000, respectively) and that the population in 1852 was as given by the state census of 1852 (264,000). For the intervening years, I interpolate on the basis of Wright's (1940, 341–42) estimates of arrivals overland and by ship at San Francisco.[39] The assumed ratios of adult men aged fifteen to forty to total population are 0.77 for 1847–52 and 0.49 for 1860. Estimates of national population are linearly interpolated from aggregate census figures; I assume that the ratio of adult men aged fifteen to forty in the nation was 0.213, the value prevailing in both 1850 and 1860.

The estimates of $\Delta(\ln w)$ and $\Delta(\ln L)$ are, respectively, as follows: from 1847–February 1848 to March–December 1848, 1.123 and 0.264; to 1849, 1.506 and 1.524; to 1850, 1.060 and 1.747; to 1851, 1.380 and 2.413; to 1852, 1.043 and 2.719; to 1850–52 average, 1.173 and 2.383; and to 1860, 1.070 and 2.393. Caution should be exercised in interpreting the elasticity estimates because of various biases inherent in the estimation procedure.[40]

Appendix 6C

Table 6C.1   Hedonic Wage Regressions: California Forts, 1847–60

	Common Laborer–Teamster	Artisan	White-Collar Worker
Variable	β	β	β
Constant	.864	1.564	1.017
	(8.165)	(12.545)	(3.993)
Monthly	−.028	−.299	.446
	(.831)	(11.942)	(2.648)
High	N.A.	.294	0.305
		(5.287)	(5.088)
Low	−.707	−.722	−.418
	(9.556)	(7.484)	(4.437)
Mexican	−.837	N.A.	N.A.
	(8.491)		
Spring	.095	−.064	−.005
	(2.733)	(1.345)	(.047)
Summer	−.311	.080	.036
	(7.572)	(1.525)	(.337)
Fall	−.019	.031	−.047
	(.549)	(.725)	(.480)

(*continued*)

	Common Laborer–Teamster	Artisan	White-Collar Worker
Teamster	.111		
	(6.560)		
Mason		−.047	
		(1.480)	
Painter		−.214	
		(3.309)	
Blacksmith		−.159	
		(6.352)	
San Francisco	.078	.062	.138
	(2.065)	(1.461)	(2.102)
Central California	.076	.155	.084
	(1.894)	(3.319)	(1.004)
Southern California	−.240	.148	−.065
	(7.186)	(3.898)	(.919)
"Field"	−.031	−.449	−.086
	(.478)	(3.103)	(.355)
1847	−.980		
	(6.748)		
1847–48			−.512
			(2.410)
1848	−.583	−.160	
	(4.995)	(1.078)	
1849	1.007	1.080	.552
	(9.891)	(5.300)	(1.686)
1850	.472	.454	.473
	(5.016)	(3.736)	(2.416)
1851	.284	.415	.357
	(3.018)	(3.332)	(1.667)
1852	.238	.216	.169
	(2.513)	(1.725)	(.897)
1853	.134	.201	.131
	(1.433)	(1.646)	(.710)
1854	−.010	.174	.084
	(.110)	(1.453)	(.460)
1855	−.088	.142	.122
	(.943)	(1.200)	(.671)
1856	−.120	.156	.143
	(1.267)	(1.303)	(.783)
1857	−.018	−.037	.175
	(.178)	(.274)	(.831)
1858	−.030	−.088	N.A.
	(.275)	(.665)	
1858–59			.163
			(.782)
1859	−.101	−.061	N.A.
	(.802)	(.412)	
R^2	.605	.488	.450

Source: See table 6.1.

Note: Left-out seasonal dummy is winter. Left-out location dummy is northern California. Left-out occupation dummies are laborers (common laborers–teamsters), carpenters (artisans). Left-out year dummy is 1860. N.A. = not applicable.

Table 6C.2   **Nominal Wage Estimates: California, 1847–60 ($)**

	Common Laborer	Artisan	White-Collar Worker
1847–February 1848	1.00	N.A.	N.A.
March 1848–May 1848	N.A.	3.83	83.33
June 1848–December 1848	4.00	N.A.	125.00
1849	7.17	12.01	210.33
1850	4.20	6.42	194.35
1851	3.48	6.18	173.07
1852	3.32	5.06	143.41
1853	3.00	4.99	138.11
1854	2.59	4.85	131.68
1855	2.40	4.70	136.79
1856	2.32	4.77	139.65
1857	2.57	3.93	143.24
1858	2.54	3.74	143.10
1859	2.37	3.83	135.01
1860	2.62	4.08	121.11

Source: See the text and app. 6A. N.A. = not applicable.

Table 6C.3   **Price Deflator and Real Wage Indices (1860 = 100)**

	Prices	Common Laborer	Artisan	White-Collar Worker
1847	142.6			
1847–February 1848		26.8	N.A.	N.A.
March 1848–May 1848		N.A.	68.3	55.3
June 1848–December 1848		122.3	N.A.	82.9
1848	124.8			
1849	166.1	164.8	177.2	104.6
1850	166.5	96.3	94.5	96.4
1851	99.6	133.4	152.1	143.5
1852	130.8	96.9	94.8	90.5
1853	107.4	106.6	113.9	106.2
1854	100.6	98.3	118.1	108.1
1855	117.2	78.2	98.3	96.4
1856	105.9	83.6	110.4	108.9
1857	108.4	90.5	88.9	109.1
1858	113.6	85.3	80.6	104.0
1859	104.2	86.8	90.1	107.0
1860	100.0	100.0	100.0	100.0

Note: N.A. = not applicable.

Antebellum Wages and
Labor Markets
A New Interpretation

Previous chapters in this book have presented new series of nominal and real wages for the antebellum period and have used the new series, as well as other data, to examine the behavior of labor markets. This chapter uses these findings and others to construct the new interpretation of antebellum wages and labor markets sketched in the introduction.

7.1 Real Wages in the Long Run

Charting economic growth before the Civil War has long occupied the attention of economic historians. For the benchmark census years of 1840 and 1860, sufficient economic data are available in the federal censuses and other documents to produce fairly reliable estimates of per capita incomes (Gallman 1966). For the period before 1840, however, there is much less certainty over the long-run growth rate of per capita income. The most recent estimates for the pre-1840 period are those of Thomas Weiss (1992), based on the so-called conjectural method (David 1967). According to Weiss (1992; and Gallman 1966), per capita income rose from $77.00 in 1820 (in 1840 dollars) to $125 in 1860, implying an average annual rate of growth of 1.2 percent per year.

To place this figure in the context of my indices of real wages, it is useful to begin by assuming that total output can be described by the aggregate production function $Q = F(K, L, T)$, where Q = output, K = capital, L = labor, and T = natural resources or raw materials. I further assume that F is Cobb-Douglas, $F = AK^\beta L^\alpha T^\delta$, where $\alpha + \beta + \delta = 1$.

If labor is paid the value of its marginal product, then

$$w = pMP_L = p\alpha Q/L,$$

where p = price of output. In rate-of-change form,

$$(\dot{w/p}) = \dot{\alpha} + (\dot{Q/L}),$$

where "•" indicates the percentage growth rate. Assuming that the aggregate output elasticity of labor (α) did not change, the real wage (w/p) should grow at the same rate as labor productivity (Q/L) in the long run if labor is paid the value of its marginal product.

Weiss (1992) has also produced new estimates of the labor force for the census years 1820–60. According to these estimates, the aggregate labor force participation rate increased from 0.328 in 1820 to 0.358 in 1860 (computed from Weiss 1992, 37; and U.S. Department of Commerce 1975, 8). Combining the estimates of labor force participation with his estimates of per capita income, it follows that output *per worker* increased from $235 in 1820 to $349 in 1860, or at an average annual rate of 0.99 percent per year.

Chapter 3 presented occupation- and region-specific indices of real wages. In chapter 5, the regional series were adjusted for differences across regions in the cost of living, and aggregate occupation-specific series were constructed. If the trend rates of growth estimated from these series are aggregated by weighting by estimates of occupation shares derived from the 1850 census, the overall growth rate of real wages is 1.01 percent per year from 1820 to 1860.[1]

If output per worker and real wages grew at approximately the same secular rate, it is reasonable to infer, as stated in the introduction, that economic growth did "trickle down," on average, to the members of the antebellum working class.[2] Pessimists who maintain that antebellum growth bypassed the working class evidently cannot base their case on a failure of real wages to rise in the long run.

It is important to keep in mind that my real wage indices pertain to daily or monthly wages while Weiss's estimates pertain to annual output. No series of average annual days worked has been produced for the antebellum period. Scattered evidence, however, suggests that seasonality declined, and annual days of labor increased, over the course of the nineteenth century (Gallman 1975; Adams 1982; Engerman and Goldin 1993).

7.2   Real Wages in the Short Run

Although real wages grew in the long run before the Civil War, my new series reveal considerable variability in the growth rate in the short run, measured over a period of years (decades or five-year periods, e.g.) or on an annual basis. Real wages grew in fits and starts, and certain periods witnessed stagnation and decline.

Although there were differences across occupations and regions, the general cyclic pattern was as follows. Real wages grew starting in the mid-1820s into the early 1830s, but then growth ceased or reversed direction in the mid- to late 1830s. Real wages then increased sharply in the early 1840s, declining somewhat in the late 1840s from their early 1840s peak, but still remaining well above levels observed in the 1820s and 1830s. Then, from the late 1840s to the mid- to late 1850s, real wages fell.

The finding that real wages fell beginning in the late 1840s is consistent with much of the previous literature on antebellum real wages and supports Robert Fogel's (1989) characterization of this final period before the Civil War as a "hidden depression" for free labor. But the relatively slow growth of real wages comparing the mid- to late 1830s to the 1820s is a novel finding and is the consequence of the improved measurements made possible by the new real wage series in this book.

Some of the variability of real wages in the short run reflects real factors that influenced either labor demand or labor supply. Because of the paucity of good annual economic time series for the antebellum period, it is difficult convincingly to measure the effect of these shocks quantitatively. But identifying plausible candidates is not so difficult.[3] For example, the Midwest experienced severe cycles in railroad construction in the 1840s and 1850s. The waves of railroad building led to periodic booms and then slumps in labor demand, putting (respectively) upward and downward pressure on wages in the labor markets affected by the construction (Fogel 1989; for a contrary view, see David 1987). Perhaps most important, the Irish potato famine and political upheaval led to a marked increase in immigration into the United States starting in the late 1840s, dramatically altering the ethnic composition of Northeastern cities and sizably augmenting urban labor supplies (Fogel 1989). From 1844 to 1856, the annual number of unskilled immigrants entering the country was 950 percent higher than the average during the 1830s; for skilled artisans, the figure was 279 percent (computed from U.S. Department of Commerce 1975, ser. C-132, C-136, p. 111). In the light of these magnitudes, it is plausible that the immigration shock was an important factor contributing to the decline in real wages in the 1850s.[4]

Nominal factors may have played an important role in generating short- and medium-run movements in real wages because cyclic movements in prices were negatively correlated with movements in real wages. If the deviation from trend of the real wage of common labor in the Northeast is regressed on the deviation from trend in the Northeastern price deflator (both variables in levels are averages over five-year periods, e.g., 1821–25 and 1826–30), the (contemporaneous) correlation between the two was -0.90 ($t = 7.64$).[5]

While I will argue below that the sign of the correlation should be taken seriously, it might be claimed that the magnitude is biased away from zero (too large in absolute value).[6] The issue is my use of wholesale prices to construct the price deflators. Specifically, if wholesale prices fluctuated more in the short run than retail prices, my real wage indices may be excessively volatile (fluctuate too much in the short run).[7]

Because of the lack of good retail price data for the antebellum period, it is difficult to respond directly to this criticism. David and Solar (1977) attempted to show that retail prices were less volatile than wholesale prices by estimating a regression of the log of their price index on the log of an index of Philadelphia wholesale prices. The regression coefficient β was positive but less than one, implying that shocks to wholesale prices were reflected in retail prices, but less than proportionately. Taken seriously, David and Solar's result would suggest that price deflators based on wholesale prices fluctuate "too much" in the short run (relative to price deflators based on retail prices). If this were true, my real wage indices would be excessively volatile. However, this inference is questionable because David and Solar's price index and the Philadelphia price index are not based on a common set of goods traded in the same location.[8] Because they are not, it is not surprising that β, as estimated by David and Solar, was less than one, even if its true value were unity.

Nevertheless, it is worthwhile exploring the possibility that retail prices were less volatile than wholesale prices. I do so by making use of my recent study of rental housing in antebellum New York, which estimated housing price indices over the period 1830–60 (Margo 1996). Specifically, I use the index numbers for 1840 and 1843, a period of substantial deflation in the general price level. My index of rents in New York City registers a fall from an index number of 86.0 in 1840 to 63.9 in 1843, or a decline of -0.297 in log terms (Margo 1996, 623). My overall Northeastern price deflator shows a decline from a peak of 118.1 in 1839 to 69.5 in 1844, or a decline of -0.534 in log terms. Suppose that the ratio of the two, 0.56 ($= 0.297/0.534$), identifies the relation between annual changes in retail prices and annual changes in wholesale prices (i.e., the value of β).[9] I use this ratio to smooth (dampen) year-to-year movements in the Northeastern price deflator. I then recompute the real wage series for common labor by dividing nominal wages by the smoothed price deflator and reestimate the regression of real wages on prices, both detrended, as described above. If this is done, the contemporaneous correlation between real wages and prices is still smaller but significantly negative, -0.83 ($t = 4.35$). In other words, even allowing for the possibility that my price deflators are excessively volatile, it would still appear that contemporaneous increases in the antebellum price level were associated with falling real wages (and vice versa).

Why would there be a negative relation between changes in real wages and changes in prices? One explanation might be that nominal wages were simply unresponsive to changes in the price level—that is, inflation or deflation had no bearing on the wage-setting process.

Using the nominal wage series and price deflators developed in chapter 3, table 7.1 shows wage and price changes over three inflationary-deflationary episodes—the price rises of the early to mid-1830s; the price deflation following the Panic of 1837; and the inflation of the late 1840s and early to mid-1850s, which culminated in the Panic of 1857. Given enough time to adjust, nominal wages moved in the same general direction—and, during inflationary periods, at approximately the same magnitude—as the price level did over these episodes. Thus, the point is not that nominal wages were totally unresponsive to changes in prices but that the response took time.[10] Simply put, changes in nominal wages lagged behind changes in prices.

The lagged response of nominal wages to prices implies that shocks to the price level could have persistent effects on real wages—real wages could be below or above their equilibrium level for some period of time (Goldin and Margo 1992a). Such persistence has been found for other historical economies, including the postbellum United States (DeCanio and Mokyr 1977) and therefore may not be very surprising. But it does raise the question as to the precise mechanisms producing the wage lag.

One possibility is imperfect information (Lucas 1981). Individuals may have confused changes in the level of prices with changes in the structure of relative prices, causing them to adjust real magnitudes (labor demand or supply) in response to deflation or inflation. Given the costs of transmitting timely price information during the antebellum period as well as the fact that the inflationary episodes involved both absolute and relative price changes (Margo 1992, 194–95), the imperfect information story is a plausible one.

In addition to confusion over relative versus absolute price changes, expectations about the course of future price changes may have played a role. To understand this point, the distinction between an *integrated* and a *stationary* time series is useful. A stationary time series returns to a fixed, or normal, level. By contrast, an integrated time series, such as a random walk, does not return to a fixed level. If the antebellum price level were thought to be a random walk, the rational expectation of tomorrow's price level would have been today's. But, if the price level were thought to be stationary, the rational expectation would be that prices would return to their fixed level sometime in the future.

Anecdotal evidence suggests that, prior to the inflation of the 1830s, antebellum employers (and workers) may have believed that the price level was generally stable, at least during peacetime.[11] In terms of the discussion presented above, the price level was expected to be stationary. Wages did not adjust immediately when prices changed because, for the most part, such price change was expected to be temporary and prices would soon return to normal. Hence, it did not pay for workers to demand immediate wage changes or for employers to implement them. Only when inflation

Table 7.1 Nominal Wage Flexibility during the Antebellum Period

	Inflation	Deflation	Inflation
Northeast			
$\Delta(\ln p)$	.334	−.513	.562
	(1830–36)	(1839–43)	(1844–57)
	.271		.462
	(1830–35/37)		(1844–57/59)
$\Delta(\ln w)$:			
Laborers	.411	−.380	.366
	(1831–37)	(1837–40)	(1847–59)
Artisans	.279	−.195	.333
	(1830–36)	(1839–44)	(1848–59)
Clerks	.216	−.085	.345
	(1830–37)	(1839–41)	(1846–56)
Average	.302	−.220	.348
Midwest:			
$\Delta(p)$	.447	−.591	.638
	(1830–36)	(1839–43)	(1844–57)
	.373		.508
	(1830–35/37)		(1844–57/59)
$\Delta(w)$:			
Laborers	.470	−.375	.420
	(1831–37)	(1839–41)	(1847–59)
Artisans	.276	−.302	.425
	(1830–37)	(1839–43)	(1847–57)
Clerks	.357	−.121	.134
	(1831–39)	(1839–41)	(1844–57)
Average	.368	−.266	.326
South Atlantic:			
$\Delta(p)$	.428	−.586	.549
	(1830–36)	(1839–43)	(1844–57)
	.314		.441
	(1830–35/37)		(1844–57/59)
$\Delta(w)$:			
Laborers	.283	−.354	.368
	(1831–37)	(1837–43)	(1846–58)
Artisans	.099	−.155	.302
	(1830–36)	(1837–46)	(1847–57)
Clerks	.439	−.240	.019
	(1831–39)	(1839–42)	(1848–57)
Average	.274	−.250	.230
South Central:			
$\Delta(p)$	.432	−.620	.564
	(1830–36)	(1838–43)	(1844–57)
	.338		.483
	(1830–35/37)		(1844–57/59)
$\Delta(w)$:			
Laborers	.077	−.295	.481
	(1831–36)	(1837–46)	(1847–60)

(*continued*)

Table 7.1   (continued)

	Inflation	Deflation	Inflation
Artisans	.262	−.232	.312
	(1830–35)	(1839–44)	(1846–58)
Clerks	.613	−.386	.423
	(1832–39)	(1839–43)	(1843–57)
Average	.317	−.304	.405
Overall average:			
$\Delta(\ln p)$	.324	−.578	.474
	(1830–35/37)		(1844–57/59)
$\Delta(\ln w)$	.315	−.260	.327

Source: Chapter 3.

Note: A "$\Delta(\ln)$" indicates the difference in the logarithm of the variable (w = nominal wage; p = price level) between dates. Beginning and end dates shown in parentheses; dates like "57/59" are unweighted averages of years (e.g., 1857, 1858, and 1859). Rows labeled *average* are unweighted averages across occupations within a census region. *Overall average* is the unweighted average across census regions (e.g., .324 is the unweighted average across census regions of $\Delta[\ln p]$ from 1830 to 1835/37).

or deflation became abundantly obvious, and persistent, would nominal wages adjust, possibly abruptly.[12] During the inflation of the mid-1830s, strikes by journeyman cabinetmakers in New York City are said to have been motivated by the fact that the "price book [giving journeymen's wages] used by their masters was more than a quarter of a century old . . . the old book failed to keep up with the cost of living" (Wilentz 1984, 231). Such shocks to prices led first to confusion, then to a revision of price expectations, and ultimately to nominal wage adjustments.

To explore the effect of nominal and real shocks further, more and better data on retail prices and on real economic activity are needed so that the timing, the amplitude, and the duration of antebellum cycles can be more accurately determined *independently* of movements in the price level (Calomiris and Hanes 1994). That said, my new wage series may have some implications for the timing of antebellum business cycles. For example, the rise in nominal wages observed in my series of nominal wages for common labor in the Northeast beginning in 1841 suggests that economic recovery after the Panic of 1837 in that region may have begun earlier than 1843, as previously thought (see, e.g., North [1961] 1966, 206).

7.3   The Consequences of Declining Real Wages: Nutritional Status and Poor Relief

All other things being equal, a short-run decline in the real wage meant a decline in purchasing power and, therefore, in living standards. The decline might be offset by working more, by drawing on savings, or by shifting into economic activities (e.g., subsistence agriculture on the frontier) that might have been insulated from downturn. But, for individuals who had access to none of these options, a substantial fall in real wages could spell economic hardship or even disaster.

I consider here two consequences of real wage declines. The first concerns nutritional status. Given that food loomed large in antebellum budgets, declines in real wages may have had negative effects on nutritional intake and possibly, therefore, nutritional status. The second concerns a strategy to avoid economic hardship in the face of a decline in real wages—namely, the decision to seek public assistance, or poor relief.

7.3.1   Real Wages and Nutritional Status

Historians have recently begun to examine trends and cycles in height and weight by age.[13] Height and weight by age are measures of *net nutrition* or *nutritional status*. Ingesting nutrients serves three purposes in the human body—sustaining current physical activity; fighting infection; and, prior to adulthood, enabling physical growth. When a child or an adolescent suffers a nutritional insult, such as disease or malnutrition, growth is typically slowed. As long as the insult does not occur too early in life and for too long a period, adult height is unaffected, although the growth period may be prolonged. While, at an individual level, height and weight are also influenced by genetic factors, such factors tend to cancel out in the aggregate, at least among the ethnic and racial groups that populated the United States in the nineteenth century (Fogel 1986; Costa 1993).

Historical research on heights is greatly facilitated by the availability of abundant military height data. Starting in the eighteenth century, armies routinely recorded the heights of soldiers to aid in identifying deserters (as well as to gauge physical prowess). In the American case, such information is usually reported in so-called muster rolls. Surviving muster rolls of army regiments, from wartime and peacetime periods, are lodged at the National Archives in Washington, D.C.

Analysis of military height data is fraught with technical difficulties. During peacetime, armies were not randomly selected from the eligible male population, and minimum height requirements were used as a screening device. However, because data on height are (approximately) normally distributed, it is possible to work out reliable techniques for inferring unbiased estimates of mean heights. In addition, the military samples usually contain enough ancillary information that, by reweighting, aggregate estimates can be produced.

Margo and Steckel (1983) analyzed one such military sample, derived from the muster rolls of the Union army. Regression analysis was used to control for a variety of factors potentially influencing height, such as occupation, year of entry into the military, and place of birth. For the purposes of this book, the most significant finding concerned the trend in adult height. Among farmers and the nonfarm rural born, there were modest secular increases in height for cohorts born between 1820 and 1834, but, for both groups, heights declined for cohorts born between 1835 and 1839 (see also Komlos and Coclanis 1997). Using data for the Ohio National Guard, Steckel and Haurin (1982) demonstrated that the decline in height continued for individuals born after 1840: comparing cohorts born in the late 1850s to those born in the late 1820s, the decline was 2.3 centimeters, slightly less than one inch—a large change by anthropometric standards (Fogel 1986, 511). Using data on West Point cadets, Komlos (1987) showed that weight for age and weight for height also declined among the relevant cohorts.

Consumption goods—more and better food, housing, shelter, and so on—that produce an increase in average nutritional status are normal goods; that is, the demand for such goods is increasing in real income. If the period 1820–60 witnessed rising per capita incomes, how is it possible for heights to have declined?

One answer invokes negative externalities of economic growth. For example, one by-product of antebellum growth was an increased rate of urbanization. But antebellum cities were death traps and disease ridden. Exposure to a virulent disease environment, holding diet constant, can impede physical growth. The results of chapters 4–6 suggest that well-functioning labor markets promoted economic growth. But high rates of labor mobility could also spread infectious disease, exposing nonmigrants to diseases to which they may not have been immune. Rural born recruits in the Union army who moved to urban areas at young ages were at greater mortality risk than the urban born, presumably because the former lacked certain immunities compared with the latter (Lee 1997). Regressions estimated by Craig, Haines, and Weiss (1997) on a sample of heights of Civil War soldiers show significant negative correlations between crude death rates in the recruit's county of origin and adult height (see also Haines 1997).

Increases in economic inequality have also been suggested as a factor behind the decline in nutritional status because height is negatively correlated with income inequality, holding per capita income constant (Steckel 1995). In certain respects, wage inequality increased before the Civil War (see the discussion later in the chapter), which may have contributed somewhat to the decline. There is also evidence that wealth inequality increased, but this is disputed by some scholars (Williamson and Lindert 1980; Soltow 1992).

Yet another explanation lays the blame on movements in relative prices. According to Komlos (1987; see also Komlos and Coclanis 1997), various features of antebellum economic development led to shifts in relative prices that had deleterious effects on physical growth. In particular, relative food prices rose, while the relative prices of other consumption goods, chiefly manufactured products (such as clothing and shoes), fell. Consumers reacted to these relative price shifts by cutting food consumption relative to other goods.[14]

Could movements in real wages per se have been responsible for the decline in antebellum heights? From a long-run perspective, the answer obviously must be no because my real wage indices show increases between the 1820s and the 1850s. However, if attention is restricted to comovements in height and real wages over certain subperiods, the answer to this question is maybe.

I say maybe because there is no *direct* evidence linking movements in height and real wages for the antebellum United States. However, Weir (1997) has shown that, in the case of nineteenth-century France, mean adult heights and real wages (measured around infancy and early childhood) were positively correlated.[15] Assuming that the French relation ultimately reflects positive income elasticities for nutrients at the household level *and* that the distribution of nutrients within households did *not* move in favor of mothers or their (young) offspring when household real incomes fell, then it is plausible to infer that a positive relation between real wages at the time of infancy and early childhood and adult height also existed in the antebellum United States.[16] Weir's regressions imply that the elasticity of adult height with respect to the real wage was 0.01, and I use this figure for my calculations.[17]

Two cases are examined. The first concerns the data for the Ohio National Guard. Cohorts born in the 1850s were 0.8 percent shorter as adults (173.6 centimeters) than cohorts born in the 1840s (175 centimeters). My real wage series for common labor in the Midwest indicates a decline in real wages from the 1840s to the 1850s of -0.132 when measured in logs (calculated from table 3A.9). This fall in the real wage can explain 16.5 percent ($= 0.00132/0.008$) of the decline in height.

The second case is the South Atlantic region in the 1830s. Comparing birth cohorts of the 1830s to those of the 1820s, Komlos and Coclanis (1997, 440) found that heights declined by -0.18 inches for white male convicts in Georgia. My real wage series for common labor in the South Atlantic region registers a decline in log terms of -0.120 from the 1820s to the 1830s (calculated from table 3A.9). According to Komlos and Coclanis's (1997, 440) regression, the mean height of white men born in the South Atlantic states in the 1820s was 68.06 inches; hence, the decline in adult height for the 1830s cohorts was 0.26 percent. The fall in the real wage explains 46.2 percent ($= 0.00120/0.0026$) of the decline in height.[18]

In view of the assumption that a French elasticity can be applied to an American setting, these calculations—particularly for the South Atlantic case—should be viewed as speculative. However, I do believe that they demonstrate that adverse short-run movements in real wages before the Civil War could have been factors contributing to what some have called an "antebellum puzzle" (Komlos 1987).

7.3.2   Real Wages and the Antebellum Welfare Explosion, 1850–60

In the 1850s, the United States experienced one of its earliest welfare explosions on record. The 1850 and 1860 Censuses of Social Statistics were the first to report the total number of persons receiving public assistance during the census year. According to the 1850 census, 5.8 per 1,000 persons received public assistance at some point during the year. By 1860, the rate had jumped to 10.2 per 1,000 persons, an increase of 76 percent (Kiesling and Margo 1997).

When a society experiences a substantial rise in welfare usage over a relatively brief period of time, the causes are typically complex. But economic factors are likely to be important, particularly in a historical setting like the antebellum United States, where many members of the working class lacked access to capital markets or could not easily avail themselves of other options (e.g., self-employment in agriculture) that might have smoothed consumption in response to a short-run economic downturn.

In this section, I briefly discuss the findings of Kiesling and Margo (1997), who used data from the eight-state sample from the 1850 and 1860 Censuses of Social Statistics (see chap. 2) to study the relation between antebellum usage of poor relief and real wage movements. Here, *real* means the nominal wage of unskilled labor deflated by the cost of board, as measured by the census in 1850 and 1860, and as used in chapters 4 and 5. The basic presumption is that the real wage so defined was a meaningful proxy for the extent to which labor income could provide an adequate diet—that is, if real wages fell, hunger became a possibility.

Because counties were generally responsible for administering poor relief before the Civil War, Kiesling and Margo (1997) specify a model of the per capita demand and supply of poor relief at the local (i.e., county) level. The key idea in the model is that demand for relief depends negatively on the real wage as defined above—thus, a fall in the real wage generates an increase in the number of persons per capita seeking public assistance. Demand depends positively on the generosity of relief, where generosity is measured by average expenditures on relief per full-time equivalent recipient: other factors held constant, greater generosity elicits a greater demand for relief (see, e.g., the discussion in Lebergott [1976]). Demand also depends on additional factors, such as the percentage foreign born and the extent of urbanization (Hannon 1996). The urban poor lacked direct access to resources in times of need. Immigrants tended to have less wealth than the native born and thus were more vulnerable to economic distress (Ferrie 1999). On the supply side, the key assumption is that the willingness of antebellum taxpayers to support others in need was limited—that is, there was a negative trade-off between generosity (as defined above) and the number (per capita) provided public assistance. Equilibrium in the model is achieved when the number of people seeking relief just equals the number the county is willing to support at a given level of generosity.

Econometric analysis supports the basic framework sketched above—namely, that the demand for relief was a positive function of generosity, supply a negative function—and also demonstrates that increases in welfare usage were positively associated with immigration and urbanization. But movements in real wages were also a critical factor because the demand for relief, as hypothesized, was a negative function of the real wage. The magnitude to the relation between welfare usage and real wages was sufficiently large that fully 30 percent of the rise in per capita welfare usage between 1850 and 1860 can be attributed to a fall in the average real wage as defined above—more than any other single factor (Kiesling and Margo 1997).

7.4   The Effectiveness of Antebellum Labor Markets

Real world economies are characterized by a never-ending stream of decisions about how to allocate labor in response to economic opportunities created by initial conditions (e.g., a regional imbalance in factor proportions) or by economic change (e.g., technical progress in manufacturing). Broadly speaking, labor markets can be judged effective when they permit these opportunities to be realized relatively quickly, in the manner suggested by standard economic models of supply and demand.

The findings of chapters 4–6 suggest that antebellum labor markets were quite effective, in the sense just described. Antebellum labor markets appear to have been at their best when facilitating the shift of labor out of agriculture. They were reasonably effective when development necessitated a geographic reallocation of labor, and they were least effective in keeping the structure of wages intact when growth caused the relative demands for workers with different skills to change.

7.4.1   Sectoral Effectiveness: Farm-Nonfarm Wage Gaps

The shift of labor out of agriculture is the hallmark of modern economic growth. Typically, labor shifts out of agriculture when technical progress and capital accumulation raises the relative demand for labor in the nonfarm sector. The antebellum economy certainly experienced a shift of labor out of agriculture. But some scholars have questioned whether this shift was too slow, causing economic growth before the Civil War to be slower than it otherwise might have been.

Chapter 4 examined the issue of sectoral effectiveness by measuring the size of wage gaps between the farm and the nonfarm sectors. The gaps in question pertained to common laborers, chosen because such workers did not possess skills specific to either sector. The existence of farm-nonfarm wage gaps for common laborers would be prima facie evidence of a lack of labor mobility between sectors.

The analysis in chapter 4 established two points. First, wage gaps were negligible when measured in nominal terms at the level of local labor markets for labor hired on an average monthly (or daily) basis. Such markets appear to have been effective, therefore, in allocating labor between farm and nonfarm uses. Second, the gaps were relatively large in nominal terms when aggregated to the level of states. However, the gaps diminished again when the wage data were adjusted for differences in the cost of living between sectors. Nonfarm labor tended to be employed in areas where the cost of living was relatively high compared with farm labor.

My results suggest that the antebellum United States did not appear to suffer from broad sectoral imbalances in the allocation of labor, unlike some other nineteenth-century economies or less-developed countries today. In essence, the antebellum market for common labor was common to both the farm and the nonfarm sectors. Economic change that resulted in higher real wages for common nonfarm labor, therefore, can be presumed to have had a similar effect on the real wages of common farm labor.

7.4.2   Geographic Effectiveness

Labor markets are effective in a geographic sense when they help guide the allocation of labor from low- to high-value locations. In responding to the initial condition of a frontier or to economic change that increased or decreased the relative demand or supply of labor in one location in relation to another, antebellum labor markets had a reasonably good, although mixed, record of success.

The United States began the nineteenth century with most of its labor force—free or slave—located on or near the Eastern Seaboard. In response both to these initial conditions and to various economic changes, primarily technical progress in distribution, labor needed to shift toward the interior—that is, settle both the Midwest and the South Central states.

In the North, real wages were initially higher in the Midwest than in the Northeast, providing the appropriate economic signal for east-west migration. As the Northern labor force shifted toward the Midwest, the real wage gap between the Midwest and the Northeast declined, as predicted by a simple economic model of the settlement process. The decline did not occur consistently in every decade, but, when it did not—such as for common labor in the 1830s—shifts in the relative demand for labor that temporarily favored the Midwest appear to have been the reason. Previous work has suggested that a regionally integrated labor market did not appear in the North until after the Civil War, but my results suggest that such a market was already well in place by the 1850s, if not earlier.

In the South, real wages were initially higher in the East South Central region than in the South Atlantic, but, in contrast to the North, the regional wage gap did not narrow before the Civil War. The demand for labor moved against the South Atlantic states; while labor did shift out of the region, the shift was neither fast enough nor large enough. Some scholars have suggested that the existence of well-functioning markets for transferring slave labor from east to west promoted a more efficient geographic allocation of free labor in the South compared with the North (Fleisig 1976; Wright 1978). The failure of the regional wage gap to narrow in the South, however, is inconsistent with this point of view.

The South also lagged behind the North in real wage growth. As a result, there emerged a real wage gap for common labor favoring the North in the 1830s. The timing of the emergence of the gap suggests an important causal role for early industrialization, which was concentrated initially in the Northeast. Although the North-South wage gap narrowed somewhat in the 1850s, the low-wage South was already a feature of the American economy before the Civil War.

Aside from questions of regional allocation, the antebellum economy was continuously beset by shocks that left wages relatively high in some labor markets and relatively low in others. One point of view is that antebellum labor markets did not respond effectively to such shocks, with the result that wage differentials between locations persisted over long periods of time. Using data from the 1850 and 1860 Censuses of Social Statistics, however, I found strong evidence of regression to the mean: a local labor market with real wages that were, say, 10 percent above average in 1850 would have real wages only 2 percent above average in 1860. Wage convergence of this sort is exactly what would be predicted if labor markets operated effectively to guide migration from low- to high-wage areas. The remaining persistence in real wage differentials across locations may very well be due to the effect of location-specific amenities (leading to low wages) or disamenities (leading to high wages).

Additional evidence of the ability of the antebellum economy to respond to geographic shocks was presented in chapter 6, which examined one of the most extraordinary natural experiments involving labor markets in nineteenth-century America—the California Gold Rush. Real wages rose sharply during the initial years of the Gold Rush and then declined once labor migrated into the state. Thus, the labor market worked in the case of the Gold Rush, although it should be kept in mind that the supply of labor into Gold Rush California was not particularly elastic when judged by late twentieth-century standards.

7.4.3 The Structure of Wages

The occupational wage series developed in this book reveal that real wages grew most rapidly for white-collar laborers and more rapidly for common laborers than for artisans. In terms of the trickle-down effects of antebellum growth, in other words, artisans fared less well than the other occupation groups.

That the real wages of artisans did not keep pace with the wages of common laborers supports a view widely held by labor historians.[19] According to this view, the growth of manufacturing, with its emphasis on the factory system, displaced the artisanal shop (Sokoloff 1984). New methods of production and labor organization led to an increased relative demand for less-skilled labor and a decline in the relative demand for artisanal skills (James and Skinner 1985). Artisans fought back in various ways—for example, by attempting to form unions—but ultimately they could not stem the tide of technological change. The end product of the shifts in relative labor demand was a decline in the skilled-unskilled wage ratio, consistent with my estimates of the more rapid growth of common than artisanal wages in the long run.[20]

But, while economic development before the Civil War did not enhance the relative wages of artisans, it did enhance the relative wages of white-collar workers. Technical progress and organizational change—the factory system—in antebellum manufacturing, along with improved transportation, led to growth in internal trade and a concomitant increase in the demand for white-collar skills to cope with the changes (Aldrich 1971). The wage evidence presented in this book suggests that, before the Civil War, the demand for such skills must have been growing more rapidly than the supply.[21]

There is also evidence that the relative wages of white-collar labor continued to remain relatively high for several decades after the Civil War. Goldin (1998; see also Goldin and Katz 1995) has recently estimated ratios of the wages of white-collar workers to those of factory operatives for the late nineteenth century. These ratios range from 1.69 for relatively low-skilled white-collar workers to 4.35 for business managers in the early 1890s (Goldin 1998).

Economic development after the Civil War produced an increase in the number and complexity of white-collar occupations, so it is somewhat difficult to make ready comparisons between Goldin's estimates of wage ratios and any based on my wage series. However, my wage series for white-collar labor are constructed to pertain to the average clerk, who was involved in record keeping and (some) management of supplies. Hence, such labor is probably most comparable to bookkeepers in the late nineteenth century, for which Goldin (1998) has also produced an estimate of the wage ratio: 2.278.

Using decadal averages of wages from the national aggregate series in chapter 5, my estimate of the white-collar to common labor ratio is 2.07 in the 1850s, about 10 percent below Goldin's estimate for late nineteenth-century bookkeepers.[22] Taken literally, the comparison suggests that the relative wage of white-collar labor remained constant, or increased slightly, from the 1850s to the late nineteenth century. The relative wage in the 1850s was lowest in the Northeast (1.90) and highest in the South Central states (2.50).[23]

Economic historians have long wondered whether a Kuznets curve existed in American history (Williamson and Lindert 1980). By *Kuznets curve,* I mean Simon Kuznets's (1955) assertion that inequality first rises, then plateaus, and finally declines over the course of economic development. If the Kuznets curve is interpreted as referring to the relative position of educated labor in the wage structure, then my results (and Goldin's) suggest that the initial, rising portion of the curve can be dated to the period 1820–60. Wage ratios then either rose slightly or remained constant between 1860 and 1900. After the turn of the twentieth century, America experienced a substantial education expansion that increased the supply of educated labor relative to demand, driving down the returns to schooling and the relative earnings of white-collar labor after World War I (Goldin and Katz 1995).

8

Postlude

This book has presented new estimates of annual time series of nominal and real wages in the United States from the 1820s to the eve of the Civil War. These series, along with related cross-sectional data, have been used to examine aspects of the economic history of free labor that have long been regarded as central to the economic, social, and political development of the United States during the first half of the nineteenth century—the standard of living and its relation to long-run growth, and short-run fluctuations, in real wages; the effect of early industrialization on the distribution of income; and the role of well-functioning factor markets (in this case, the market for free labor) in promoting economic development.

Although the primary purpose of this book has been to illuminate the economic history of the antebellum period, it is useful to recognize that many of the historical issues have important parallels with current concerns. For example, the American wage structure has widened considerably since 1970, as the demand for better-educated workers has grown vastly relative to the demand for less-educated workers (Katz and Murphy 1992). This widening of the wage structure has occurred against a backdrop of relatively slow growth in average real wages, high rates of immigration, and (until recently) explosive growth in the welfare system that scholars have linked to adverse movements in the real wages of less-educated workers (Blank 1997).

The results of this book demonstrate that such changes are not unique in American history. The antebellum period witnessed a widening of the wage structure in favor of white-collar labor and periods of stagnation in real wages, one of which (the 1850s) was associated with a wave of immigration and a rapid increase in reliance on poor relief, prompted, in part, by adverse movements in the real wages of unskilled labor. Yet, in the long run, the benefits of antebellum economic development were manifested in higher real wages on average, as has been true of economic development in the twentieth century. History also teaches that most change in the American income distribution generally has been episodic rather than permanent. While the antebellum rise in the relative wages of white-collar labor evidently continued after the Civil War, eventually the supply of educated labor expanded in the early twentieth century, leading to a fall in the returns to white-collar skills.

Economic analyses of less-developed and transition economies today increasingly emphasize the allocative effectiveness of factor markets, such as the market for labor, as an important institutional engine of economic growth. The evidence presented in this book clearly suggests that, in certain key respects, the economic growth of the United States was enhanced by well-functioning labor markets relatively early in its history. Perhaps the most fundamental structural change of modern economic growth—the shift of labor out of agriculture—appears to have gone smoothly before the Civil War, in the sense that wage gaps between the farm and the nonfarm sector were unimportant. In a geographic sense, too, the integration of American labor markets was in progress before the Civil War, although there were important developments in the opposite direction—the emergence of the low-wage South—that would not be reversed until the twentieth century. In short, economists seeking good historical examples of the importance of labor markets in early development need look no further than the antebellum United States.

Modern economic development, it is said, has produced a variety of labor market institutions that make nominal wages less flexible over the business cycle, thereby prolonging the consequences of adverse economic shocks. The results of this book suggest that, if a golden age of totally flexible wages ever existed in American history, it was not during the antebellum period, when labor markets appear to have been far closer to the textbook norm of competition than they are today. Nominal wages before the Civil War *were* flexible in response to sustained nominal or real shocks, but not immediately so.

Documenting and explaining change in historical economies is the primary task of economic history. But economic history can also serve a useful function for a current audience because events in the past—even the distant past—may share commonalities with events in the present as well as shaping the fundamental constraints on economic decisions in the present. Careful scrutiny of past economic change, such as during the antebellum period, provides a context for interpreting economic change in later periods of American history and, in doing so, renders such change less mysterious.

Notes

Chapter 1

1. Throughout this book, designations used to refer to the various regions of the United States carry their modern denotations, with slight amendments that reflect the political realities of the period (e.g., *Virginia* includes current-day West Virginia) or as noted.

Chapter 2

1. The survey is meant, not to be exhaustive, but rather to discuss the major studies.

2. A rise in the real daily (or monthly) real wage may not imply a rise in the *annual* standard of living, if annual days of work decline sufficiently and the decline is involuntary (i.e., unemployment, see chap. 7) or if the rise in the wage compensates for more adverse working conditions (see chap. 3). If neither condition obtains, however, real consumption can increase and the worker is better off.

3. The manuscript 1850 Census of Manufactures and the manuscript and published 1860 Census of Manufactures provide additional wage evidence for manufacturing; these can be combined with the 1820 census and the McLane Report to produce estimates of average annual wages in manufacturing for four years (see Sokoloff and Villaflor 1992). Because of geographic limitations in the census, the Sokoloff-Villaflor series cover only the Northeast.

4. The absence of firm weights led Abbott (1905) and Hansen (1925) to choose the Aldrich over the Weeks Report. Lebergott (1964), however, made a persuasive case that the Weeks Report was superior to the Aldrich Report; its coverage was better, it was less affected by sampling variability, and the weighting problem could be solved by using the census figures as benchmarks.

5. For a recent study of cyclic fluctuations in wages in the late nineteenth century using the Aldrich Report, see Hanes (1993).

6. For example, if one is interested in using the Weeks Report to measure changes in the wages of common labor before 1840, there is only *one* usable observation for the period 1830–32.

7. Coelho and Shepherd present no other occupation-specific estimates at the regional level, apparently because the regional sample sizes were too small (see Coelho and Shepherd 1976, 217, n. 31). They do, however, aggregate the entire sample to the national level and produce money wage series for the other four occupations (see their app. table A2).

8. If the regional price deflators are used, however, the decline is larger in the Northeast (in percentage terms) than in the Midwest (see Coelho and Shepherd 1976, table 4, p. 213).

9. The conclusion that the real wages of engineers in the Mid-Atlantic and East North Central regions rose in the 1850s is not very robust. In the Mid-Atlantic case, there was no upward trend in the real wages of engineers between 1851 and 1859 and then an 11 percent increase between 1859 and 1860. In the East North Central states, there was supposedly a 30 percent increase in the real wages of engineers between 1851 and 1852 but no change between 1852 and 1860. Given the small number of engineers in the Weeks Report sample for the 1850s (there are only eighteen observations for the entire country in 1851 and nineteen in 1852), Coelho and Shepherd's (1976, 217, n. 31) caution that the skilled occupation groups in the Weeks data "may not be as homogenous as they appear at first glance," and the absence of an upward trend in the 1850s, there is every reason to be skeptical that a real wage increase occurred.

10. Using an unweighted average of the New England and Mid-Atlantic decadal average real wages as the base, the regional gap in real wages between the East North Central states and the Northeast was 8 percent for common laborers and 8.5 percent for engineers (calculated from Coelho and Shepherd 1976, tables 6–7, pp. 218–19).

11. The same conclusion is affirmed in an analysis-of-variance-type regression of the full sample (the regression controls for occupation and region) that, unfortunately, does not allow skill differentials to vary across regions (i.e., interactions between the occupation and the regional dummies) (see Coelho and Shepherd 1976, table 8, p. 220). In the case of engineers and common laborers, the Weeks Report data suggest that skill differentials were similar in the Northeast and the East North Central states in the 1850s but were substantially higher in the South Central states in the late 1850s; on the basis of decadal averages, the ratio of engineers' to laborers' pay was 1.69 in the 1850s in the Northeast and the East Central states but 2.28 in the East South Central states (the figure for the East South Central states pertains to 1857–60 only) (see Coelho and Shepherd 1976, tables 6–7, pp. 218–19).

12. Scattered quotations are available for other types of workers, including engineers, painters, and cooks (Smith 1963, 301), but Smith makes no use of these in his analysis.

13. Smith (1963, 299, 301) noted that he was able to produce monthly wage series for three geographic sections of the canal, but, unfortunately, the published article reports only annual series for the entire canal.

14. If the base year is 1828 instead of 1830, real wages for both common laborers and carpenters increased in the 1830s.

15. Lebergott (1964, 150) provided "best guesses" at real wage movements over medium-length periods (such as 1835–50). Like Coelho and Shepherd (1976), Lebergott (1964, p. 150) also argued that real wages fell in the 1850s.

16. The exact nature of the disagreement between Zabler and Adams is somewhat unclear, at least as far as carpenters are concerned. The ratio of the pay of house carpenters to that of common laborers averaged 1.25 in Philadelphia in the 1820s; as noted in the text, the corresponding ratio for the iron industry was 1.22.

17. Had the cost of living been the same in Philadelphia and rural eastern Penn-

sylvania, a Philadelphia carpenter would have had to work only 46 percent of the year (= 0.57/1.25), or roughly 141 days (based on a 310-day workyear). Had the cost of living been 50 percent higher in Philadelphia, annual earnings would have been equalized by working 68 percent of the year or an annual unemployment rate of 32 percent.

18. Unfortunately, there is no wage quotation for common labor in 1820, but a decline in the money wage for common labor is evident comparing the late 1810s to the early 1820s (from $1.00 to $0.75 per day).

19. Adams also argues (1968, 413) that the use of wholesale instead of retail prices exacerbates annual fluctuations in real wages, but he provides no evidence supporting this position.

20. For example, the growth rate of real wages for ships' carpenters was 4.6 percent per year from 1821 to 1830 but only 1.6 percent per year from 1820 to 1830.

21. However, unemployment was high in the early 1840s, consistent with Adams's argument. Also, suppose the relative price of goods other than food and shelter declined in the 1850s to a degree sufficient to offset the rise in the budget share for food and shelter. Then labor welfare could be higher even though leisure fell.

22. To explain the absence of real wage growth, Adams (1986, 637) speculates that the supply curve of labor to the farm sector in Maryland may have been close to perfectly elastic during the period. Even if this were true, however, it does not imply an absence of real wage growth because the supply price to agriculture would depend (as Adams recognizes) on the opportunity cost of labor in the nonfarm sector. Thus, if real wages were rising outside Maryland agriculture, the supply price to the farm sector would also rise, assuming that the two labor markets were integrated.

23. Taking 1820–29 as the base decade (= 100), the index number for w/p (the real wage) for 1850–55 was 100.8.

24. Sokoloff (1986a, 23) reaches a similar conclusion; he deflates Rothenberg's nominal wage series by the David-Solar price index, thereby producing real wage gains from the 1820s to the 1850s.

25. The basis for this belief is unclear since, as David and Solar (1977, 61) point out, there is "considerable obscurity surround[ing] the number and distribution of establishments" in the Massachusetts data.

26. As noted previously, Lebergott's figures are weighted averages of the state estimates published in the 1850 and 1860 volumes; the weights are the census counts of common laborers in each state.

27. Note that, by construction, the nominal wage appears in both the numerator and the denominator of the David-Solar real wage index, which may dampen its volatility. This effect is probably not large since housing costs are assumed to be roughly 15 percent of the total household budget.

28. Hoover (1960) constructed a retail price index for the period 1851–80 using retail prices from the Weeks Report.

29. Williamson and Lindert did not actually report a separate index for skilled labor; rather, they report a series of skill differentials (the ratio of skilled to unskilled wages). The relevant series is given as "urban skilled workers" in app. D of Williamson and Lindert (1980, 307).

30. Williamson (1975, 36) does argue, however, that nominal wage gaps between farm and nonfarm common labor declined from the 1810s to the 1830s in Massachusetts and thus that his series overstates the growth in unskilled pay prior to 1830.

31. There is some confusion between Williamson (1975) and Williamson and Lindert (1980) over the use of Layer's series. According to the notes to table 9 in Williamson (1975, 37), Layer's series was used for the period 1834–49, Layer being

"preferred to Abbott . . . since the Aldrich sample is too small and inconsistent prior to 1850." According to the text of Williamson (1975, 36) and the notes to app. G of Williamson and Lindert (1980, 320), Layer's series was used only through 1839. In what follows, I assume that Williamson and Lindert (1980) is the authoritative discussion.

32. The growth rate is calculated from decadal averages of index numbers of real wages for 1820–29 and 1850–59 (Williamson and Lindert 1980, app. G, p. 319). The ratio of the 1850s index number to the 1820s index number was 1.576 ($= 89.1/56.5$). Taking logarithms, and dividing by 30 (the number of years between 1825 and 1855, the midpoints of the respective decades), gives a growth rate of the skill differential of 1.52 percent per year.

33. According to Brady, the cost of living rose by about 9 percent from 1834 to 1836, compared with an approximately 30 percent increase in the wholesale price level (see Margo 1992, 189).

34. If one uses Brady's (1966) data, substitutes wholesale prices for coffee and tea, and excludes clothing items with extremely steep price declines, the revised David-Solar price index shows an increase in the cost of living between 1834 and 1836 of about 18 percent. As pointed out in chap. 3, the David-Solar real wage index shows too high a level in the late 1830s because the numerator is based on data from an unusually high wage location. Part of the reason, therefore, why the David-Solar real wage index registers a decline in the early 1840s is a consequence of the biased level in the late 1830s. However, the price deflator is also responsible, as evinced in table 2.1 above. Price indices based on wholesale prices, such as Williamson and Lindert's (1980) or those developed in chap. 3, register dramatic declines in the early 1840s, in excess of declines in nominal wages, thereby causing real wages to rise. In chap. 7, I argue that nominal wages were rigid in the short run before the Civil War, partly on the basis of the episode of the early 1840s (see also Goldin and Margo 1992b). If retail prices declined less than wholesale prices—and, in particular, according to the pattern revealed by the David-Solar price index—then real wages might conceivably have fallen. However, as noted in the text (see also chaps. 3 and 7), there are good a priori reasons to doubt that wholesale prices, particularly for basic food items like flour, were substantially more variable than retail prices.

35. Weiss's (1992, 26) variant A estimate of per capita income grows at an average annual rate of 1.21 percent per year between 1820 and 1860. Using Weiss's figures on the total labor force, the aggregate labor force participation rate increased from 0.328 in 1820 to 0.358 in 1860, or an average annual rate of growth of 0.22 percent per year. Thus, output per worker grew at 0.99 percent per year, considerably slower than the growth rates implied by the real wage series.

36. For an excellent general history of the Quartermaster's Department, see Risch (1962).

37. The ability of post quartermasters to hire civilians varied over time. Normally, it would appear, the hiring of civilians had to be approved at some level, even if directly authorized by the post's commanding officer. General Order no. 43, issued in 1851, made obtaining such authority much more difficult; it forbade the hiring of civilians for any purpose except as authorized by army division headquarters (Prucha 1953, 168). Although the number of civilians hired in the 1850s clearly fell in certain regions (see, e.g., table 2.2 below in the case of forts in the South Atlantic region), it did not in others.

38. By *gaps,* I mean that not every type of worker (e.g., teamsters) was hired at every post in every month. The idiosyncratic nature of the army's demand for civilian labor (e.g., no carpenter could be found among the troops) is the most likely explanation for the gaps, although it is certainly possible that some civilians were hired but that no administrative record survives.

39. For an exhaustive survey of the available records, see Heppner and John (1968).

40. Workers at arsenals were frequently paid by the piece, and output seems to have been recorded on a daily basis. Hence, the records are voluminous and difficult to use. The naval records are similar to the *Reports* but tend to be more voluminous, and the locations tend to more or less duplicate those from the *Reports*.

41. Payrolls were also collected from forts in Florida between 1835 and 1842, forts in Texas during the Mexican War, and forts in the Far West. With the exception of forts in California (see chap. 6), data from these forts are not used in this book.

42. The extract from the full sample used in chap. 3 differs in that certain forts and wage outliers are excluded and attention restricted to particular occupation groups, but the broad distributional patterns are the same.

43. This number, however, overstates the amount of independent information in the sample because some workers were hired for longer periods of time than a month and therefore appear more than once in the sample.

44. The temporal detail in the table understates the degree to which certain time periods are under- or overrepresented; when the data are disaggregated by year, some years are severely underrepresented. As a result, it is necessary in some cases to pool data across years, which means that some of the resulting wage estimates must be interpolated (see chap. 3).

45. The unusually large number of observations for Kansas pertains only to the 1850s.

46. For example, Smith (1963) provided series for only common laborers, carpenters, masons, and teamworkers.

47. Of free males aged fifteen and over reporting nonfarm occupations in the 1850 census, fully 43.2 percent were either carpenters, clerks, laborers, masons and plasters, painters and glaziers, or teamsters (computed from DeBow 1854, 126–28).

48. For an analysis of the data on agricultural yields in 1860, see Schaefer (1983).

49. The specific instructions for collecting the wage data stated nothing more than that "the information called for in the six columns is so simple and so plainly set forth in the headings that it is deemed unnecessary to add thereto" (DeBow 1853, xxv).

50. Such activities can be inferred from the occupation information in the *Reports*. For example, a white-collar worker might be designated as a "clerk in the quartermaster's department" or an "assistant to quartermaster"; since the post quartermasters were involved in record keeping and so forth, it seems reasonable to infer that their civilian employees assisted them in such activities.

51. It is clear that post quartermasters had to compete with private-sector employers when they attempted to hire civilians (see, e.g., Prucha 1953, 166). Ruhlen (1964, 19) cites a report describing the construction of an early Nevada fort: "At the time the post was located a great competition for mechanics, materials, &c was created by the settlement and building of the several cities of Carson, Silver, and Virginia."

Chapter 3

1. For example, a tight specification would allow wages to vary over time according to a linear time trend rather than dummy variables for each year (see the text). The coefficient of the time trend is an estimate of the average annual rate of growth. This growth rate may be estimated accurately but at the cost of ignoring annual movements in wages around the trend.

2. It is important to note that this is a pooled time-series cross-sectional regression as opposed to a panel regression. In a panel setup, observations—or, rather, individuals—would be followed through time. To follow individuals through time, it would be necessary to link them across years using some identifying feature, such as a name. Although names were sometimes included on the payrolls, the reporting of names was irregular enough (especially for common laborers) that panel estimation proved infeasible.

3. In logs, the value of X^* in period j is $X^*\beta + \delta_j$, while the value in period k is $X^*\beta + \delta_k$. Thus, the relative value of the bundle in the two periods is $(X^*\beta + \delta_j) - (X^*\beta + \delta_k) = \delta_j - \delta_k$, which does not depend on X or β, as stated in the text.

4. Twenty-six days is the standard figure used in such conversions (see Lebergott 1964, 245).

5. Compared with modern-day wage regressions, the list of X variables is very small; in particular, it does not control for work experience, which, on the basis of modern evidence, might be expected to have an effect on wages. The assumption in constructing the wage series is that the distribution of *unobserved* characteristics does not vary over time. If it does—e.g., if workers at the forts were, on average, more experienced in the 1850s than in the 1820s and wages were a positive function of experience—then the growth rates of the series would be biased upward. To get at this issue, it would be necessary to trace observations through time or else link the payrolls to another source that would provide proxies for unobserved characteristics, such as the manuscript Censuses of Population of 1850 or 1860. However, any such linked sample would be small in size and could not be used to construct annual wage series.

6. Regressions for the South were also estimated excluding slaves; however, to produce nominal wage series from these regressions requires much more interpolation (see the text regarding the procedure to produce the nominal wage series) than if slaves are included. Because almost all slave artisans at South Central forts were employed in the 1830s, it was not possible to allow the coefficient of slave status in this regression to vary across decades.

7. Fishback and Kantor estimate the wage premium for unemployment risk in a hedonic regression. Their regression also includes dummy variables for pay periods (whether the worker was paid weekly or monthly). As argued in the text (see also Fishback and Kantor 1992, 832), the coefficients on these dummy variables also capture unemployment risk. Fishback and Kantor's conclusion, however, that workers were less than fully compensated for unemployment risk is based on coefficients of days lost in the hedonic regression, *controlling* for the pay period; thus, they may be underestimating the degree to which workers were compensated for unemployment risk.

8. Lebergott (1964, 245–50) provides evidence on the day wage premium for a variety of occupations. In agriculture, the premium stood at about 46 percent in 1869, drifting down to 29 percent at the turn of the century. In Pennsylvania ironworks in the early 1830s, twenty-six times the day wage was 36 percent higher than the average monthly wage. Labor contracts for seamen provide some of the most revealing evidence; Lebergott shows that monthly wages were significantly lower on longer-distance voyages—until the replacement of steam for sail, which cut the length of voyages significantly.

9. In such cases, rations were valued at $0.12 or $0.20, depending on internal evidence in the reports (see Margo and Villaflor 1987, 878).

10. Alternatively, slaves may have been more costly to supervise than free labor and may also have been less likely to bring tools to the job, and both these factors would be reflected in a lower wage.

11. Choosing an X^* is not necessary if one wishes merely to calculate a nominal

wage index; such an index can be computed directly from the coefficients of the time-period dummies because the dependent variable is measured in logarithms (see Margo 1992). However, if one wishes to produce a nominal wage *series* (i.e., dollar values), it is necessary to choose a value of X^*.

12. The fort location weights are similar to those in Margo (1992).

13. It is worth noting that the nominal wage indices can be computed from the nominal wage series simply by dividing each wage by the appropriate 1850 benchmark.

14. These data can be found in "Naval Hospital Payrolls," Bureau of Yards and Docks, Record Group 71, National Archives. It is important to note that these workers were building hospitals and other buildings at the yard, *not* ships (ship carpenters earned a premium above ordinary carpenters).

15. The coefficient estimates are as follows: 1835: skilled, -0.236; 1836: skilled, -0.167; unskilled, -0.206; 1837: skilled, -0.218.

16. If Pittsburgh observations are allocated to the Midwest, the nominal wages of white-collar workers in the Midwest grew at an average annual rate of 1.77 percent (based on the decadal averages for the 1820s and 1850s), compared with 1.24 percent per year if Pittsburgh observations are allocated to the Northeast. If the Pittsburgh observations are excluded from the Northeast, the nominal wages of white-collar workers in the Northeast increase at an average annual rate of 1.18 percent per year (based on the decadal averages for the 1820s and 1850s), compared with an average annual rate of 1.43 percent per year if Pittsburgh observations are included in the Northeastern samples. The upshot is that white-collar wages in Pittsburgh increased comparatively rapidly (relative to other locations in the Northeast) and thus that their inclusion (exclusion) raises (lowers) the regional growth rate.

17. For details on the construction of the price indices for 1821–56, see the appendix to Goldin and Margo (1992b). Extending the original Goldin-Margo price indices to 1860 followed the procedures described in the Goldin and Margo paper. Some slight additional modifications were made to trend in the price indices for the 1850s, making use of the 1850 and 1860 census data on the weekly cost of board.

18. In this respect, they are similar to the price deflators employed in various studies of antebellum real wages, such as Williamson and Lindert (1980; see also chap. 2 below).

19. There is also the problem of properly pricing the services provided by goods that are affected by technological progress, a problem that I do not address. Nordhaus (1997) argues that conventional real wage series, such as those developed in this book, systematically understate growth rates in living standards by failing to account for the value of such services properly.

20. Lebergott (1964, 548) reported price index numbers for 1830, 1840, 1850, and 1860. I substituted the good-specific retail price change between 1830 and 1860 for the decadal average of the respective subindex in my Northeastern price deflator. Thus, e.g., Lebergott's calculation shows a decline in the retail price of textiles of 26 percent (from an index number of 100 in 1830 to an index number of 74 in 1860), whereas the cotton subindex of my price deflator declines by 12.5 percent from the 1830s to the 1850s. I do not substitute Lebergott's price index for coffee since this shows a rise over the period, compared to a decline in the wholesale price. It is important to note that, had I averaged Lebergott's figures between successive census years (e.g., 1830 and 1840) to produce decadal midpoints and used the midpoints instead to infer the bias, the bias would have been smaller.

21. As noted in chap. 2, the Hoover housing price index is problematic because it is based on company housing (see Lebergott 1964).

Chapter 4

1. The proof is very simple. Suppose that aggregate labor supply is fixed at $\underline{L}$. Efficiency requires that production be at a point on the production possibilities frontier. In the two-sector model in the text, the value of output is

$$pF(L_A, T) + G(\underline{L} - L_A, K),$$

where F is a production function for agriculture, G is a production function for nonagricultural output, T (land) and K (capital) are specific (fixed) factors, and p is the relative price of farm output. V is maximized when

$$pF_L = G_L$$

or when $\text{VMP}_F = \text{VMP}_G$. Note that this formulation assumes that both economic activities (can) take place at the same time, with the result that the opportunity cost of labor in one sector (e.g., agriculture) is the value of the marginal product in the other sector. Suppose, instead, that production were seasonal, specifically, that the marginal product of labor in sector i was zero for some portion of the relevant time period (e.g., a year). Seasonal cycles can be said to mesh perfectly if, when the marginal product in sector i is zero, the marginal product in sector j is positive (and vice versa). With perfect seasonal cycles, labor is no longer mobile between the two sectors; rather, it moves between, say, nonparticipation (leisure) and one or the other sector, depending on the time of year. While seasonality was certainly important during the antebellum period and there was some meshing of the agricultural and nonagricultural cycles (see, e.g., Earle 1992; Engerman and Goldin 1993), it would be incorrect to claim that it was perfect, in the sense discussed above.

2. Implicit in the model is the assumption that the demand for both goods is perfectly elastic—i.e., p_{nf}/p_f (f = farm, nf = nonfarm) is a constant. If, instead, the relative demand for nonfarm goods were an inverse function of the relative price, an improvement in technology could drive down the value of the marginal product in the nonfarm sector, and labor would migrate into the farm sector.

3. In the so-called Harris-Todaro model, the resulting wage difference between the formal and the informal sectors adjusts to compensate workers for the cost of unemployment (see Williamson 1991).

4. Weiss's (1992, 24–25) major revisions for the early decades of the century involve the reallocation of slave labor (attributed by Lebergott to agriculture) to the nonfarm sector, while his revisions at midcentury involve the reallocation of substantial numbers of common laborers to farming. Because the revisions to the early years have more of an effect on the South than on the North, while his revisions for midcentury are more uniform in their geographic effect, Weiss's figures imply a slower pace of industrialization outside the South than previously thought.

5. Or, indeed, at all. According to Field (1978), the puzzle is why industrialization would take hold in such a land-abundant economy as the United States.

6. The labor that was vented off the farm was, according to Field (see also Goldin and Sokoloff 1984), children and, especially, young women. Migration to the frontier was difficult and costly for adult males, all the more so for young women (but, for evidence that hired hands who were young might also migrate long distances on their own in search of work, see Schob 1975). Young women who might work as domestics on farms were forced to seek work in manufacturing. A serious problem for Field's argument, however, is the fact that industrialization apparently raised the earnings of young women relative to those of adult males, while the

opposite would have been true if Field's model were correct (see Goldin and Sokoloff 1984).

7. For example, Simkovich (1993) explicitly assumes the absence of wage gaps in his analysis of Field's argument (see, e.g., his fig. 3).

8. In this respect, far better data are available for studying postbellum wage gaps (see, e.g., Hatton and Williamson 1991). Lebergott (1964) produced extensive estimates of farm, common, and manufacturing wages for the antebellum period, but he did not use them for the purpose of estimating wage gaps.

9. All Bidwell and Falconer's wage comparisons refer to farm labor paid by the month or by the day and "mechanics" paid by the day, even though mechanics were certainly skilled laborers by the standards of the day.

10. The nonfarm wage series used to construct the Vermont wage ratio was drawn from the Aldrich Report of the 1890 census and does not appear to be specific to Vermont (see the notes to Williamson and Lindert 1980, table E, p. 313), although it is specific to the Northeast. Since Vermont farm wages were relatively low by Northeastern standards, particularly in the 1830s (see Lebergott 1964, 539), it is likely that Williamson and Lindert's estimates of the Vermont wage gap are biased upward.

11. Williamson and Lindert (1980, 72 and app. E) claim that their Massachusetts common wage pertains to urban labor, but nowhere does Wright (1889) give any information about the geographic location of the common laborers whose wage rates he collected for his sample.

12. Later in the chapter, however, I show that Williamson and Lindert's analysis of the published 1850 data was faulty and that their conclusion that (aggregate) nominal wage gaps "were trivial" cannot be sustained.

13. Comparing the wages of farmhands with those of carpenters or mechanics (à la Bidwell and Falconer 1925) would confuse a true wage gap with one produced by differences in human capital. Ideally, we would have a sample of individuals employed in both sectors and use hedonic regression to control for worker characteristics, but such samples are not available for the antebellum period. For an example of such a study, see Hatton and Williamson (1991).

14. The harvest was an apparent exception. Harvest labor was paid a wage premium, evidently because the supply of labor to the farm sector during the harvest was less than perfectly elastic (see Schob 1975; and Rothenberg 1992). The farm wage data analyzed here refer to monthly labor, whereas harvest labor was typically hired by the day or the task (Schob 1975).

15. Twenty-six days per month is the standard figure assumed for full-time work during the antebellum period (see Schob 1975; or Lebergott 1964).

16. Ideally, I would use county-level estimates of the number of hired hands and (unskilled) nonfarm laborers, but these are simply not available. It is debatable whether slaves should be excluded from the weighting scheme since slave labor was hired out into nonfarm (or even farm) tasks (see Fogel and Engerman 1974). To test the sensitivity of the results to the inclusion of slave labor, I recomputed the Southern sample averages (the adjusted row) for 1850, excluding slave labor as follows. First, slaves were excluded from the count of the farm labor force of each state (North Carolina, Virginia, Kentucky, and Tennessee), as given by Weiss (1992, 53). Next, I estimated the nonfarm slave labor force, assuming that the agricultural slave labor force was 0.74 times the total slave labor force (see Weiss 1992, 54). Finally, using Weiss's (1992, 37) estimates of the total labor force, the free nonfarm labor force was computed for each state. Using these weights, the adjusted farm wage was $14.50 and the adjusted nonfarm wage $16.46 for the Southern sample in 1850, very similar to the figures reported in table 4.1 below.

17. For example, the use of manufacturing labor in place of my estimate of nonfarm labor would not change the substantive results.

18. The use of β may be more appropriate since it gives more weight to counties with relatively more employment in the nonfarm sector, which was expanding over time in settled areas (but see n. 16 above).

19. Weights for arbitrarily defined local economies (e.g., ones that cut across county or state boundaries) would require computations based on the manuscript Censuses of Agriculture and Manufacturing, computations that, while technically feasible, are well beyond the scope of this chapter. It should be noted that the use of census political units (e.g., counties, states, census regions) in the analysis of market integration has a long history in the literature (see also chap. 5). For example, state per capita income data have formed the basis of numerous studies of labor market integration, such as Williamson and Lindert (1980).

20. The Northern aggregate gaps are larger than the state-specific gaps because of weighting; in computing the mean farm wage, more weight is given (via the distribution of improved acres) to the frontier states, where the farm wage was relatively low compared with, say, Massachusetts.

21. However, it is quite likely that nonfarm labor within counties was concentrated in towns or cities, where the cost of living was higher than in rural areas. As I later demonstrate, the aggregate wage gap declines once cost-of-living differences are taken into account. I cannot replicate this analysis, however, within counties because I lack suitable sector weights (e.g., improved acres) at the minor civil division (MCD) level. Thus, use of the β weights probably overstates the true within-county gap.

22. This regression is estimated at the minor civil division level, pooling the data across states and over time (seventy-nine MCDs reported a monthly common wage instead of a daily wage). The dependent variable is the log of the common wage; state dummies, a dummy for 1860, and a dummy for the misreported observations are the independent variables. It would be desirable to estimate a similar regression for farm labor, but the number of misreported observations on the farm wage was judged to be too small (ten observations) to obtain a reliable estimate.

23. The adjustment factor shifts the distribution of farm wages closer to the distribution of nonfarm wages, thereby closing the wage gap, on average (and throughout the distribution). Since the adjustment factor is constant, it does not compress either distribution, as I suspect county-specific adjustment factors would.

24. Studies of labor market integration have frequently had to rely on food prices to adjust for geographic differences in the cost of living (see, e.g., Rosenbloom 1990; and chap. 5 below).

25. Defining an *urban* county as one that had at least one urban area with population greater than ten thousand, the cost of board was higher, on average, in such counties by 34 percent in 1850 and 25 percent in 1860 (these estimates were derived from regressions of the log of the weekly cost of board on the urban dummy, also including state dummies).

26. Williamson and Lindert's estimates compare the daily wage of farm labor with board and the daily wage of common labor with board. Williamson and Lindert (1980, 31) assert that, because both wages include board, "cost of living differences are unlikely to matter much." However, in equilibrium, the difference between the daily wage with and without board should approximate the value of board.

27. Williamson and Lindert's estimates of daily wages of common and farm labor at the regional level and for various states are taken directly from Lebergott (1964), who produced them from the average wages reported in the 1850 census. The regional estimates are weighted averages of the state-level wage figures. In the

case of the common laborer, the weight is Lebergott's estimates of the number of nonfarm laborers; in the case of the farm wage, the weight is Lebergott's estimate of the number of free white farmers.

28. Williamson and Lindert converted monthly farm wages to daily farm wages using an adjustment factor derived from table A-30 in Lebergott (1964, 546). Lebergott's table gives estimates of monthly and daily wages with board, both purportedly for farm labor, in 1832. Williamson and Lindert's adjustment factor is simply the ratio of the monthly to the daily wage. But Lebergott's text (pp. 258, 267–68), table A-23 (p. 539), and table A-25 (p. 541) make it clear that the *monthly wage* in his table A-30 refers to farm labor and the *daily wage* to common labor. As Lebergott (p. 267) notes, the ratio of the day wage of common labor to the monthly wage of farm labor in 1832 was approximately the same as the ratio prevailing in 1850.

29. I assume that the average female wage was 55 percent of the average male wage; this ratio is derived from fig. 3.1 in Goldin (1990, 62). Assuming the same female-male wage ratio for each county, I derive an estimate of the male wage on the assumption that w_m is a weighted average of the male and the female wage, the weight being the proportion female.

30. This procedure was used for each state except Tennessee, where it resulted in implausible nonfarm weights. In the case of Tennessee, the common wage was aggregated using census figures on the manufacturing labor force.

Chapter 5

1. Coelho and Shepherd's (1976) regional series begin in the 1850s. On capital market integration before the Civil War see Bodenhorn and Rockoff (1992).

2. Per capita incomes in the East South Central region, however, were nearly twice as high as in the South Atlantic or West South Central regions.

3. A related explanation involves liberal policies toward the disposal of public land, which effectively subsidized western movement (see, e.g., Fogel and Rutner 1972; Temin 1969; or Lebergott 1985).

4. On the other hand, the implicit assumption is that the "weekly cost of board to laboring men"—the census definition of the concept—meant the same thing to all respondents; i.e., the quantity of food purchased by the weekly expenditure was (approximately) the same in all parts of the country. If board meant much fancier meals in, say, New York City than in rural Iowa, this assumption would be false.

5. The weekly cost of board divided by the weekly wage (without board) is an estimate of the budget share for food. If the weekly wage for common and farm labor is estimated by multiplying the daily wage without board by six days per week (the daily wage for farm labor is the monthly wage plus the [imputed] value of board divided by twenty-six days of work), the mean value of the budget share is 0.39, or 39 percent. This might seem low, but it must be remembered that this is an estimate for a single male, without dependents, working full-time. Allowances for unemployment and dependents would push the budget share up into the range observed for working-class households during the period.

6. Note that board is used in this manner only for the benchmark (i.e., 1850) deflator. Changes in the relative price indices over time also reflect changes in nonfood prices because nonfood prices are included in the indices (see chap. 3 below; and Goldin and Margo 1992a).

7. To derive the estimate of the relative (Midwest-Northeast) cost of living in 1851, I multiply the benchmark for 1850 (= 0.77) by the ratio of the Midwest-Northeastern price deflators for 1851.

8. I use farmers as well as laborers because chap. 5 found that the wages of farm and common laborers were similar. The implicit assumption is that the ratio of farm laborers to total farmers in each region were similar.

9. The timing of the convergence in relative wages in the North contrasts somewhat with Ross's (1985, 43) assertion that migration "in the late 1820s and 1830s brought the artificially high wages of the labor scarce frontier . . . more in line with lower eastern wage levels."

10. By *other forces,* I mean the effects of factor price equalization. It is well known that falling costs of internal transport produced convergence in output prices between the Midwest and the Northeast (Berry 1943), and it is plausible to argue that factor price equalization occurred in response to output price convergence (O'Rourke and Williamson 1994; Slaughter 1995).

11. Specifically, the aggregate North-South gap (in logs) was -0.027 for 1821–30, 0.103 for 1831–40, 0.175 for 1841–50, and 0.076 for 1851–60.

12. In choosing the North over the South, unskilled immigrants were, according to my findings, migrating to those places where real wages were higher on average. Skilled immigrants in the 1840s, however, would have enjoyed higher real wages in the South (see table 5.3) and, thus, must have avoided the South for other reasons (e.g., slavery or the climate).

13. Booming conditions in the cotton market may also explain some of the narrowing of the North-South wage gap in the 1850s (see Fogel 1989).

14. That is, $0.045 = [\exp(0.0152 - 0.0141) \times 40] - 1$. For artisans redistribution added 3.6 percent over four decades, for common laborers 2.8 percent.

15. An alternative approach to measuring the effect of migration on aggregate wage growth is to allow the regional occupation shares to change but to fix the wage gaps at their initial level. For the purpose of illustration, I fix the wage gaps at their average levels for the period 1825–30. Recomputing the aggregate series under this assumption, and then reestimating the trend growth rates as in table 5.5 ($\ln w = \alpha + \beta T$), the resulting β's are 0.00174 for common laborers, 0.00226 for artisans, and 0.00183 for white-collar workers. These rates imply much larger effects of migration; e.g., migration raised the growth rate of common wages by 16.7 percent ($= 0.00174/0.0104$). The larger effects result because the alternative approach does not permit wage convergence to occur as a consequence of internal migration.

16. If w/p is computed relative to the state average and all variables are in logs, this is equivalent to adding terms like $\beta w/p_{\mu 50} + w/p_{\mu 60}$ for each state to the right-hand side of the regression, where μ = the state average. Since these terms are the same for all counties in a state, an equivalent procedure is to include a full set of state dummies.

17. The growth rate of population is log (population 1860/population 1850). The change in urbanization is a dummy variable that takes the value 1 if the county had an urban area of population ten thousand or more in 1860 but not in 1850.

18. Perhaps the best way to control for amenities or disamenities would be through county fixed effects (dummy variables), but this would require additional years of data. On the other hand, offsetting the bias in β toward zero is a bias toward -1 because of measurement error in the real wage. On the assumption that the errors in measurement are concentrated in the tails of the distribution, the effects on the estimate of β can be gauged by trimming the data, i.e., excluding observations with high or low values of $\ln(w/b)_{1850}$. For example, if the regression for common/farm labor is subjected to a 10 percent trim (the bottom and top 10 percent of observations are excluded on the basis of their values of $\ln[w/b]_{1850}$), the estimate of $\beta = 0.779$, similar to the estimate for the full sample.

19. According to the regression coefficient, about 80 percent of the relative wage

gap for a typical county was eliminated within a decade. This is much faster than, e.g., the speed at which the Midwest-Northeast wage gap was eliminated over the period 1820–60 (see table 5.2).

20. The weight $\gamma_j = s_j/s$, where s_j is Weiss's estimate of the total labor force (Weiss 1992, 37) less his estimate of the number of slaves in the farm labor force (Weiss 1992, 53). This overstates the free labor force in the South because some slaves were engaged in nonagricultural pursuits. However, experiments with different weights that also netted out estimates of nonagricultural slaves produced virtually identical deflators.

21. The regional adjustment factor is the unweighted average of the ratio (Σ $\delta_{jk}b_{jk})/b_j$ for the two states in each region in the eight-state sample (chap. 2), where k indexes counties, b_{jk} is the weekly cost of board at the county level (from the manuscript census returns), and δ_{jk} is the county's share of the state population. The adjustment factors differ from unity, indicating that, properly weighted, the average cost of board within states differed from the state averages published in the 1850 census.

Chapter 6

1. The California Gold Rush was not the only gold rush of the nineteenth century, but it was certainly the most famous. For a good general history of nineteenth-century gold rushes, see Marks (1994).

2. The Sutter's Mill discovery was actually not the first in California. Small amounts of gold were found in southern California near Los Angeles in 1842. The gold was quickly recovered by experienced Mexican miners, and a search for additional gold ensued, but none was found (Lavender 1976, 3).

3. According to Wright (1940, 342), forty-two thousand migrants are estimated to have arrived overland, while another thirty-nine thousand arrived by ship at San Francisco. In 1850, fifty-five thousand are alleged to have arrived overland, thirty-six thousand by sea. However, approximately twenty-seven thousand departed by sea in 1850 (the number departing in 1849 is unknown); whether they left permanently is not known. The estimates of arrivals by land derive primarily from newspaper reports and must be regarded as extremely rough. Records of ship arrivals were kept at the San Francisco customhouse and are presumably more accurate.

4. The share of miners per person in 1850 is biased upward because of damage to the manuscript census returns from a few nonmining areas, including San Francisco. However, adding the population counts from the 1852 state census to the denominator would still produce a substantial decline in miners per capita between 1850 and 1860.

5. The 1850 population figure is biased downward because of fire damage to the census manuscripts for San Francisco and other counties.

6. Evidently, sending clothes to Hawaii for cleaning (presumably to be picked up on the miner's next trip to San Francisco) could be cheaper than buying a new shirt or trousers or paying inflated prices for cleaning in San Francisco. Caughey (1948, 35) notes that the price of a coarse shirt in 1849 was $16.00, apparently high enough to make the cost of transporting dirty shirts to Hawaii for washing economically feasible.

7. A Dutch disease model is used to study the effects of supply-side shocks, usually the discovery of natural resources, on other sectors of an economy (e.g., manufacturing) (see Corden and Neary 1982). The name *Dutch disease* comes from the fact that the rise in the price of oil in the early 1970s apparently caused

resources to flow into oil production in countries like the Netherlands, at the expense of manufacturing.

8. By assuming equal endowment shares, I am relegating property rights issues (who owns the gold) to the background. For an analysis of property rights issues, see Umbreck (1977) and Clay and Wright (1998).

9. An alternative, essentially equivalent model divides the population of a gold rush economy into three groups: capitalists (owners of K), workers, and mine owners (owners of ore). The capitalists and mine owners hire labor in a competitive market. Aggregate demands for X and Z are then the sum of the group-specific demands (the incomes of the capitalists and mine owners are the rents accruing to K and O). There will be a balanced trade condition similar to the budget constraint in the text.

10. The maximization problem is

$$\max_{X, Z, L_x} U(X, Z)$$

subject to

$$p_x X + p_z Z = p_x F(L_x, K) + g(L - L_x)S,$$

where F is the production function for X, K is capital, and S is the endowment of gold ore. The first-order conditions are

$$U_x / U_z = p_x / p_z,$$
$$p_x F_L = g'S.$$

11. For example, $h = p_x^\beta p_z^{1-\beta}$, where β is the share of income devoted to X (recall that the price deflators developed in chap. 3 take this form).

12. The opposite would be true if demand for labor in the local sector fell, but this cannot happen if X is a normal good.

13. Capital might also be attracted if, in the new equilibrium, L_x is higher than initially.

14. That is, with specialization, there would be a marginal worker who, in the initial equilibrium, would be indifferent between harvesting gold and producing the local good.

15. Alternatively, individuals might believe (erroneously) that the gold rush will last forever and then be surprised by its end.

16. By *convex adjustment costs*, I mean that, at any time t, the marginal cost of moving L^* units of labor into the gold rush economy is increasing in L^*. Convex adjustment costs are frequently analyzed in dynamic models of labor demand (see, e.g., Hamermesh 1993; Carrington 1996).

17. By *long-run equilibrium value*, I mean the value of w in the absence of adjustment costs. With adjustment costs, there is no constant equilibrium value of w for all dates t in the interval (t, t').

18. That is, there is option value to waiting if the returns to migration are uncertain (see Dixit and Pindyck 1994). The transport costs of migration are sunk because the good (transportation) is perishable; however, for evidence that some migrants took goods with them to sell in the gold fields, which would be a way of recouping some of the sunk costs, see Caughey (1948, 98).

19. Such a belief would be rational if, as was the case in California, property rights to the gold were not established ex ante. In other words, if property rights had been established, it is plausible that some migration would have been delayed, producing a less elastic labor supply response. I am grateful to Lee Alston for this point.

20. See also Fraser (1983), who argues that the introduction of money by army quartermasters into the local indigenous economies of the Southwest had effects on local prices.

21. In particular, the time series are too short to distinguish between the effects of the real shock—the discovery of gold—on wages and any effects of the increase in the money stock.

22. Gerber (1997) has recently constructed annual nominal and real wage indices for California during the Gold Rush using such anecdotal evidence. Gerber's indices differ significantly in terms of the nature of the data and the manner of construction from those presented in this chapter. In particular, Gerber presents a single wage index meant to capture the average nominal daily wage covering a variety of occupations. Each occupation is weighted according to occupation shares derived from the 1850 census. However, the number of occupations included in the average differs from year to year (e.g., two in 1848, fifteen in 1853). Thus, Gerber's index is not a true fixed-weight index (in a true fixed-weight index, the same occupations would be represented every year); fluctuations in the average from year to year are almost certainly introduced when new occupations are added, not a desirable characteristic for a wage index. Gerber produces his real labor cost series by dividing the nominal wage index by Berry's overall wholesale price index. Although year-to-year movements in Berry's overall index and the price deflator are similar, the downward trend in prices from 1847 to 1860 is more pronounced in Berry's overall price index. The overall index includes nonconsumption goods (unlike the price deflator developed in this chapter), and thus its use as a price deflator to produce a real wage series is questionable—hence, presumably, Gerber's term *real labor cost.*

Prior to 1850, Gerber's data derive principally from the personal correspondence of miners and travel accounts. The 1850 estimate is based on the federal census, while those for 1851–60 derive from scattered figures reported in the newspapers *Alta California* and *San Francisco Prices Current.* Wage quotations from southern California were excluded from Gerber's index on the grounds that wages were lower in the southern part of the state, implying that "the state was not a well-integrated economic region" (Gerber 1997, 5). While my regressions also reveal that wages were lower in southern California, the payrolls themselves clearly demonstrate that labor could still command impressive pay by national standards, such as the herdsmen employed at the fort at San Diego who earned $100 per month in 1850, a figure far in excess of wages for similar work elsewhere in the United States. This suggests that southern California locations were not immune to the wage effects of the rush (and, therefore, should not be excluded from the sample on a priori grounds). The number of wage quotations in Gerber's sample is extremely small—e.g., the 1847 estimate was apparently based on only two wage quotations, that for 1848 on six (Gerber 1997, 24).

It is difficult to determine the accuracy of wage quotations contained in letters and other testimony of migrants (or even in newspapers) in the light of the known hyperbole characteristic of accounts of the early years of the rush. A large sample of wage observations from payroll records, such as those used in this chapter, would seem clearly preferable for constructing wage indices because such data record actual wage payments, unlike the quotations evidently underlying Gerber's index.

In any event, comparisons of the nominal and real wage series presented here with those by Gerber are difficult to make because of the very different methods of construction. However, the basic findings are very similar. Gerber finds that real wages peaked in 1849; my real wage series for common laborers and artisans (the occupations examined by Gerber) also peak in 1849. Gerber also finds, as do I, that the Gold Rush permanently raised real wages in California (according to his real labor cost index, real wages were 4.9 times higher in 1860 than in 1847) and that the wage effects of the rush were largely over by the mid-1850s. Using my estimates of labor supply (see app. 6B), Gerber's wage series also imply an inelastic supply of labor into California in the late 1840s ($\varepsilon = 0.15$ from 1847 to 1848, $d[\ln L]$ is my estimate of the change in labor supply from 1847–February 1848 to March–December 1848, and $d[\ln w]$ is the change in Gerber's [1997, 17] index of real labor cost from 1847 to 1848), followed by a flattening (e.g., $\varepsilon = 1.85$ from 1847 to 1852).

23. For example, common laborers hired at army installations in the San Francisco Bay area could command up to $120-$150 per month in 1850 and $5.00–$6.00 per day, while some carpenters were paid up to $12.00 per day (although most were paid less, $10.00 per day). According to the manuscript Census of Social Statistics for San Francisco, day laborers earned $6.00 per day and carpenters $9.42 (quoted in Gerber 1997, 5). San Francisco wages were higher than the averages estimated for the entire state, which indicates the importance of having a large sample covering a variety of locations rather than a few isolated locations that may or may not be representative of the average.

24. Hispanic status is inferred from name or from ancillary remarks in the payrolls; as noted in chap. 2, the reporting of names in the payrolls is haphazard, particularly at larger forts.

25. Coman (1912, 2:317) also suggests that nominal wages of carpenters fell by 1853, but, unfortunately, she provides no source citations for her wage quotations.

26. To construct the deflator, I used Berry's annual price indices (budget shares in parentheses) for candles (0.098), coffee (0.075), flour (0.150), hams (0.189), raisins (0.033), rice (0.003), cotton sheeting (0.260), sugar (0.085), tobacco (0.025), and butter (0.133). The price deflator is a geometric weighted average of the commodity-specific indices, with weights equaled to the budget shares, as above.

27. The drop in prices in 1848 may reflect the sudden exodus of population from San Francisco for the gold fields. According to Coman (1912, 2:257), real estate prices fell sharply in 1848 in the immediate aftermath of the exodus, and the price deflator suggests that the same may have been true of other prices.

28. Berry drew his price quotations from newspapers, and therefore the bulk of the quotations pertain to urban prices (chiefly, San Francisco). Since most goods were transported to the camps from San Francisco (or Sacramento), retail prices at the camps would include transport costs as well as other markups (Coman 1912, 2:271). However, because of the dependence on urban areas for supply, there is no reason to believe that prices at the mining camps followed a vastly different annual pattern than that indicated by Berry's data.

29. The growth rate of real wages for common labor in California over the period from 1847–February 1848 to 1860 was 10.1 percent per year, compared with 1.9 percent per year for 1847–60, as computed from my aggregate national real wage series for common labor (see chap. 5).

30. Using the state-level figures on the weekly cost of board (from Kennedy 1864, 512) and on the daily wages of common laborers without board (from Lebergott 1964, 541), I compute

$$r = (w_c/b_c)/(w_n/b_n)$$

for 1860, where w is the wage, b is the weekly cost of board, c refers to California, and n refers to the rest of the United States (excluding the West): $r = 0.99$ (note that r is the same measure of real wages as used in chap. 5). Taken at face value, the calculation suggests that real daily wages in California for common laborers on the eve of the Civil War were virtually identical to real wages elsewhere. Similar results were found for male manufacturing workers in 1879 by Rosenbloom (1996, 644); not until the late nineteenth and early twentieth centuries did a sizable real wage gap in favor of the West open up (Rosenbloom 1996).

31. As noted in sec. 6.1, East Coast ships did occasionally trade manufactured goods for furs in pre–Gold Rush California, but their small numbers and infrequent stops make it difficult to maintain in any meaningful sense that pre–Gold Rush California was integrated into the American economy (see Coman 1912, 1:165).

32. For example, using the real wage series for common labor for California, the national aggregate series in chap. 5, and the observation (see n. 30 above) that real wages of common labor in California in 1860 were essentially the same as in the rest of the country, the average real wage of common labor in California over the period 1850–52 was 12.5 percent higher than the national average. If the calculation is made for 1849, the real wage gap in favor of California was 56.1 percent.

33. Estimates for 1850 and 1860 of capital in manufacturing (in current dollars) and of population are from DeBow (1853) and Kennedy (1862). Nominal capital per person is deflated by Berry's overall price index (1984, 235, col. 1). Improved acres and wheat output are from Kennedy (1862, 196, 200). For further discussion of the emergence of California agriculture during the Gold Rush period, see Gerber (1993).

34. The elasticity of labor supply appears to have been somewhat smaller in the case of the Australian Gold Rush. According to Maddock and McLean (1984, 1065), real wages in Victoria increased by 85 percent between 1850 and 1852. Maddock and McLean do not report labor quantities, but using population or net migration (see Maddock and McLean 1984, 1048) as a substitute yields elasticities ranging from 1.3 (population) to 1.7 (net migration). My estimates of the medium-run labor supply elasticity into Gold Rush California (e.g., 1848–51) are in the same range as Rosenbloom's (1991, 435) estimate ($\varepsilon_{Lw} = 1.96$) for common labor in the building trades in the late nineteenth century, which is derived from cross-city differences in wages and employment.

35. The assumption that daily hours of work in Gold Rush California did not increase biases the elasticity downward, compared with the Alaska figure. However, daily hours of work in Gold Rush California would have had to increase to more than twenty-four hours per day—obviously impossible—to equal the Alaska elasticity.

36. It is possible that my estimates of the labor supply elasticities into Gold Rush California are biased upward because of uncertainty. Some individuals may have been attracted to California by the (small) prospect of striking it rich rather than by the average returns to migration; faced with an alternative decision in which the prospective argonaut was guaranteed the average returns, the decision would have been to stay in the East (or wherever the place of origin).

37. However, it is easy to overstate the degree to which the antebellum labor supply was less flexible than today's in response to geographically localized shocks to labor demand. The evidence on real wages and labor supply elasticities in this chapter suggests that labor supply adjustment to the discovery of gold per se was essentially completed by the early to mid-1850s, the traditional dating of the end of the rush, lasting five to seven years. Recent work by Blanchard and Katz (1992) has examined the adjustment process of state economies to shocks to labor demand over the post–World War II period. According to Blanchard and Katz (1992, 33), the effects of shocks on labor supply to the average state take six to seven years to dissipate, similar to the duration of the adjustment period in the case of the Gold Rush. Blanchard and Katz also find that much of the short-run

adjustment to negative demand shocks comes in the form of higher unemployment rather than lower wages. Two years after a negative shock to labor demand of 1 percent, wages fall by about 0.2 percent, compared with about a 0.25 percent decline for labor supply, implying a short-run labor supply elasticity of 1.25, compared with my estimate of 1.01 for California between 1847 and 1849.

38. However, my estimate for common laborers in 1850 of $4.20 per day is reasonably close to the census figure of $5.00 per day. Readjusting my estimate for artisans for 1850 so that it refers solely to carpenters produces a daily wage of $6.95, compared with the census estimate of $7.60.

39. Wright (1940, 342) estimates that between 4,200 and 6,350 individuals arrived overland, which I arbitrarily average at 5,000. There are no records of arrivals by ship at San Francisco for this year, so I assume zero arrivals. However, there must surely have been some arrivals by ship, which implies that my estimate of the short-run elasticity is biased downward. For 1849, I sum Wright's estimate of overland arrivals plus 27 percent of reported arrivals; the 27 percent adjustment is the ratio of departures (by sea) to arrivals in 1850 (thus, I am assuming that all departures by sea were permanent). For 1851, I add arrivals by land and sea in both 1850 and 1851, again assuming that 27 percent of arrivals by sea in 1851 were permanent. Finally, I multiply the population estimates for 1847–52 by 0.77, the assumed ratio of adult men aged fifteen to forty to the total population. All figures are rounded to the nearest hundred. Note that I am assuming that all men in this age group in California were in the labor force (labor force participation rates for adult men of all ages in 1850 were close to 90 percent [see Weiss 1992]) or, equivalently, that the labor force participation rate in California did not change much over the Gold Rush (if it rose, then my labor supply elasticities are biased downward). The labor supply estimates for California are as follows: 1847–February 1848, 11,500; March–December 1848, 15,400; 1849, 55,800; 1850, 71,600; 1851, 144,800; 1852, 203,300; and 1860, 186,200.

40. The 1850 federal census estimate of population is understated because of damage to certain census manuscripts. The understatement produces a downward bias in my estimate of the labor supply elasticity for that year.

Chapter 7

1. The occupational shares are 0.71 for unskilled laborers, 0.21 for artisans, and 0.08 for white-collar workers. To obtain these shares, I first summed the number of common laborers, teamsters, and artisans in the building trades (carpenters, masons, plasterers, painters, and glaziers) and clerks reported in the 1850 census (DeBow 1854, 126–28). The unskilled labor share is the share of common laborers and teamsters in the total (= 924,255/1,301,807); the artisan share is the share of building tradesmen in the total (276,229/1,301,807); the white-collar share is the share of clerks in the total (101,325). Adding in additional white-collar or artisanal occupations does not alter the substantive results.

2. To be fair, my aggregate real wage series exclude certain groups—the most important being slaves and free female labor—that contributed to the growth of total output, along with a variety of occupations not represented in the army data.

3. Poor harvests in the Northeast in the mid-1830s and in Europe in the early 1850s may be other examples of (negative) real shocks (see Sokoloff and Villaflor 1992). According to Sokoloff and Villaflor, the demand for labor fell as a result of the agricultural supply shock in the 1830s, producing declines in real wages of farm labor (and, by inference, common labor) in the mid-1830s (see chap. 3, table

3A.9). However, the price level began rising in the early 1830s, well before the alleged harvest failures (see table 3A.3 above; and Temin 1969).

4. The differential rates of growth of skilled and unskilled immigrants suggest that the skill differential ought to have risen in the Northeast in the 1850s, that being where the majority of immigrants arrived; in fact, the differential did increase by 9.2 percent comparing the 1850s to the 1840s (see chap. 3).

5. If the regression is estimated in first-differences, the coefficient is -0.90 ($t = 7.73$).

6. The correlation might also be biased away from zero because the nominal wage series were constructed from hedonic regressions that did not fit the data perfectly; hence, some of the year-to-year movement in real wages reflects the prediction error of the hedonic regressions (Williamson 1992). However, it should be kept in mind that the hedonic method is simply a way of producing an average; if, according to the regression, wages on average did not keep pace with prices during periods of inflation, it follows that, at the individual level, some wages moved in the opposite direction.

7. In general, antebellum consumers had three sources of retail supply: general stores, public markets, and direct purchases from manufacturers. For perishable items, often obtained from public markets, it is reasonable to assume that price fluctuations were felt directly (and immediately) by consumers regardless of the source of supply. Manufacturers supplied wholesale markets as well as consumers, so it is reasonable to suppose that, in these cases, annual price fluctuations at the wholesale and retail levels were similar. General stores obtained goods directly from wholesale markets or from jobbers. General stores tended to replenish their stocks twice a year or so; because there were few, if any, contractual mechanisms to hedge price risk, it is reasonable to assume that antebellum retailers passed on *some* portion of wholesale price fluctuations. However, if the retail markup were more stable than wholesale prices, retail prices would fluctuate less than wholesale prices. This would be true, e.g., if general stores possessed some local monopoly power. On antebellum wholesale and retail marketing, see Jones (1937).

8. This is particularly true for the nonbenchmark years for which David and Solar interpolated using prices in Vermont for goods not regularly traded in wholesale markets.

9. Effectively, I am assuming that the price of housing relative to that of other goods did not change between the late 1830s and the early 1840s.

10. However, there is evidence of downward rigidity of nominal wages: wage cuts in the early 1840s were slightly less than half price declines. Unemployment is thought to have been high in the early 1840s, and the downward rigidity may be an important reason why (but see Temin 1969).

11. *Stable* here does not necessarily mean "constant," only that deviations from the "normal" price level are well understood (as in the case of seasonality) or long-term trends (as in the Midwest, where the long-term trend in prices was upward).

12. Note that abrupt adjustments *are* evident in the wage series. For example, nominal wages of common labor jumped sharply in 1837 in the Northeast and Midwest and declined sharply in both regions in 1840.

13. The historical literature on height is now voluminous. A representative recent selection of papers may be found in Steckel and Floud (1997).

14. Komlos has tried to bolster his case by presenting estimates of food consumption that suggest declines for the relevant cohorts, although this has been disputed by Robert Gallman (1996) (for a reply, see Komlos [1996]).

15. Specifically, Weir (1997, 179) shows that median adult height at age twenty is positively and significantly correlated with the real wage at approximately age

twenty. For the sake of argument, I will assume that the effect would be the same if the real wage were measured from birth to age four.

16. It is reasonable to assume a positive income elasticity of demand for nutrients on the basis of the French results because Weir (1997, 173) shows that real wages and per capita meat consumption were positively related at the department level.

17. I use Weir's (1997, table 5.4, col. 2b) regression, which reports the coefficient of a pooled time-series cross-sectional regression of median adult height (age twenty) on the real wage. All variables are measured at the department level. To convert the coefficient (16.88) into an elasticity, I use the average height of the 1843 birth cohort (1,647.2 centimeters), the midyear of birth years covered in Weir's study. Thus, the elasticity of height with respect to the real wage is 0.01 (= 16.88/1,647.2).

18. However, Komlos and Coclanis also show that heights continued to decline among the birth cohorts of the 1840s, when, according to my estimates, real wages in the South Atlantic were higher than they were in the 1830s. The only way to explain the reversal of the correlation in the 1840s is to argue that the sharp rises in real wages in the early 1840s are not an indication of rises in labor welfare but a consequence of nominal wage rigidity that produced rising unemployment.

19. The finding that the ratio of artisans' pay to common laborers' pay fell before the Civil War appears to contradict evidence put forth by Williamson and Lindert (1980). Williamson and Lindert present two series of skilled-unskilled wage ratios, the first constructed from data collected by Carroll Wright (1885) and the second a linked series constructed by splicing together certain of the wage series discussed in chap. 2. Both series, which pertain primarily to artisans, show substantial increases in artisan-unskilled wage ratios from the 1820s to the 1850s, the opposite of my findings. Elsewhere, however, it is demonstrated that the increase evident in the series based on the Carroll Wright data is a consequence of failing to control for changes in the composition of Wright's sample over time and that the increase evident in the linked series is a consequence of too low a level of skilled wages in the 1820s. For a detailed discussion of these points, see Margo and Villaflor (1987).

20. Habakkuk (1962, 23) asserted that the "premium on artisan skills was generally lower in America than England in the early nineteenth century." My findings do not support Habakkuk. According to Williamson (1985, 13), the skill differential for artisans (ser. 4H, building trades) compared to nonfarm common laborers (ser. 2L) was 1.51 in the 1820s (this is an unweighted average of the skill differentials for 1819 and 1827). My estimate for the American Northeast (Habakkuk's focus since he was concerned with industrialization) is 1.67 for the 1820s (this is the ratio of the decadal average daily wage for artisans to that for common laborers, from chap. 3). (See also Adams 1968.)

21. Here a caveat is in order. Recall from chap. 3 that I am not able to control for years of work experience in the hedonic wage regressions. It is possible that the rising return to white-collar labor reflects changes in the composition of the sample such that the average clerk was more experienced later in the period than earlier. If this were true, and if experience had a positive effect on wages (as it does today), then I would be overstating the extent to which the white-collar skill differential grew during the antebellum period.

22. The ratio for the nation as a whole is computed from the national series of nominal wages in chap. 5. A monthly wage for common labor is computed by multiplying the daily wage by twenty-six days. This overstates the monthly common wage because no adjustment is made for an unemployment risk premium (see chap. 3); hence, the wage ratio is biased downward. Goldin's estimates (see also

Goldin and Katz 1995, table 5) are based on annual earnings. If, as seems plausible, white-collar workers labored for more days per year than common laborers, my estimate of 2.07 for the 1850s would be biased downward on an annual, as well as a monthly, basis.

23. Goldin and Katz (1995) also report much higher wage ratios for the South than for the rest of the United States.

References

Abbott, Elizabeth. 1905. The wages of unskilled labor in the United States, 1850–1900. *Journal of Political Economy* 13 (June): 321–67.

Adams, Donald R. 1968. Wage rates in the early national period: Philadelphia, 1785–1830. *Journal of Economic History* 28 (September): 404–26.

———. 1970. Some evidence on English and American wage rates, 1790–1830. *Journal of Economic History* 30 (September): 499–520.

———. 1973. Wage rates in the iron industry: A comment. *Explorations in Economic History* 11 (Fall): 89–94.

———. 1975. The residential construction industry in the early nineteenth century. *Journal of Economic History* 35 (December): 794–816.

———. 1982. The standard of living during American industrialization: Evidence from the Brandywine region, 1800–1860. *Journal of Economic History* 42 (December): 903–17.

———. 1986. Prices and wages in Maryland, 1750–1850. *Journal of Economic History* 46 (September): 625–45.

———. 1992. Prices and wages in antebellum America: The West Virginia experience. *Journal of Economic History* 52 (March): 206–16.

Adams, T. M. 1939. *Prices paid by farmers for goods and services and received by them for farm products, 1790–1871.* Burlington: Vermont Agricultural Experiment Station.

Aldrich, Mark. 1971. Earnings of American civil engineers, 1820–1859. *Journal of Economic History* 31 (June): 407–19.

Aldrich, Nelson W. 1893. *Wholesale prices, wages, and transportation.* 52d Cong., 2d sess., S. Rept. 1394. Washington, D.C.: U.S. Government Printing Office.

Atack, Jeremy, and Fred Bateman. 1987. *To their own soil: Agriculture in the antebellum North.* Ames: Iowa State University Press.

————. 1991. Did the U.S. industrialize too slowly? University of Illinois, Department of Economics. Typescript.

Bateman, Fred, and Thomas Weiss. 1981. *A deplorable scarcity.* Chapel Hill: University of North Carolina Press.

Berry, Thomas Senior. 1943. *Western prices before 1861.* Cambridge, Mass.: Harvard University Press.

————. 1984. *Early California: Gold, prices, trade.* Richmond, Va.: Bostwick.

Bezanson, Anne, Robert D. Gray, and Miriam Hussey. 1936. *Wholesale prices in Philadelphia, 1784–1861.* Philadelphia: University of Pennsylvania Press.

Bidwell, Percy W., and John I. Falconer. 1925. *History of agriculture in the Northern United States, 1620–1860.* Washington, D.C.: Carnegie Institution.

Blanchard, Olivier J., and Lawrence F. Katz. 1992. Regional evolutions. *Brookings Papers on Economic Activity,* no. 1:1–75.

Blank, Rebecca M. 1997. *It takes a nation: A new agenda for fighting poverty.* Princeton, N.J.: Princeton University Press.

Bodenhorn, Howard, and Hugh Rockoff. 1992. Regional interest rates in antebellum America. In *Strategic factors in nineteenth century American economic history: A volume to honor Robert W. Fogel,* ed. C. Goldin and H. Rockoff. Chicago: University of Chicago Press.

Brady, Dorothy. 1966. Price deflators for final product estimates. In *Output, employment, and productivity in the United States after 1800* (NBER Studies in Income and Wealth, vol. 30), ed. D. S. Brady. New York: Columbia University Press.

Calomiris, Charles W., and Christopher Hanes. 1994. Consistent output series for the antebellum and postbellum periods: Issues and preliminary results. *Journal of Economic History* 54 (June): 409–22.

Carrington, William J. 1996. The Alaskan labor market during the Pipeline era. *Journal of Political Economy* 104 (February): 186–218.

Caughey, John Walton. 1948. *Gold is the cornerstone.* Berkeley: University of California Press.

Clay, Karen, and Gavin Wright. 1998. Property rights and California gold. Stanford University, Department of Economics. Typescript.

Coelho, Phillip, and James Shepherd. 1974. Differences in regional prices: The United States, 1851–1880. *Journal of Economic History* 34 (September): 551–91.

————. 1976. Regional differences in real wages: The United States, 1851–1880. *Explorations in Economic History* 13 (April): 203–30.

Coffman, Chad, and Mary Eschelbach Gregson. 1998. Railroad development and land values. *Journal of Real Estate Finance and Economics* 16 (March): 191–204.

Cole, Arthur H. 1938. *Wholesale commodity prices in the United States, 1700–1861.* Cambridge, Mass.: Harvard University Press.

Coman, Katherine. 1912. *Economic beginnings of the Far West.* 2 vols. New York: Macmillan.

Commons, John R., et al. 1918. *History of labor in the United States.* New York: Macmillan.

Corden, W. Max, and J. Peter Neary. 1982. Booming sector and de-industrialization in a small open economy. *Economic Journal* 92 (December): 825–48.

Costa, Dora L. 1993. Height, wealth, and disease among the native-born in the rural, antebellum North. *Social Science History* 17 (Fall): 354–83.

Crafts, N. F. R. 1985. *British economic growth during the Industrial Revolution.* Oxford: Oxford University Press.

Craig, Lee. 1991. The value of household labor in antebellum Northern agriculture. *Journal of Economic History* 51 (March): 67–82.

Craig, Lee, and Elizabeth Field-Hendry. 1993. Industrialization and the earnings gap. *Explorations in Economic History* 30 (January): 60–80.

Craig, Lee A., Michael R. Haines, and Thomas Weiss. 1997. The short and the dead: Agricultural surpluses, mortality, and stature in the antebellum United States. North Carolina State University, Department of Economics. Typescript.

Craig, Lee A., Raymond B. Palmquist, and Thomas Weiss. 1998. Internal improvements and land values in the antebellum United States: A hedonic approach. *Journal of Real Estate Finance and Economics* 16 (March): 173–89.

David, Paul. 1967. The growth of real product in the United States before 1840: New evidence, controlled conjectures. *Journal of Economic History* 27 (June): 151–97.

———. 1987. Industrial labor market adjustments in a region of recent settlement: Chicago, 1848–1868. In *Quantity and quiddity: Essays in U.S. economic history,* ed. Peter Kilby. Middletown, Conn.: Wesleyan University Press.

David, Paul, and Peter Solar. 1977. A bicentenary contribution to the history of the cost of living in America. In *Research in economic history,* vol. 2, ed. P. Uselding. Greenwich, Conn.: JAI.

DeBow, J. D. B. 1853. *The seventh census of the United States: 1850.* Washington, D.C.: Robert Armstrong, Public Printer.

———. 1854. *Statistical view of the United States, embracing its territory, population—white, free colored, and slave—moral and social condition, industry, property, and revenue; the detailed statistics of cities, towns, and counties, being a compendium of the seventh census.* Washington, D.C.: Robert Armstrong.

DeCanio, Steven, and Joel Mokyr. 1977. Inflation and the wage lag during the American Civil War. *Explorations in Economic History* 14 (October): 311–36.

Dixit, Avinash, and Robert S. Pindyck. 1994. *Investment under uncertainty.* Princeton, N.J.: Princeton University Press.

Earle, Carville. 1992. *Geographical inquiry and American historical problems.* Stanford, Calif.: Stanford University Press.

Easterlin, Richard. 1960. Interregional differences in per capita income, population, and total income, 1840–1950. In *Trends in the American economy in the nineteenth century,* ed. Committee on Research in Income and Wealth. Princeton, N.J.: Princeton University Press.

Engerman, Stanley, and Claudia Goldin. 1993. Seasonality in nineteenth century labor markets. In *Economic development in historical perspective,* ed. D. Schaefer and T. Weiss. Stanford, Calif.: Stanford University Press.

Ferrie, Joseph. 1997. Migration to the frontier in mid-nineteenth century America: A re-examination of Turner's "safety valve." Northwestern University, Department of Economics. Typescript.

———. 1999. *Yankeys now: Immigrants in the antebellum U.S., 1840–1860.* New York: Oxford University Press.

Field, Alexander James. 1978. Sectoral shifts in antebellum Massachusetts: A reconsideration. *Explorations in Economic History* 15 (April): 146–71.

Fishback, Price, and Shawn Kantor. 1992. "Square deal" or raw deal? Market compensation for workplace disamenities, 1884–1903. *Journal of Economic History* 52 (December): 826–48.

Fleisig, Heywood. 1976. Slavery, the supply of agricultural labor, and the industrialization of the South. *Journal of Economic History* 36 (September): 572–97.

Fogel, Robert W. 1986. Nutrition and the decline in mortality since 1700: Some preliminary findings. In *Long-term factors in American economic growth* (NBER Studies in Income and Wealth, vol. 51), ed. S. L. Engerman and R. E. Gallman. Chicago: University of Chicago Press.

———. 1989. *Without consent or contract: The rise and fall of American slavery.* New York: Norton.

Fogel, Robert W., and Stanley L. Engerman. 1974. *Time on the cross.* Boston: Little Brown.

Fogel, Robert W., and Jack Rutner. 1972. The efficiency effects of federal land policy, 1850–1900. In *The dimensions of quantitative research in history,* ed. W. O. Aydelotte, A. G. Bogue, and R. W. Fogel. Princeton, N.J.: Princeton University Press.

Foster, George G., ed. 1848. *The gold regions of California.* New York: Dewitt & Davenport.

Fraser, Robert W. 1983. *Forts and supplies: The role of the army in the economy of the Southwest, 1846–1861.* Albuquerque: University of New Mexico Press.

Galenson, David, and Clayne Pope. 1992. Precedence and wealth: Evidence from nineteenth century Utah. In *Strategic factors in nine-*

teenth century American economic history: A volume to honor Robert W. Fogel, ed. C. Goldin and H. Rockoff. Chicago: University of Chicago Press.

Gallman, Robert E. 1960. Commodity output, 1839–1899. In *Trends in the American economy in the nineteenth century* (NBER Studies in Income and Wealth, vol. 24), ed. W. Parker. Princeton, N.J.: Princeton University Press.

————. 1966. Gross national product in the United States, 1834–1909. In *Output, employment, and productivity in the United States after 1800* (NBER Studies in Income and Wealth, vol. 30), ed. D. S. Brady. New York: Columbia University Press.

————. 1975. The agricultural sector and the pace of economic growth: U.S. experience in the nineteenth century. In *Essays in nineteenth century economic history,* ed. D. C. Klingaman and R. K. Vedder. Athens: Ohio University Press.

————. 1996. Dietary change in antebellum America. *Journal of Economic History* 56 (March): 193–201.

Gerber, James. 1993. Origins of California's export surplus. *Agricultural History* 67 (Fall): 40–57.

————. 1997. Agricultural expansion during the Gold Rush: California grain farming as a "booming" lagging sector. San Diego State University, Department of Economics. Typescript.

Goldin, Claudia. 1990. *Understanding the gender gap: An economic history of American women.* New York: Oxford University Press.

————. 1992. Comment. In *American economic growth and standards of living before the Civil War,* ed. R. Gallman and J. Wallis. Chicago: University of Chicago Press.

————. 1998. Egalitarianism and the returns to education during the great transformation of American education. Harvard University, Department of Economics. Typescript.

Goldin, Claudia, and Lawrence Katz. 1995. The decline of non-competing groups: Changes in the premium to education, 1890 to 1940. Working Paper no. 5202. Cambridge, Mass.: National Bureau of Economic Research.

Goldin, Claudia, and Robert A. Margo. 1992a. The great compression: The U.S. wage structure at mid-century. *Quarterly Journal of Economics* 107 (February): 1–34.

————. 1992b. Wages, prices, and labor markets before the Civil War. In *Strategic factors in nineteenth century American economic history: A volume to honor Robert W. Fogel,* ed. C. Goldin and H. Rockoff. Chicago: University of Chicago Press.

Goldin, Claudia, and Kenneth Sokoloff. 1982. Women, children, and industrialization in the early Republic: Evidence from the manufacturing censuses. *Journal of Economic History* 42 (December): 741–74.

———. 1984. The relative productivity hypothesis of industrialization. *Quarterly Journal of Economics* 99 (August): 461–88.

Goodman, David. 1994. *Gold seeking: Victoria and California in the 1850s.* Stanford, Calif.: Stanford University Press.

Grosse, Scott. 1982. On the alleged antebellum surge in wage differentials: A critique of Williamson and Lindert. *Journal of Economic History* 42 (June): 413–18.

Habakkuk, H. J. 1962. *American and British technology in the nineteenth century.* Cambridge: Cambridge University Press.

Haines, Michael R. 1989. Consumer behavior and immigrant assimilation: A comparison of the United States, Britain, and Germany, 1889/1890. Working Paper no. 6, Series on Historical Factors in Long Run Growth. Cambridge, Mass.: National Bureau of Economic Research.

———. 1997. Health, height, nutrition, and mortality: Evidence on the "antebellum puzzle" from Union army recruits for New York State and the United States. Colgate University, Department of Economics. Typescript.

Hamermesh, Daniel. 1993. *Labor demand.* Princeton, N.J.: Princeton University Press.

Hanes, Christopher. 1993. The development of nominal wage rigidity in the late 19th century. *American Economic Review* 83 (September): 732–56.

Hannon, Joan. 1996. Explaining nineteenth century dependency rates: Interplay of life cycles and labor markets. St. Mary's College, Department of Economics. Typescript.

Hansen, Alvin. 1925. Factors affecting the trend in real wages. *American Economic Review* 15 (March): 27–42.

Hatton, Timothy, and Jeffrey G. Williamson. 1991. Wage gaps between farm and city: Michigan in the 1890s. *Explorations in Economic History* 28 (October): 381–408.

Heppner, Francis, and Harry John. 1968. Wage data among nineteenth century military and naval records. Washington, D.C.: National Archives and Record Service. Typescript.

Hirsch, Susan E. 1978. *Roots of the American working class: The industrialization of crafts in Newark, 1800–1860.* Philadelphia: University of Pennsylvania Press.

Hoover, Ethel. 1958. Wholesale and retail prices in the nineteenth century. *Journal of Economic History* 17 (September): 298–316.

———. 1960. Retail prices after 1850. In *Trends in the American economy in the nineteenth century* (NBER Studies in Income and Wealth, vol. 24), ed. W. Parker. Princeton, N.J.: Princeton University Press.

James, John, and Jonathan Skinner. 1985. The resolution of the labor scarcity paradox. *Journal of Economic History* 45 (September): 513–40.

Jones, Fred Mitchell. 1937. *Middlemen in the domestic trade of the United States, 1800–1860.* Urbana: University of Illinois Press.

Katz, Lawrence F., and Kevin M. Murphy. 1992. Changes in relative wages, 1963–1987: Supply and demand factors. *Quarterly Journal of Economics* 107 (February): 35–78.

Kennedy, Joseph C. G. 1862. *Preliminary report on the eighth census, 1860.* Washington, D.C.: U.S. Government Printing Office.

———. 1864. *Population of the United States in 1860.* Washington, D.C.: U.S. Government Printing Office.

Kiesling, Lynne, and Robert A. Margo. 1997. Explaining the rise in antebellum pauperism, 1850–1860: New evidence. *Quarterly Review of Economics and Finance* 37 (Summer): 405–17.

Komlos, John. 1987. The height and weight of West Point cadets: Dietary change in antebellum America. *Journal of Economic History* 47 (December): 897–927.

———. 1996. Anomalies in economic history: Toward a resolution of the "antebellum puzzle." *Journal of Economic History* 56 (March): 202–14.

Komlos, John, and Peter Coclanis. 1997. On the puzzling cycle in the biological standard of living: The case of antebellum Georgia. *Explorations in Economic History* 34 (October): 433–59.

Kuznets, Simon. 1955. Economic growth and income inequality. *American Economic Review* 45 (March): 1–28.

———. 1966. *Modern economic growth.* New Haven, Conn.: Yale University Press.

Laurie, Bruce. 1980. *Working people of Philadelphia, 1800–1850.* Philadelphia: Temple University Press.

Lavender, David. 1976. *California: A bicentennial history.* New York: Norton.

Layer, Robert G. 1955. *Earnings of cotton mill operatives, 1825–1914.* Cambridge, Mass.: Harvard University Press.

Lebergott, Stanley. 1964. *Manpower in economic growth: The American record since 1800.* New York: McGraw-Hill.

———. 1976. *The American economy: Income, wealth, and want.* Princeton, N.J.: Princeton University Press.

———. 1985. The demand for land: The United States, 1820–1860. *Journal of Economic History* 45 (June): 181–212.

Lee, Chulhee. 1997. Socioeconomic background, disease, and mortality among Union army recruits: Implications for economic and demographic history. *Explorations in Economic History* 34 (January): 27–55.

Licht, Walter. 1995. *Industrializing America: The nineteenth century.* Baltimore: Johns Hopkins University Press.

Lindert, Peter, and Jeffrey G. Williamson. 1982. Antebellum wage widening once again. *Journal of Economic History* 42 (June): 419–22.

Lotchin, Roger W. 1974. *San Francisco, 1846–1856: From hamlet to city.* New York: Oxford University Press.

Lucas, Robert. 1981. *Studies in business cycle theory.* Cambridge, Mass.: MIT Press.

Maddison, Angus. 1987. Growth and slowdown in advanced capitalist economies: Techniques of quantitative assessment. *Journal of Economic Literature* 25 (June): 649–98.

Maddock, Rodney, and Ian McLean. 1984. Supply-side shocks: The case of Australian gold. *Journal of Economic History* 44 (December): 1047–67.

Margo, Robert A. 1992. Wages and prices during the antebellum period: A survey and new evidence. In *American economic growth and standards of living before the Civil War,* ed. R. Gallman and J. Wallis. Chicago: University of Chicago Press.

———. 1996. The rental price of housing in New York City, 1830–1860. *Journal of Economic History* 56 (September): 605–25.

———. In press. Regional wage gaps and the settlement of the Midwest. *Explorations in Economic History.*

Margo, Robert A., and Richard Steckel. 1983. Heights of native born whites during the antebellum period. *Journal of Economic History* 43 (March): 167–74.

Margo, Robert A., and Georgia C. Villaflor. 1987. The growth of wages in antebellum America: New evidence. *Journal of Economic History* 47 (December): 873–95.

Marks, Paula Mitchell. 1994. *Precious dust: The American Gold Rush era, 1848–1900.* New York: Morrow.

McLane, Louis. 1833. *Documents relative to the manufactures in the United States, collected and transmitted to the House of Representatives, in compliance with a resolution of Jan. 19, 1832. By the secretary of the Treasury in two volumes.* Washington, D.C.: Duff Green.

Mitchell, Wesley Clair. 1908. *Gold, prices, and wages under the greenback standard.* Berkeley, Calif.: University of California Press.

Nordhaus, William D. 1997. Do real-output and real-wage measures capture reality? The history of lighting suggests not. In *The economics of new goods,* NBER Studies in Income and Wealth, vol. 58, ed. Timothy F. Breshnahan and Robert J. Gordon. Chicago: University of Chicago Press.

North, Douglass C. (1961) 1966. *The economic growth of the United States, 1790–1860.* Reprint, New York: Norton.

O'Rourke, Kevin, and Jeffrey G. Williamson. 1994. Late nineteenth century Anglo-American factor price convergence: Were Heckscher and Ohlin right? *Journal of Economic History* 54 (December): 1–25.

Parke, Charles Ross. 1989. *Dreams to dust: A diary of the California Gold Rush.* Edited by James E. Davis. Lincoln: University of Nebraska Press.

Pope, Clayne L. 1992. Adult mortality in America before 1900: A view from family histories. In *Strategic factors in nineteenth century American economic history: A volume to honor Robert W. Fogel*, ed. C. Goldin and H. Rockoff. Chicago: University of Chicago Press.

Prucha, Francis Paul. 1953. *Broadax and bayonet: The role of the United States army in the development of the Northwest, 1815–1860*. Lincoln: University of Nebraska Press.

———. 1969. *The sword of the Republic: The United States army on the frontier, 1783–1846*. Lincoln: University of Nebraska Press.

Risch, Erna. 1962. *Quartermaster support of the army: A history of the corps, 1775–1939*. Washington, D.C.: U.S. Army, Center of Military History.

Rosen, Sherwin. 1972. Hedonic prices and implicit markets. *Journal of Political Economy* 82 (March): 34–55.

Rosenberg, Charles E. 1962. *The cholera years: The United States in 1832, 1849, and 1866*. Chicago: University of Chicago Press.

Rosenbloom, Joshua. 1990. One market or many? Labor market integration in the nineteenth century United States. *Journal of Economic History* 50 (March): 85–108.

———. 1991. Occupational differences in labor market integration: The United States in 1890. *Journal of Economic History* 51 (June): 427–39.

———. 1996. Was there a national labor market at the end of the nineteenth century? New evidence on earnings in manufacturing. *Journal of Economic History* 56 (September): 626–56.

Ross, Steven J. 1985. *Workers on the edge: Work, leisure, and politics in industrializing Cincinnati, 1788–1890*. New York: Columbia University Press.

Rothenberg, Winifred. 1979. A price index for rural Massachusetts, 1750–1855. *Journal of Economic History* 39 (December): 975–1001.

———. 1988. The emergence of farm labor markets and the transformation of the rural economy: Massachusetts, 1770–1855. *Journal of Economic History* 48 (September): 537–66.

———. 1992. *From market places to a market economy: The transformation of rural Massachusetts, 1750–1850*. Chicago: University of Chicago Press.

Ruhlen, George. 1964. Early Nevada forts. *Nevada Historical Quarterly* 7, nos. 3–4:1–64.

Schaefer, Donald. 1983. The effect of the 1859 crop year upon relative productivity in the antebellum cotton South. *Journal of Economic History* 43 (December): 851–65.

Schob, David E. 1975. *Hired hands and plowboys: Farm labor in the Midwest, 1815–1860*. Urbana: University of Illinois Press.

Secretary of the Interior. 1866. *Statistics of the United States (including mortality, property, etc.) in 1860*. Washington, D.C.: U.S. Government Printing Office.

Simkovich, Boris A. 1993. Agriculture and industry in the new Republic: Explaining America's structural transformation, 1800–1860. Harvard University, Department of Economics. Typescript.

Slaughter, Matthew. 1995. The antebellum transportation revolution and factor-price convergence. Working Paper no. 5303. Cambridge, Mass.: National Bureau of Economic Research.

Smith, Walter B. 1963. Wage rates on the Erie Canal, 1828–1881. *Journal of Economic History* 23 (September): 298–311.

Sokoloff, Kenneth. 1984. Was the transition from the artisanal shop to the non-mechanized factory associated with gains in efficiency? Evidence from the U.S. manufacturing censuses of 1820 and 1850. *Explorations in Economic History* 21 (October): 351–82.

———. 1986a. Productivity growth in manufacturing during early industrialization: Evidence from the American Northeast, 1820–1860. In *Long term factors in American economic growth* (NBER Studies in Income and Wealth, vol. 51), ed. S. L. Engerman and R. Gallman. Chicago: University of Chicago Press.

———. 1986b. The puzzling record of real wage growth in early industrial America: 1820–1860. University of California, Los Angeles, Department of Economics. Typescript.

Sokoloff, Kenneth, and Georgia C. Villaflor. 1992. The market for manufacturing workers during early industrialization: The American Northeast, 1820 to 1860. In *Strategic factors in nineteenth century American economic history: A volume to Honor Robert W. Fogel,* ed. C. Goldin and H. Rockoff. Chicago: University of Chicago Press.

Soltow, Lee. 1992. Inequalities in the standard of living in the United States, 1798–1875. In *American economic growth and standards of living before the Civil War,* ed. R. Gallman and J. Wallis. Chicago: University of Chicago Press.

Soltow, Lee, and Edward Stevens. 1981. *The rise of literacy and the common school in the United States: A socioeconomic analysis to 1870.* Chicago: University of Chicago Press.

Steckel, Richard. 1983. The economic foundations of East-West migration during the nineteenth century. *Explorations in Economic History* 20 (January): 14–36.

———. 1995. Stature and the standard of living. *Journal of Economic Literature* 33 (December): 1903–40.

Steckel, Richard, and Roderick Floud, eds. 1997. *Health and welfare during industrialization.* Chicago: University of Chicago Press.

Steckel, Richard, and Donald R. Haurin. 1982. Height, nutrition, and mortality in Ohio, 1870–1900. Ohio State University, Department of Economics. Typescript.

Stone, Alfred Holt. 1909. Free contract labor in the antebellum South. In *The South in the building of the nation: Southern economic history,* vol.

5, ed. J. C. Gallagh. Richmond, Va.: Southern Historical Publication Society.

Sullivan, William A. 1955. *The industrial worker in Pennsylvania, 1800–1840.* Harrisburg, Pa.: Pennsylvania Historical and Museum Commission.

Taylor, Alan M. 1996. Convergence and international factor flows in theory and history. Working Paper no. 5798. Cambridge, Mass.: National Bureau of Economic Research.

Taylor, George R. 1951. *The transportation revolution, 1815–1860.* New York: Rinehart.

Temin, Peter. 1969. *The Jacksonian economy.* New York: Norton.

———. 1971. Labor scarcity in America. *Journal of Interdisciplinary History* 1 (Winter): 251–64.

Turner, Frederick Jackson. 1920. *The frontier in American history.* New York: Holt.

Umbreck, John. 1977. California Gold Rush: A study of emerging property rights. *Explorations in Economic History* 24 (July): 197–226.

U.S. Department of Commerce. 1975. *Historical statistics of the United States.* Washington, D.C.: U.S. Government Printing Office.

Ware, Norman. 1924. *The industrial worker, 1840–1860.* New York: Houghton Mifflin.

Warren, George F., and Frank A. Pearson. 1933. *Prices.* New York: Wiley.

Weeks, Joseph D. 1886. *Report on the statistics of wages in manufacturing industries with supplementary reports.* Washington, D.C.: U.S. Government Printing Office.

Weir, David R. 1997. Economic welfare and physical well-being in France, 1750–1990. In *Health and welfare during industrialization,* ed. R. Steckel and R. Floud. Chicago: University of Chicago Press.

Weiss, Thomas. 1992. U.S. labor force estimates and economic growth, 1800–1860. In *American economic growth and standards of living before the Civil War,* ed. R. Gallman and J. Wallis. Chicago: University of Chicago Press.

Wilentz, Sean. 1984. *Chants democratic: New York City and the rise of the working class, 1788–1850.* New York: Oxford University Press.

Williamson, Jeffrey G. 1975. The relative costs of American men, skills, and machines: A long view. Discussion Paper no. 289–75. University of Wisconsin, Madison, Institute for Research on Poverty.

———. 1985. *Did British capitalism breed inequality?* London: Allen & Unwin.

———. 1991. *Inequality, poverty, and history.* New Haven, Conn.: Yale University Press.

———. 1992. Comment. In *American economic growth and standards of living before the Civil War,* ed. R. Gallman and J. Wallis. Chicago: University of Chicago Press.

————. 1995. The evolution of global labor markets since 1830: Background evidence and hypotheses. *Explorations in Economic History* 32 (April): 141–96.

Williamson, Jeffrey G., and Peter H. Lindert. 1980. *American inequality: A macroeconomic history.* New York: Academic.

Wright, Carroll. 1885. *Sixteenth annual report of the Bureau of Statistics of Labor.* Boston: State Printer.

————. 1889. *Comparative wages, prices, and the cost of living.* Boston: Wright & Potter.

Wright, Doris Marion. 1940. The making of cosmopolitan California: An analysis of immigration, 1848–1870. *California Historical Quarterly* 19 (December): 323–43.

Wright, Gavin. 1978. *The political economy of the cotton South: Households, markets, and wealth in the nineteenth century.* New York: Norton.

————. 1986. *Old South, new South.* New York: Basic.

Zabler, Jeffrey F. 1972. Further evidence on American wage differentials, 1800–1830. *Explorations in Economic History* 10 (Fall): 109–11.

Index

DATE DUE